RELIGION IN THE PRIMARY SCHOOL
A partnership between church and state?

RELIGION IN THE PRIMARY SCHOOL

A partnership between church and state?

Leslie J. Francis

Senior Research Officer, Culham College Institute for Church Related Education

Collins

Collins Liturgical Publications
8 Grafton Street, London W1X 3LA

Collins Liturgical in USA
Icehouse One – 401
151 Union Street, San Francisco, CA 94111-1299

Collins Liturgical in Canada
Novalis, Box 9700, Terminal,
375 Rideau St, Ottawa, Ontario K1G 4B4

Distributed in Ireland by
Educational Company of Ireland
21 Talbot Street, Dublin 1

Collins Liturgical Australia
PO Box 316, Blackburn, Victoria 3130

Collins Liturgical New Zealand
PO Box 1, Auckland

First published 1987

Typographical design Colin Reed
Typeset by Burgess & Son (Abingdon) Ltd
Printed in Great Britain by Bell and Bain Ltd, Glasgow

CONTENTS

FOREWORD

This research project was established in 1983 by the Culham College Institute for Church Related Education, the Gloucester Diocesan Education Committee and the Gloucestershire Local Education Authority, in association with the Clifton Catholic Diocesan Schools Commission. The stimulus came from the Green Paper, *A Future in Partnership*, published by the National Society of the Church of England, and the fortieth anniversary of the 1944 Education Act. The intention was to design an empirical study to look closely at the partnership between church and state in the state maintained system of education.

Having collected data, the researcher has to decide whether simply to present them or whether also to run the risk of interpreting them. The relationship between empirical research and theoretical interpretation is both complex and delicate. Some of my previous studies have presented the data objectively and left interpretation in the hands of the reader; this study both presents the data and provides an interpretative context. This is a personal interpretation and must not be thought to represent the views of the sponsoring bodies.

I am grateful to those key people who helped to design and to establish the research project in Gloucestershire: the Reverend George Humphrey (religious education adviser to both the Anglican diocese and the local education authority), Mrs Marianne Atkinson (diocesan schools officer), the Reverend Canon Roger Grey (diocesan director of education) and to Father Patrick Purnell and Father Harry Stratton (Catholic National Catechetical Association). I am also grateful to the 267 headteachers and 4,948 pupils who completed questionnaires for me; without their help there would be no data to report and interpret.

My thanks are also due to the Department of Education and Science and the Welsh Office for making available some statistical data; to the team of people who prepared the questionnaires for computer analysis; to Helen Piper for assistance with computing; to Marianne Atkinson, Sue Chapman, Geoffrey Duncan, John Gay, David Lankshear, Kathleen Mills, Michael Nott, Helen Piper and Christine Wright for commenting on various drafts of the manuscript; to Kim Luckett for so ably preparing the manuscript for printing.

Culham College Institute
February 1987

Leslie J. Francis

1 INTRODUCTION

From a distance one primary school looks very much like another, the only distinguishing feature seeming simply to be the period when the school was built. Closer inspection, however, reveals another key difference, this one written into the school name on the noticeboard. Some are county schools; others are Church of England controlled, Church of England aided or Catholic aided schools.

Throughout England, 34% of the primary schools, including middle schools deemed primary, are associated with the Anglican or Catholic churches. In the shire counties as a whole the proportion rises to 37%, while in seven of the shire counties more than half of the primary schools are church-related. All of these schools, county and church schools alike, are part of the one system of state maintained education.

It is not simply through the name boards on certain schools that the churches exert an influence on the shape of state maintained primary education in England. According to the letter of the law, religious education is compulsory throughout all state maintained schools and the churches have a voice in preparing the syllabuses of religious education. According to the letter of the law, "the school day in every county school and every voluntary school shall begin with collective worship". Of course, what actually happens inside the school cannot always be accurately predicted from the name board outside or from detailed knowledge of the law.

Amy, John, Ruth, Patrick, Sarah and Abu are all nine year old children living in one of the shire counties. They all attend a state maintained primary school. Where they differ is both in the type of school they attend and in the religious atmosphere of their homes.

Amy's parents are not church-goers, nor are they believers. They did not have Amy baptised as a baby. The option, they say, is open for her to make up her own mind when she is an adult. They do not send her to church. Amy's neighbourhood school is a county school, where she meets a lot of religion. She begins every school day by singing a hymn, hearing a passage from the bible and joining in the Lord's Prayer. She comes home from school one day singing a hymn from the school hymn book. Her parents listen to the words, 'O Jesus, I have promised to serve thee to the end', and begin to wonder what effect school religion is having on her.

John's parents are not really church-goers either, although they regard themselves as good Christians. They had John baptised at the Methodist chapel and they usually go to a service in the chapel at Christmas and harvest time. For a year or two John went to the Methodist Sunday school, but now that he is nine he feels that he has grown out of this. John's neighbourhood school is a Church of England controlled school. The vicar is chairman of the governors and a frequent visitor to the school. He takes an assembly once a week and has the top class for religious education. Through school the vicar spotted that John had a good voice and asked him to join in the parish church choir. John's parents are pleased and feel that it will be good for him; now they go to occasional services in the Anglican church rather than the Methodist chapel.

Ruth's parents are closely involved in the local Anglican church. Her mother teaches in the Sunday school and her father sings in the choir. They were concerned to find a Christian education for their daughter. Living in a suburban area, they are in easy reach of a Church of England aided, a Catholic and a county school. First, they went to talk with the headteacher of the Church of England aided school. He explained that his school was there primarily to serve the local neighbourhood. Recognising that most of the pupils were not from church-going homes, he made a conscious point of not emphasising the church-related character of the school. Ruth's parents decided to send her to the Catholic school where they recognised an explicitly church-related environment.

Patrick's mother and father had grown up in Catholic communities and attended Catholic schools. His mother continues to be a regular mass-goer; his father has lapsed. As a baby, Patrick was baptised a Catholic. The nearest Catholic school is some 10 miles away. His mother felt torn between expressing loyalty to Patrick's church and loyalty to the community in which he was living and growing up. In the end she decided not to take Patrick away from other children in the community in order to send him to a denominational school.

Sarah's parents are Jehovah's Witnesses. They take their religion seriously and are bringing up Sarah in the same faith. They find the religious provision of state maintained schools offensive and they have exercised their right to withdraw Sarah from the religious life of the school. Sarah's school is a county school where an assembly takes place three mornings every week. Sarah sits in the classroom alone while the other children share in a common activity and sometimes she feels very isolated and lonely.

Abu's parents are practising Muslims who are bringing Abu up in the

Muslim faith. Abu lives in an area where there are a number of other Muslim families. The neighbourhood school is a Church of England controlled school; today about one in five of the pupils are Muslims. The curriculum and the religious life of the school tries to take the presence of these non-Christian pupils fully into account.

What, then, is the place of religion in the primary school today? How much can we generalise from the experiences of Amy, John, Ruth, Patrick, Sarah and Abu? What are primary schools doing in religious education and how much influence do the churches really have in determining the shape of religious education? How are primary schools interpreting the law's requirement to hold a daily assembly and how close is the relationship between assemblies and the worship of the churches? Are church schools different from county schools and, if so, what form do these differences take? How has the present situation of church involvement in primary education come about? And where should this relationship be going in the future? These are the questions which the present book sets out to address.

Chapter two sets the historical context. The present situation can only be properly understood by an appreciation of the historical processes through which it has evolved. The original initiative in creating the present educational system came from the churches, not from the secular authorities. This historical legacy played a crucial role in shaping the 1944 Education Act which formulated the present partnership between church and state within the state maintained system of schools.

Chapter three sets the theoretical context. Since the 1944 Education Act considerable changes have taken place in educational thinking on the three key religious provisions of the act, namely religious education, school worship and church schools. This chapter summarises the way in which new educational thinking has changed the character of religious education, challenged the place of school worship and questioned the appropriateness of church schools.

Change in educational theory, however, is not the same thing as change in educational practice. It is one thing to know what is being said about the changing place of religion in education, it is another matter to discover what is happening in practice. The main body of this book describes a research project which sets out to discover precisely how the partnership between church and state in education is being interpreted and implemented in one shire county.

Chapter four deals with the mechanics of the survey. It discusses the design of the project, the development of two research instruments for use among headteachers and among fourth year junior pupils, how these two instruments were administered, and the kind of responses they received.

Chapters five through eight analyse the headteachers' questionnaires in order to provide detailed profiles of county, Catholic, Church of England aided and Church of England controlled schools. They illustrate just how much the religious character of state maintained primary schools can still be related to the historic foundation of the school. Each of these chapters concludes with a summary and interpretation.

Chapters nine through eleven explore the differences in emphasis between village, town and suburban schools respectively. They illustrate just how much the religious character of state maintained primary schools can vary from one location to another. The second half of these chapters moves away from statistical generalisations to provide four succinct profiles of individual schools: county, Catholic, Church of England aided and Church of England controlled. In writing these profiles the anonymity of the individual schools has been totally preserved.

Chapter twelve steps up the power and sophistication of the statistical procedures to attempt two things. First, it identifies more precisely the features which characterise some schools as more church-related than others. Then it assesses the importance of various factors in determining whether individual schools display these features of church-related education or not. As a consequence of this kind of analysis, chapter twelve is able to make some predictions about the changes which are likely to occur in the religious emphases of primary schools during the coming years. This chapter also poses in a particularly poignant way some key problems and questions about the future of the partnership between church and state in the provision of a state maintained system of schools.

Chapters thirteen and fourteen turn attention from the schools to the pupils. After all, no description of schools can be complete without taking the pupils into account. Chapter thirteen begins by introducing the religious background of the pupils. It examines their personal habits of church attendance, the church attendance of their parents and their personal attitudes towards Christianity. It examines the influence of home, church and environment on shaping the pupils' attitudes. Then chapter fourteen addresses the key question as to whether church schools influence the religious development of their pupils.

Finally, chapter fifteen summarises the main conclusions to emerge from the study and challenges the churches to face the need to adapt their educational theory in the light of real changes in the secular educational climate.

2 CHURCH AND STATE

Church initiative

The main antecedents of the present system of primary schools were two voluntary societies founded at the beginning of the nineteenth century, the British and Foreign School Society and the National Society. Both were inspired by religious principles and it was religion which kept them apart.

The British and Foreign School Society emerged in 1814 from the Royal Lancasterian Society and was supported primarily by non-conformists and liberal Anglicans. British schools were established to promote "the education of the labouring and manufacturing classes of society of every religious persuasion". Religious instruction in British schools was confined to scripture and "general Christian principles". It was one of the society's original rules that,

> The lessons for reading shall consist of extracts from the holy scriptures; no catechism or peculiar religious tenets shall be taught in the schools, but every child shall be enjoined to attend regularly the place of worship to which its parents belong.

The National Society was founded in 1811 as a direct response to the Royal Lancasterian Society and had the backing of the great body of Anglicans. National schools were established to promote "the education of the poor in the principles of the established church". Religious instruction in National schools was to include the doctrines, catechism and liturgy of the established church.

In its early days the National Society was willing to be liberal in its outlook and made allowances for children whose parents objected to the religious instruction given in the schools. The Royal Commission of 1818 made it clear that at this stage,

> The church catechism is only taught and attendance at the established place of worship only required of those whose parents belong to the establishment.

Later, however, National schools generally took a harder line and insisted on attendance for religious instruction and attendance at an Anglican church on Sunday as conditions of entry to the school.

Very soon the greater resources of the National Society, in association with the parochial clergy, enabled it to draw ahead of the British and Foreign School Society. By 1830 the National Society had established 3,678 schools, educating approximately 346,000 children.

During this early period school provision for Catholic children was particularly inadequate, due largely to the relatively small number of middle class subscribers and the large number of poor immigrants from Ireland. Catholic children were forbidden to attend schools where the Authorised Version of the bible was used.

The state did not enter the field of public education until 1833, and then it did so not by establishing state schools, but by distributing public funds to the National Society and the British and Foreign School Society. A government grant of £20,000 was distributed between the two societies to assist with school building. The government grant was essentially in "aid of private subscription", being available only to those voluntary bodies which could raise the first half of building costs and guarantee to meet all future running costs. Because of the greater voluntary resources available to the Church of England, by 1839 about 80% of the state grant went to Anglican schools.

In 1839 a committee of the Privy Council was set up "to superintend the allocation of any sums voted by Parliament for the purpose of promoting education". Between 1833 and 1870 the state continued to contribute to public education solely through the administrative system provided by voluntary societies. In 1847 the state was spending £100,000 on education, a decade later it was spending £500,000. In 1847 it was spending public money only on school buildings; a decade later it was contributing towards teachers' salaries, the provision of apparatus and, by means of capitation grants, towards the annual income of the schools.

With the provision of state grants, the number of schools established under the sponsorship of the two societies continued to grow. By 1851 there were 17,015 Church of England schools with nearly 956,000 pupils, and 1,500 non-conformist schools with 225,000 pupils. When other church groups saw that these public funds were available for church related schools, they began to establish administrative machinery to claim their share of the state's beneficence.

In 1843 the Methodist Conference decided to enter the field of providing voluntary day schools and accepted its first state grant in 1847, on being assured that this acceptance would not preclude them opposing similar assistance for Catholic schools. Wesleyan policy was midway between that of the two existing societies. Unlike the National Society, the Wesleyan Society found no difficulty in accepting a conscience clause to accommodate children of other denominations; unlike the British and

Foreign School Society, the Wesleyan Society insisted on including denominational instruction.

When the Catholic authorities applied for state aid in 1846, this was refused. However, in 1847 the Catholic Poor School Committee was established and after some delay, was recognised as an authority able to receive grants from the state. The Catholic church was now ready to promote the principle of establishing a separate school system. The Westminster Synod, meeting in 1852, declared:

> No congregation should be allowed to remain without its schools, one for each sex. Where the poverty of the people is extreme, we earnestly exhort you, beloved children, whom God has blessed with riches... to take upon yourselves lovingly this burden.... Indeed, wherever there may seem to be an opening for a new mission, we should prefer the erection of a school, so arranged as to serve temporarily for a chapel, to that of a church without one.

In urban areas it was possible for different denominations to establish their own schools, provided that they could afford to do so. In rural districts, however, the National Society often had a form of monopoly, when the Anglican school was the only one available. Nonconformist parents, understandably, often objected to their children being forced to attend lessons on the prayer book and catechism. In her book, *Church and State in English Education* (1963), Marjorie Cruickshank comments on this problem:

> Perhaps nothing in the educational controversies of the nineteenth century did more to inflame denominational bitterness than the Anglican refusal to concede rights of conscience, for it bred deep resentment and distrust which were to rankle in dissenting hearts for many years to come. Herein lay the problem of the single school area, where there was only one school and that a church school.

By 1860 the Committee of Council on Education had taken one important step towards meeting this denominational problem by beginning to refuse grants for proposed schools in what would become single school areas unless a conscience clause were included in the constitution of the school.

During the 1850s and 1860s there was widespread discussion about future educational developments and a wide disparity of views about the relationship of church and state initiative. The *voluntaryists*, consisting mainly of nonconformists, advocated the non-intervention of the state in education: all should be left to voluntary enterprise. They objected strongly to paying for the support of Anglican or Catholic religious instruction. The *radicals* advocated a wholly secular system of education: religious instruction should be left to the churches. Anglican opinion was already divided. One Anglican group supported the voluntaryists' view and advocated that education was entirely the responsibility of the church; another Anglican group advocated continued co-operation between church and state. One Anglican group supported the radical view and advocated that secular education and religious instruction should be kept quite separate; another Anglican group maintained that the two could not be separated out. The Catholic church became even more strongly convinced of the evils of 'united education'.

1870 Education Act

The problem with leaving the development of a national system of schools to voluntary initiative was that provision was erratic over the country as a whole. Despite the increased state grants, many children were still not being taught. According to the Newcastle Commission, published in 1861, "one of the chief failures" of the existing system was that it "did not touch the districts which required most assistance". The poor areas which could least well raise voluntary subscriptions also least qualified for government grants.

The 1870 Elementary Education Act recognised that compromise was essential and made provision for two different types of school. On the one hand, the schools founded by the voluntary societies were permitted to continue and given official entitlement to grants-in-aid. On the other hand, local school boards were established to build schools in areas where voluntary provision was inadequate. Board schools were intended to make good the gaps in the voluntary system, not to replace that system.

The possibility of the establishment of board schools spurred the voluntary bodies to increase their share in the national provision of schools. The act gave the voluntary societies a period of grace "not exceeding six months", to present plans for making good the deficiencies with the help of the existing state building grants. After the completion of those schools for which plans were approved, such grants would cease.

According to the act, voluntary schools could continue to provide denominational religious teaching. Board schools could decide whether or not to include religious teaching, but when they decided to do so it was to be in accordance with the 'Cowper-Temple clause', which stated that,

> No religious catechism or religious formulary which is distinctive of any particular denomination shall be taught in any school provided by a school board.

The Cross Commission in 1888 revealed that very few board schools took advantage of their right to exclude all religious instruction. The Birmingham school board tried to do this in 1873 and for six years permitted religious instruction to be given only outside school hours, by clergymen or others who were not concerned with the secular instruction, and who paid to use the classroom. This situation produced such opposition that from 1879 bible reading by the headteacher, without note or comment, was permitted.

Different school boards interpreted the Cowper-Temple clause in a variety of ways. Many boards opted for undenominational teaching of one kind or another, explicitly going beyond the Cowper-Temple requirements. The Sheffield board instructed its teachers,

> Not only to adhere strictly to the terms of the fourteenth section of the Education Act which provides that no 'religious formulary which is distinctive of any religious denomination shall be taught in the school', but also to abstain from all denominational teaching.

On the other hand, the Manchester board argued that denominational instruction could indeed be given in board schools as in voluntary schools, the difference being merely that in board schools "you must not use a catechism or formulary".

Anglican views on the acceptability of board schools as an adequate alternative to church schools varied widely. Bishop Fraser of Manchester was reported in 1875 as prepared to transfer his church schools to the public authority. Archdeacon Denison refused even to accept the conditions of state aid for a church school and continued for almost half a century to run his own village school efficiently, without a grant, without a conscience clause and without the interference of Her Majesty's Inspectors.

While the 1870 Education Act enabled voluntary schools and board schools to develop side by side, the financial provisions of the act favoured the board schools. The churches found it increasingly difficult to keep pace with the school boards and to maintain educational standards. According to Murphy (1971), in 1880 the average expenditure in board schools was forty-two shillings for each child, compared with thirty-five shillings in Anglican, Wesleyan and British schools and thirty shillings and six pence in Catholic schools. During the thirty years after the 1870 Education Act nearly 14,000 voluntary schools were transferred to school boards and by the end of the nineteenth century voluntary schools were closing at the rate of 60 a year, while many more were struggling for survival. Nevertheless, voluntary provision still accounted for 71% of the nation's schools and provided 52.5% of the school places.

The 1902 Education Act established greater parity between voluntary and board schools. Under the 1902 Education Act the councils of the counties and county boroughs became local education authorities, as also did some of the larger borough and urban district councils, though with restricted powers. Education thus became one of the local services for which the councils were responsible, rather than the responsibility of a body outside the main system of local government. The new local education authorities took over the educational administration of the board schools; they were also given control over secular education in voluntary schools. Board schools were renamed 'provided' schools; voluntary schools were renamed 'non-provided' schools. The significant feature of this act is that both provided and non-provided schools were to receive rate aid. It was this rate aid for Catholic as well as Anglican schools which provoked a violent opposition from Free Churchmen.

Between 1902 and 1944 the dual system continued, in spite of the churches' increasing financial difficulty in maintaining their commitment to schools and in spite of the Fisher Education Bill's abortive attempt to introduce a unitary system in 1921. By the time of the 1936 Education Act, the partnership between the church and state had become so much part of the English educational system that local education authorities were empowered to enter further into agreements with the churches to assist financially towards the erection of church senior schools.

1944 Education Act

The partnership between church and state in state maintained education as we know it today is a direct result of the 1944 Education Act, which set out to reconstitute the educational system after the Second World War. At the heart of its thinking was provision of secondary education for all. To make this possible a large number of schools required extension, modernisation and re-equipment; new senior schools were needed. On the one hand, the churches could not afford to maintain their voluntary schools and to bring them up to the new standards required. On the other hand, the state could not afford to buy up the church schools and was reluctant to annex them. In short, the denominational schools presented a major political problem.

The fact that the churches owned a high proportion of the nation's schools placed them in a strong position to influence the 1944 Education Act. At the same time, the churches were divided on their understanding of the future of voluntary schools. Catholic opinion insisted on retaining the full denominational character of their schools and remained clearly in favour of separate Catholic schools for Catholic children. The main body of Free Church opinion advocated the replacement of the dual system by a unified state system. They argued that the Christian presence in education could best be preserved through non-denominational religious education in state schools. Some Anglicans also took this line. Bishop Brook of St Edmundsbury and Ipswich, for example, argued that,

> It is my conviction that so far as religious education is concerned it is neither buildings, syllabuses, nor timetables that matter most. What matters is that the teachers in all the schools whether voluntary or county shall be Christian men and women.

Others, like Bishop Kirk of Oxford, took a completely different line:

> Undenominationalism is the first step on the road to complete irreligion, and . . . true religion is only possible by virtue of active and loyal membership in a worshipping community. Our church schools are essential means towards making our witness effective; we must not let them go.

Prolonged negotiations resulted in another compromise between church and state, affecting both the future of church schools and the place of religion in county schools.

As far as the place of religion in county schools is concerned, the 1944 Education Act made three very important points. First, the act made religious instruction obligatory in all county schools and specified that this religious instruction shall be,

> In accordance with an agreed syllabus . . . and shall not include any catechisms or formulary which is distinctive of any particular religious denomination.

Second, the act made school worship obligatory by specifying that,

> The school day in every county school and in every voluntary school shall begin with collective worship on the part of all pupils in attendance.

In the case of county schools the collective worship "shall not . . . be distinctive of any particular denomination". Although religious instruction and collective acts of worship had been a major feature of the English educational scene, they had never previously been made a statutory obligation.

Third, the fifth schedule of the act defined the procedure for preparing and bringing into operation an agreed syllabus of religious instruction. It lays down that the local education authority must convene a conference to bring together representatives from the churches, the local education authority and teachers. This procedure, therefore, gives the churches a key role in agreeing the form of religious instruction to be provided in county schools.

At the same time, the act reaffirmed the legal provision for parents to withdraw their children from worship and religious instruction:

> If the parent of any pupil in attendance at any county school or any voluntary school requests that he be wholly or partly excused from attendance at religious worship in the school, or from attendance at religious instruction in the school, or from attendance at both religious worship and religious instruction in the school, then, until the request is withdrawn, the pupil shall be excused such attendance accordingly.

The act also made provision for parents to withdraw their children from school, under certain conditions, to receive denominational religious instruction, if this can be appropriately arranged.

As far as church schools are concerned, the 1944 Education Act continued the dual system and strengthened it. Voluntary schools were individually given the choice between 'aided' or 'controlled' status. This choice enabled schools which could afford to retain a high level of independence to do so, while those that either could not afford or did not desire to retain such a high level of independence could nevertheless retain something of their church-related character.

The aided school approximated the status of the non-provided school, and involved the churches in continued financial liability. The managers or governors of an aided school were responsible for the capital expenditure on alterations required by the local education authority to keep the premises up to standard, for external repairs to the school building, improvements and extensions to existing school buildings. Government grant aid was made available to meet 50% of these costs. Subsequent legislation raised the grant to 75% in 1959, 80% in 1967 and 85% in 1974. Under the 1944 Education Act government grants were also available for providing new aided schools under certain conditions. The local education authority is responsible for all other running costs of the aided school, including teachers' salaries, repairs to the interior of the building, the playground and playing fields, and for the erection and maintenance of buildings used exclusively for the school medical and meals services. In return for their continued financial involvement, the churches retained the right to appoint a majority of the school managers or governors and to provide denominational religious instruction and denominational worship. If the managers or governors of an aided school decide that they no longer wish or can afford to maintain aided status, the school may become controlled.

The controlled school gave the churches reduced rights, but involved no ongoing financial liability. In this case, the churches retained the right to appoint a minority of the school managers or governors. Religious instruction is given according to the agreed syllabus, but parents may ask for denominational teaching "during not more than two periods each week". Provided the teaching staff of the controlled school exceeds two, up to one fifth of the staff can be "selected for their fitness and competence to give such religious instruction". These are called 'reserved teachers'. The daily act of worship can also be denominational in character. Once a voluntary school has accepted controlled status, the act makes no provision whereby the school could become aided.

A third category of voluntary school provided for in the 1944 Education Act is the 'special agreement' school. This category continued to honour the arrangements negotiated between local education authorities and the churches as a result of the 1936 Education Act, the implementation of which had been interrupted by the war. For most practical purposes the provisions regarding religious instruction, worship, finance and school management are basically the same as for aided status, except in relation to the appointment of staff.

The Catholics in 1944 rejected controlled status completely. Just two small Catholic schools accepted the irreversible designation of controlled status. Murphy (1971) accounts for these two anomalies "as the result of an administrative oversight". While the Catholic community continued to feel that the financial arrangements of aided status were unfair to a religious minority who, in conscience, could not accept the implications of controlled status, the Catholic church worked hard to finance a national network of aided schools.

As far as Church of England schools were concerned, the choice between aided and controlled status was left in the hands of the governors or managers of each church school. They needed to weigh up the advantages of aided status against the cost and their ability to meet that cost. While Church of England schools are autonomous, the diocese is in the position to offer advice, guidance and financial aid. In the absence of an agreed central policy on the comparable merits of aided and controlled status, each diocese formulated its own recommendations, which the school governors within its area could choose to follow or to ignore, at least as far as their independent sources of finance would permit. Some dioceses, like London, Southwark and Blackburn, opted heavily for aided status; other dioceses, like Bristol, York, Coventry and Lichfield, opted mainly for controlled status.

Religious Consensus

The 1944 Education Act designed an educational system appropriate for a Christian or church-related society. While some of the denominational controversies which had beset the 1870 and the 1902 Education Acts still survived, there was also a new feeling of religious consensus. What made sense of the 1944 Education Act were the key ideas that England was a Christian country and that the churches had a particular right and responsibility to share with the state in shaping the education of the nation's children.

The specific provisions of the 1944 Education Act highlight nine key religious assumptions. These assumptions have looked different from different denominational perspectives and at different times during the intervening years since 1944. They are, however, worth spelling out in some detail, since they are at the heart of the idea of the educational partnership between church and state as conceived in 1944 and now their current interpretation determines precisely what that partnership is like in practice.

First, the act made obligatory a daily act of collective worship in all county and voluntary schools. The churches' assumption was that religious worship is not only compatible with, but an essential component of, the school's educational task. When schools promote religious worship, even undenominational worship, they are helping to prepare their pupils for a place in the worshipping congregations of the churches. Schools and churches share the same hymns, the same language of prayer and the same tradition of reading from scripture.

Second, the act made religious instruction a compulsory subject in all county and voluntary schools. The churches' assumption was that all state maintained schools have a responsibility to teach religion. At the time of the act no sophisticated distinction existed between the churches' confessional teaching and the schools' non-confessional teaching of religion. Many Anglicans, therefore, felt that the rationale behind teaching religion in county schools was so close to their own objectives that there was less need to retain church schools.

Third, the act gave the churches a key role in preparing the agreed syllabuses of religious instruction. The churches' assumption was that religious instruction in county schools was as much a theological question as an educational question. The churches wanted a significant hand in determining what religious instruction should look like in county schools and the opportunity to make sure that denominational interests did not infiltrate what was supposed to be a non-sectarian programme. Many Anglicans felt that agreed syllabus teaching was an appropriate foundation on which they could build denominational teaching through church and Sunday school.

Fourth, the act safeguarded parents' rights to withdraw their children from religious instruction, from religious worship or from both, whether they attended a county or a voluntary school. The churches' assumption was that these withdrawal clauses protected the rights of a minority. The majority of parents would want to accept the religious worship and the religious instruction which the churches helped to shape. The minority who desired the protection of the withdrawal clauses were more likely to do so because of sectarian interests, rather than secularist persuasion.

Fifth, the churches felt secure in their continued involvement in training teachers to staff county and church schools. The churches' assumption was that they should influence the teachers who in turn would influence the pupils in school. Many Anglicans felt that church money was better invested in training colleges than schools. Some, indeed, expressed this view with missionary fervour and zeal.

Sixth, the act enabled the churches to maintain controlled schools without continuing financial liability. A number of Church of England schools welcomed controlled status. In controlled schools the church appoints some of the managers, the daily worship can be denominational in character and the *clergy continue to have contact. By accepting controlled status in many neighbourhood single-school areas, the Church of England was assuming that it was still appropriate for denominational worship to take place in schools which exist primarily to serve all the children of an area, whatever the religious persuasion of their homes.

Seventh, the act enabled the churches to choose which of their schools they wished to maintain as more distinctively church-related through aided status. Aided status gives the churches control over the majority of the managing body and the right to provide denominational religious instruction throughout the school, in addition to the daily denominational act of worship. A number of Church of England schools in single school areas opted for aided status. By accepting aided status for schools which it proposed to run on a neighbourhood model the Church of England was assuming that it was still appropriate for the church to determine the church-related character of local area schools. Unless parents deliberately withdrew their children from religious instruction and religious worship, the clergy could assume the right to teach them denominational doctrine and to lead them in denominational worship, whatever the religious persuasion of their homes.

Eighth, the act enabled the churches to develop a distinctive system of denominational aided schools, to serve the needs of religious communities, rather than neighbourhoods. In this situation parents were only likely to send their children to the school if they accepted the religious emphasis of the school. The Catholic church opted exclusively to develop schools of this nature; the Anglican church also developed a few schools along these lines, as did the Jewish community. The churches' assumptions here are of a completely different order. Instead of trying to influence the religious formation of the nation's children, they are seeking to serve the needs of their own particular religious community and making the assumption that the general educational system is unable to meet these needs adequately. This assumption is in accord with religious minorities, rather than religious majorities.

Ninth, provisions under the 1944 Education Act gave parents the opportunity to ask for free transport for a reasonable distance to enable their children to attend a school of the denomination they desired. The churches' assumption was that a variety of religious provisions would exist within different schools and that parents should be able to choose the school that would best suit their religious needs. This assumption, like the previous one, concerns the churches' protection of the rights of their own members, not their intention to influence the rest of the nation.

Since 1944, both educational and church-related thinking in the specific areas of religious education, school worship and church schools, and more generally about the relationship between religion and education, have changed and developed. It is the intention of the next chapter to review these changes and developments and to assess their implications for the churches' assumptions underlying the 1944 Education Act.

3 RELIGION AND EDUCATION

The close relationship between church and school assumed by the 1944 Education Act has been questioned in a variety of ways. This chapter focuses on five key issues: developments in educational theory, the implications of secularisation, changes in religious education, challenges to school worship and the church school question. The aim of the chapter is to make clear the direction in which contemporary thinking is moving and to highlight the implications for the churches' educational thinking.

Educational theory

Since 1944, the academic study of education has emerged as an autonomous discipline in its own right and, by the 1980s, some educationalists were making the strong case that the churches could no longer assume their former right to influence educational theory and practice. This case is expressed most strongly in the writings of Paul Hirst, Professor of Education at the University of Cambridge, and is summarised in two key papers.

In the first paper, published in *Learning for Living* in 1972, Hirst argues that the concept of 'Christian education' is a contradiction in terms. On this account, the theologian is precluded from making a distinctive contribution to *educational* theory. In the second paper, published in the *British Journal of Religious Education* in 1981, Hirst extends the argument to church schools. On this account, the church school is precluded from making a distinctive contribution to *educational* practice. The main strand in Hirst's argument rests on his understanding of what is to count as education; another strand rests on his analysis of the educational implications of secularisation.

Hirst's first point is that "there has already emerged in our society" a concept of education, according to which education constitutes an area of discourse autonomous in its own right. Hirst (1976) illustrates what he means by this autonomy by developing the parallel between education and science. He argues that,

> Just as intelligent Christians have come to recognise that justifiable scientific claims are autonomous and do not, and logically cannot, rest on religious

beliefs, so also, it seems to me, justifiable educational principles are autonomous. That is to say that any attempt to justify educational principles by an appeal to religious claims is invalid. I am anxious that the terrible story of the long battle which Christianity waged and lost over science and religion be no longer repeated in the area of education and religion.

For Hirst, to speak of Christian education is a misleading anachronism.

Hirst's second point draws a distinction between a *primitive* and a *sophisticated* concept of education. The primitive concept is "concerned with passing on to children what we believe, so that they in turn come to believe it to be true". The sophisticated concept is not "determined by what any group simply believes but by what on publicly acknowledged rational grounds we can claim to know and understand". The goal of the sophisticated concept of education is to develop "a rationally autonomous person whose life is self-directed in the light of what reason determines".

Hirst argues that, because of their religious beliefs, Christians are involved in the primitive concept of education. It is, however, the sophisticated concept of education which has a place in schools and which excludes the possibility of a distinctively Christian contribution to the curriculum. Hirst argues that according to the sophisticated view of education,

> The character of education is not settled by any appeal to Christian, Humanist or Buddhist beliefs. Such an appeal is illegitimate, for the basis is logically more fundamental, being found in the canons of objectivity and reason, canons against which Christian, Humanist and Buddhist beliefs must, in their term and in the appropriate way, be assessed. When the domain of religious beliefs is so manifestly one in which there are at present no clearly recognisable objective grounds for judging claims, to base education on any such claims would be to forsake the pursuit of objectivity.

Hirst's third point is to develop a distinction between *education* and *catechesis*: "In catechesis . . . the aim is from the stance of faith, the development of faith". Hirst argues that when the churches are in business to educate, they need to play by the same rules as secular schools; when the churches are involved in catechesis, they cannot be said to be engaging in education. While theologians may contribute to the theory and practice of catechesis, they are firmly excluded from being allowed a contribution to the theory and practice of education.

Hirst's fourth point is that church schools need to take seriously the distinction between education and catechesis. According to his argument, the two activities obey different rules and are in fact logically incompatible. A school undertaking both activities would find itself "at one and the same time committed to trying to develop commitment to reason and commitment to a particular faith". The consequence of attempting to combine these incompatible activities would be confusion for both pupils and teachers.

While Hirst does not pursue his case to its logical conclusion of arguing that church schools, like Christian education, are necessarily a contradiction in terms, he does wish to impose stringent limitations on the church school. According to Hirst, the important condition that can legitimate church schools being involved both in education and catechesis is that these two activities are "sharply separated within the school, being self-consciously and deliberately presented to the pupils as clearly different in character and objectives". In practice, this means separating the two activities both in time and place and by the use of quite different personnel to mark out the differences between those involved in 'teaching' and 'preaching'.

Thus, Hirst is not simply arguing that there are difficulties either in formulating a coherent theological understanding of education or in putting this understanding to work through church schools. He is arguing that the very *logic of education* outlaws the possibility of the churches having a distinctive contribution to make to educational theory and practice.

Hirst's position has done much to undermine the church's confidence and authority in engaging in educational debate. At the same time, the churches in England have tended to accept and agree with the secularisation of the concept of education. The British Council of Churches working party on *The Child in the Church* (1976), for example, distinguished clearly between the concept of *education* and the concept of *nurture*: nurture, it is argued, is the responsibility of the churches, while education is the proper task of the schools.

If Hirst's arguments about the logic of education are accepted, they seriously challenge the assumption underlying the 1944 Education Act that the churches have a right to help shape the nation's educational system.

Secularisation

At the time of the 1944 Education Act, the churches assumed that they were helping to shape an educational system for a Christian country. The second strand in Hirst's case, his analysis of the educational implications of secularisation, questions this assumption. This line of argument implies that, even if the churches had a logical right to contribute to educational debate, their contribution is unlikely to be welcomed or taken seriously by a secular world. The power of this argument rests on perceptions about just how far English society has marched down the road towards secularisation.

The concept 'secularisation' is defined by Bryan Wilson in *Religion and Secular Society* (1966) and *Religion in Sociological Perspective* (1982), as "that process by which religious institutions, actions, and consciousness, lose their social significance". While he is under no illusion about a past golden age when all people were devoutly religious, Bryan Wilson maintains that "by most criteria, the social significance of religion for the conduct of human life was greater than it is now". Similarly, David Lyon's book, *The Steeple's Shadow* (1985), argues that the steeple's shadow has shrunk drastically:

'Secularisation' sums up a strikingly significant aspect of modern life. Unlike previous times, and unlike many non-advanced societies, the warp and woof of social life contains little explicit reference to religion (at least as conventionally defined).

Alan Gilbert chose to call his study of the secularisation of modern society, *The Making of Post-Christian Britain* (1980). Gilbert's view is that,

A post-Christian society is not one from which Christianity has departed, but one in which it has become marginal. It is a society where to be irreligious is to be normal, where to think and act in secular terms is to be conventional, where neither status nor responsibility depends upon the practice or profession of religious faith. Some members of such a society continue to find Christianity a profound, vital influence in their lives, but in so doing they place themselves outside the mainstream of social life and culture.

In many ways indices of church membership, church attendance and public opinion surveys confirm this view of secularisation. A relevant survey is that undertaken by the European Value Systems Study Group and reported in *Values and Social Change in Britain* (Abrams, Gerard and Timms, 1985). According to this survey in Britain as a whole, over 70% of the population seldom or never read the bible and no more than one person in seven attends church weekly. David Gerard sums up the implications of the survey for the churches as follows.

The age profile of the churches is untypical of the population. There is a tendency to emphasise frail and elderly church members as far as ministry and services are concerned as opposed to evangelisation among the young. . . . The narrow contemporary appeal of the teaching authority of the churches, the relative irreligiosity of young adults and the potential fragility of the moral consensus clearly confront the churches with a formidable challenge.

By concentrating on the whole of Britain, David Gerard's analysis actually presents a picture more favourable to the churches than he would have found if he had isolated England from the rest of Britain. Peter Brierley's analysis in the *UK Christian Handbook* (1986) identifies higher levels of church membership in Wales and Scotland than in England. According to Brierley's figures, in 1980 church membership in England embraced just 12% of the population; in 1985 it had fallen further to 11%.

While statistics of church attendance seem to support Hirst's view about secularisation, a number of commentators remind us of the danger of defining religion too narrowly. John Habgood in his *Church and Nation in a Secular Age* (1983) writes,

> From a sociological perspective active churchgoers form the tip of a huge religious iceberg. They are simply the most visible and articulate part of a much wider phenomenon.

The submerged part of the iceberg Habgood characterises as folk religion, which he defines as the "unexpressed, inarticulate, but often deeply felt, religion of ordinary folk". These are the people who would not describe themselves as church-going Christians, "yet feel themselves to have some sort of Christian allegiance".

In support of this view, the European Value Systems Study Group's survey revealed that more than three-quarters of British people expressed a belief in God, three-fifths identified themselves as religious persons and half regularly felt the need for prayer, meditation or contemplation. Similarly, David Hay's study, *Exploring Inner Space* (1982), reports that 62% of the people interviewed in Nottingham during the mid 1970s reported religious experiences.

One of the key supporters of this religious iceberg theory is Edward Bailey in his pursuit of "implicit religion", or "the religion of the people". In his chapter in Tony Moss's book, *In Search of Christianity* (1986), Bailey maintains,

> What we do have evidence for, however, is a doggedly persistent faith in 'Christianity', not seen as a set of dogmas but as symbolising an intrinsic faith or spirit.

In support of his view, Bailey cites the continued parental quest for infant baptism, even among those who are not regular church-goers.

If Bailey is correct in pointing to infant baptism as a useful index of implicit or folk religion, the churches need to take seriously the statistical trends in this area. My own recent study, *Rural Anglicanism* (1985), shows that in a rural diocese as recently as 1956 nearly two-thirds (63%) of babies were being baptised in Anglican fonts; by 1983 the proportion had fallen to one-third (33%).

If the social significance of religion in English society has been significantly eroded and if Hirst is right in his analysis of the educational implications of secularisation, a serious challenge is presented to the assumptions underlying the 1944 Education Act that the educational system is being designed for a Christian nation.

Religious education

At the time of the 1944 Education Act, the churches assumed that it was appropriate to make religious education obligatory in all state maintained schools. Although not specified in the act, it is clear from the parliamentary debates that 'religious education' implied 'Christian education'. For example, Mr Chuter Ede, Parliamentary Secretary to the Board of Education, said in his speech replying for the government,

> There is, I think, a general recognition that even if parents themselves have in the course of life encountered difficulties that have led them into doubts and into hesitations, they do desire that their children shall have a grounding in the principles of the Christian faith as it ought to be practised in this country.

The post 1944 agreed syllabuses made explicit both the Christian content and the evangelistic function of religious education. The introduction to the 1949 *Cambridgeshire Syllabus of Religious Teaching for Schools* states that:

> Parliament has decided that instruction in the Christian religion shall be a recognised and indispensable part of our public system of education.

The Birmingham agreed syllabus, reissued in 1962, stated that,

> We speak of religious education, but we mean Christian education.... The aim of Christian education in its full and proper sense is quite simply to confront our children with Jesus Christ.

The agreed syllabuses produced or adopted by local education authorities after the 1944 Education Act were a solid course of biblical study or church history. The material is organised according to theological considerations. Shape is given to the syllabuses by tracing the history of the Judaeo-Christian religion through sections like 'the fall of the kingdom', 'the exile' and 'the reconstruction of Palestine'.

During the second half of the 1960s, the first major revolution took place in religious education, which led to the development of a new type of agreed syllabus, pioneered by the West Riding of Yorkshire in 1966. Behind this first revolution stood the psychological research of Ronald Goldman in his two books, *Religious Thinking from Childhood to Adolescence* (1964) and *Readiness for Religion* (1965). The new syllabuses were child centred rather than subject centred, theme based rather than bible based. Shape is given to the syllabuses by themes like 'wells and water', 'sheep and shepherds' and 'Christian festivals'. Although this new generation of syllabuses changed the shape of religious education, they did not as yet change its purpose: religious education still remained confessional in its intention.

During the early 1970s, the second major revolution took place in religious education; this time both the shape and purpose of the subject were affected. Behind the second revolution stood an alignment between educational philosophy and the philosophy of religion. The educational philosopher was arguing that it is not an appropriate function for secular schools to adopt the confessional approach towards religious education which attempts to initiate the young into the beliefs and practices of the worshipping community. At the same time, philosophers of religion, like Professor Ninian Smart (1968, 1969), were changing the academic stance of the university faculties of theology. Smart advanced a clear distinction between the objective study of religion and the transmission of religious faith.

The key document to promote this new view of religious education was the Schools Council Working Paper 36, *Religious Education in Secondary Schools* (1971), which consciously adopted Smart's phenomenological approach to the study of religion as the platform on which to build a rationale for religious education in state maintained schools. This working paper draws a clear distinction "between the role of the school in religious education and the role of the church, home, synagogue or mosque". It argues that religious education should "take account of the presence of non-Christian groups and to promote understanding and goodwill between people of varying religious convictions", and that children should be "introduced to some of the living religions of the world at an earlier stage than hitherto".

By 1970 the rapid changes taking place in thinking about religious education encouraged Cambridgeshire (1970), Essex (1970) and Hampshire (1971) to promote something less formal than an agreed syllabus. For example, the Cambridgeshire handbook of suggestions for teachers contains the following introduction, "these suggestions are not in any way a new syllabus: they are to be considered as part of continuing curriculum development". The emphasis was moving away from the problem of reaching an agreement between the churches on what they held in common, to teachers' participation in the development of a school subject. At the same time other faith communities were being included in the drafting conference.

When the Birmingham syllabus and handbook came out in 1975, it was being argued that religious education should be seen as an intrinsically valid educational activity, justified by its particular contribution to preparation for life in a contemporary society. The Birmingham syllabus argued that in the secondary school there should be a detailed study of at least one religious tradition in all its dimensions:

> Each pupil should have the right to choose for himself the subject of this study from the following options: Christianity, Hinduism, Islam, Judaism and Sikhism. In addition to this detailed study some further study of one or more of these options should be undertaken, including Christianity if this is not the religion chosen for detailed study. All secondary school pupils should also study one, at least, of the non-religious stances for living.

A popular and influential syllabus during the 1980s is the one produced by Hampshire in 1978 and subsequently adopted by many other local education authorities, including Gloucestershire. According to this syllabus,

> The principal aim of religious education in schools within the public sector is to enable pupils to understand the nature of religious beliefs and practices and the importance and influence of these in the lives of believers.

While the Hampshire syllabus agrees that religious education will be based largely on the study of Christianity, as the "religious faith which has most influenced our culture", it also emphasises that,

> It is no part of the responsibility of a county school to promote any particular religious stand-point, neither could an exclusively Christian content do justice to the nature of the subject.
>
> Religious education is concerned with making pupils aware of experiences and concepts basic to all religions. It is also concerned with investigating the visible features of particular religious and non-religious belief systems. But it must go deeper, evoking sympathetic appreciation of the meanings and values enshrined within such systems; and, with older pupils, critically examining them.

The new syllabuses produced by the Inner London Education Authority in 1984 and by Manchester in 1985 repeat Hampshire's phrase that "it is not part of the responsibility of the county school to promote any particular religious stand-point". According to the London syllabus,

The aim is to help young people to achieve a knowledge and understanding of religious insights, beliefs and practices, so that they are able to continue in, or come to, their own beliefs and respect the right of other people to hold beliefs different from their own.

According to the Manchester syllabus,

The principal aim of religious education in county and voluntary controlled schools is to enable pupils to reflect upon and respond to the religious and spiritual beliefs, practices, insights and experiences that are expressed in human-kind's search for meaning in life.

If the new agreed syllabuses are right in drawing a firm distinction between religious education in secular schools and Christian nurture in churches, they seriously challenge the assumption underlying the 1944 Education Act that religious instruction in the school can help to promote the Christian formation of young people. While religious education remains on the school timetable, it is no longer doing what the churches thought it would do in 1944. Moreover, if religious education is to be justified on purely educational criteria, the role of the churches in shaping agreed syllabuses becomes much less clear than it seemed in 1944.

School worship

At the time of the 1944 Education Act, the churches assumed that it was appropriate to make worship obligatory in all state maintained schools. Contemporary literature on school worship discussed the school as a worshipping community of committed Christians and underlined the close relationship between school and church. For example, the Cambridge Syllabus (1949) offers the exhortation:

The teacher must strive by his own demeanour, as in the presence of God, to create a sense of worship and enable the children to feel that he is really praying the prayers which he speaks.

C.L. Berry's book, *The Teacher's Handbook* (1946), explains:

Religious worship, in secondary schools, as everywhere else, must be nothing less than the rendering unto Almighty God of the honour, veneration and – most perfect of all worship – the adoration which is due to Him as Creator and Redeemer, and the love which is due to Him as Himself Eternal love.

By the end of the 1960s, however, clear warning notes were being sounded about school worship. The Plowden Report, *Children and their Primary Schools* (1967), continues to affirm that the act of worship offers children an opportunity to find "a religious expression of their life in school". At the same time, the report recognises that,

> In a school of mixed religious or non-religious backgrounds, it is essential that the assembly should be conducted in such a way that as large a part of the school community as possible, both teachers and children, can take part in it without offence being given to anyone's conscientious scruples.

The most sustained criticism of school worship is expressed by John Hull's book, *School Worship: an obituary* (1975), which concludes that in the county school,

> Real tension has developed between the aims of education and the nature of worship, to such a degree that compulsory worship in daily assembly stands out as an anachronism, inadequate as worship and ill-related to the needs and concerns of the school and the society in which it is situated.

For Hull, this conclusion emerges not from antagonism to the Christian faith, but rather from commitment to it.

The main argument in Hull's case is not dissimilar from that advanced by Paul Hirst and discussed above. Hull argues that in today's society the concept of education needs to be clearly distinguished from related concepts, like training, instruction, indoctrination, evangelisation, nurture and catechesis. Education, Hull argues, is essentially a critical process:

> Education into a subject implies knowledge of the principles of knowledge (knowing why what is alleged to be known is known, and knowing how to know more).

Worship, on the other hand, Hull argues, logically entails certain beliefs and the acceptance of those beliefs as true. As processes worship and education are, therefore, fundamentally different and logically incompatible:

> Nurture prepares for belief, evangelisation summons belief, instruction implies belief, catechesis strengthens belief and worship assumes belief. But education scrutinises belief. It is clear, then, that worship and education cannot take place concurrently.

33

B

Alongside this main argument, Hull develops five subsidiary arguments. First, he analyses the implications for school worship of the recent changes in religious education, discussed in the previous section. While the 1944 Education Act assumed that school worship and religious education went hand in hand, the changing face of religious education has caused a sharp separation between the two activities. Worship entails the acceptance of beliefs, while the new religious education is not concerned with what the pupils believe to be true but with their understanding of the grounds for belief and disbelief. Thus, school worship and religious education have not only drifted apart, they have become incompatible.

Second, Hull reviews the way in which schools have tried to respond to changes in educational theory and in religious education by secularising school worship. In this case worship is removed from its theological beliefs and we are left with the psychological affinities, such as "reverence, trustfulness, joy or a meditative attitude towards life". Hull argues that this approach only serves to "disguise the nature of the changes that are taking place" and in fact concedes the demise of real worship within the school.

Third, Hull speculates about the implications of trends in the psychology of religious development for school worship. He argues that if worship logically entails certain beliefs, it is important for those who are involved in worship to be able to grasp and understand these underlying beliefs. Thus, "if children cannot grasp the underlying doctrine" it is inappropriate for that doctrine to be affirmed in worship.

Fourth, Hull argues that cultural and religious pluralism in county schools places the whole question of school worship in a sharper focus. The application of the withdrawal clauses to accommodate those of other faiths is "odious and divisive". The idea of holding separate assemblies for different faith groups within the one school is "contrary to the role of assembly and indeed of the county school itself as a cohesive agent in a mixed society". The solution of devising eclectic acts of worship drawing on a range of religious traditions contradicts the idea of real worship "which presupposes loyalty".

Fifth, Hull argues that trends in secularisation have now thoroughly undermined any assumption that schools can claim to be Christian communities. Real school worship, he argues, only makes sense on the assumption that schools remain faith communities.

If Hull's arguments about the incompatibility of school worship and the county school are accepted, they seriously challenge the assumption underlying the 1944 Education Act that the churches have a right to demand a daily act of worship in all state maintained schools.

Church schools

At the time of the 1944 Education Act, some churches assumed that it was appropriate to continue to promote church schools as part of the state maintained system. The two denominations to take advantage of this provision are the Church of England and the Catholic church.

The Church of England understood these provisions as an opportunity to retain as much as possible of its historic stake in education. Table 3.1 shows that the Church of England's investment in schools is mainly in the primary sector. As the school population rose between 1949 and 1974 the proportion of state maintained primary places provided by Anglican schools in England and Wales fell steadily from 22.5% to 16.3%. Since 1974, in a situation of falling primary rolls, the Anglican church's contribution gradually crept up again to 16.9%. Looked at from another perspective, in 1953 35.3% of primary schools belonged to the Church of England or the Church of Wales. By 1963 the proportion had fallen to 31.1% and by 1973 to 25.6%. In other words, during twenty years, the number of Anglican primary schools in England and Wales had been reduced from 8,251 to 5,860.

According to figures provided by the Department of Education and Science and the Welsh Office, at January 1985, the Anglican church had 5,095 primary schools and 88 middle schools deemed primary, providing 16.9% of the state maintained primary places in England and Wales. At the same time, the Anglican church had 160 secondary schools and 84 middle schools deemed secondary, providing 4.1% of the state maintained secondary places in England and Wales.

The Catholic church understood the provisions of the 1944 Education Act as an opportunity to expand its school places. In particular the Catholic church decided to develop a network of church secondary schools to match its provision of primary places. Overall, the proportion of state maintained school places in Catholic schools grew from 7% in 1947 to 9.4% in 1969. Catholic schools were providing 350,495 places in 1947, 496,528 places in 1957, 679,377 places in 1967 and reached their peak with 798,960 places in 1976.

According to figures provided by the Department of Education and Science and the Welsh Office, at January 1985, the Catholic church had 1,960 primary schools and 17 middle schools deemed primary, providing 9.3% of the state maintained primary places in England and Wales. At the same time, the Catholic church had 438 secondary schools and 41 middle schools deemed secondary, providing 8.8% of the state maintained secondary places in England and Wales.

The philosophies underlying the involvement of the Church of

England and the Catholic church in church schools are quite different. These different philosophies clearly reflect the different historical roots from which the two systems have developed.

A key statement on the Anglican philosophy of church schools is the *Durham Report* (1970). This report sharpens the distinction between the Church of England's *domestic* and *general* functions in education. The domestic function characterises the inward-looking concern to "equip the children of the church to take their place in the Christian community". The general function characterises the outward-looking concern "to serve the nation through its children". The *Durham Report* recognises that historically the two roles were "indistinguishable, for nation and church were, theoretically, one, and the domestic task was seen as including the general".

The *Durham Report* goes on to recognise that "nowadays no one would pretend to claim that nation and church are coextensive" and recommends that,

> The church should for the present see its continued involvement in the dual system principally as a way of expressing its concern for the general education of all children and young people rather than as a means for giving 'denominational instruction'.

The report underlines this point again by recommending that "religious education, even in a church aided school, should not be seen in domestic terms".

This emphasis on the church's general function in education has helped to consolidate the notion of the Church of England working in close partnership with the state. The Green Paper, *A Future in Partnership* (1984), argues that the idea of *partnership* should be stressed in preference to the *dual system* and that the *voluntary* aspects of church schools should be stressed in preference to *denominationalism*. The emphasis of this paper is on arguing for a balance of power in state maintained education over an increasing trend towards educational dominance by central government. The church is seen as one component, alongside other political, community, parental and professional bodies, in an educational partnership which offsets the claims of central government in determining educational policy and practice. It is argued that the maintenance of church schools gives the church an institutional credibility in this context. Today the Church of England sees its rationale for involvement in education to be in terms of balance, partnership and voluntarism, rather than in terms of denominationalism, religious distinctiveness or the dual system.

In the Church of England, documents like the *Durham Report* and *A Future in Partnership* are able to make recommendations, but not to impose policy. The individual dioceses are also able to make recommendations, but not to impose policy. In practice, the governors of each church school have considerable freedom to shape the school's identity. This means that the balance between the general and the domestic aims in education varies from diocese to diocese and from school to school. Some Church of England aided schools operate admissions policies on denominational criteria; some Church of England aided and controlled schools operate as neighbourhood schools while continuing to maintain varying degrees of denominational emphasis; other Church of England aided and controlled schools operate as neighbourhood schools which are very difficult to distinguish from county schools.

In the Catholic church, the classic formula for church schools has been 'Every Catholic child from a Catholic home to be taught by Catholic teachers in a Catholic school'. Insistence on this basic view by religious leaders is now couched in far less assertive terms than earlier this century. In 1929 Pope Pius IX's encyclical letter 'Divini Illius Magistri' confirmed:

> The prescriptions of canon law which forbid Catholic children on any pretext whatsoever to attend . . . schools open indiscriminately to Catholics and non-Catholics alike.

By way of contrast, the 'Declaration on Christian Education' issued from the second Vatican Council (Abbott, 1966) reminded parents of,

> their duty to entrust their children to Catholic schools, when and where this is possible, to support such schools to the extent of their ability, and to work along with them for the welfare of their children.

In the document *The Catholic School* (1977), the Sacred Congregation for Catholic Education replaces the note of command with that of reasoned argument in favour of the Catholic school.

The report to the Bishops of England and Wales, *Signposts and Homecomings* (1981), recognises that Catholic education should be confined neither to the years of compulsory schooling nor to the Catholic school. At the same time, the report reaffirms the identity of the Catholic school as "a believing and integrated Christian community". It argues that,

> Within a Catholic school the ultimate distinctive element is that its life is based on the vision of Christ in which all learning, growing, service, freedom and

relationships are seen as part of a growth in the knowledge, love and experience of God. In other words there is a deliberate hope that the experience of belonging to this school will encourage personal commitment to Jesus Christ.

Today the church school system is undergoing increasing scrutiny and criticism not only from secular bodies but from within the churches themselves. To the objections raised by the British Humanist Association, the Socialist Education Association, the Runnymede Trust and the Swann Report must be added the voices of the Catholic Commission for Racial Justice, Christians Against Racism and Fascism, and the Church of England's Partners in Mission Consultation.

The British Humanist Association has campaigned against church schools within the state maintained system for a number of years. Their pamphlet, *Religion in Schools* (1967), argues strongly that the dual system is an anachronism and accuses the church of abusing its privileged position by indoctrination. The British Humanist Association argues that the state should not be involved in financing and recognising the religious teaching of individual churches or religious bodies. They urge that religion should be left to the home and to the church, without either support or interference from the state, and that church aided schools should be "taken over as county schools or left to the church to finance without state aid".

Church schools come under close scrutiny from the Socialist Education Association in their discussion document, *The Dual System of Voluntary and County Schools* (1981). An appendix marshalling the case against church schools focuses on two primary objections. The first objection concerns the problem of religious privilege in a pluralist society. This objection acknowledges that, if certain churches are permitted to operate voluntary schools, every sect and faith should be allowed the same privilege. It is argued that this would lead to "divisive sectarianism and some of the difficulties already evident in a place like Northern Ireland". The second objection concerns the political problem of privilege itself within a socialist educational system. This objection argues that "the continuing existence of the segregated voluntary school sector will frustrate the achievement of the truly comprehensive system".

The Socialist Education Association's more recent document, *All Faiths in All Schools* (1986), reports that the majority of those who sent comments on the original document supported the view expressed in this appendix. The new report proposes:

> The eventual establishment of a new unified system of maintained schools, in which voluntary schools – without sacrificing their ethos and individual

approach – could gradually develop the capacity to educate a greater diversity of intake from their own local communities, and where county schools – without sacrificing their unifying secular approach – could gradually develop the capacity to meet more widely the religious and cultural needs of their intakes.

Another set of questions about church schools comes from the direction of racial discrimination. Ann Dummett and Julia McNeal's study, *Race and Church Schools* (1981), sponsored by the Runnymede Trust, argues that the Christian reference of church schools can hamper the development of multi-racial institutions in areas where "the black community was not Christian". Similarly, Christians Against Racism and Fascism state that "in some areas church schools have become white enclaves using religion as a means of discrimination".

The Catholic report, *Learning from Diversity* (1984), takes the discussion of the problem of church schools in a multi-racial, multi-cultural society one stage further.

Many Catholic schools have a pupil population which is predominantly white. As a result many Catholic children have an educational experience which is, in this respect, narrow. They do not have the opportunity to mix with black children nor do they have the opportunity to mix with children of other Christian denominations or of other faiths. Moreover the predominantly white Catholic school in a racially mixed area can be seen as a 'white island' and a divisive anomaly in an area which faces the difficult task of struggling to become a cohesive multiracial and multicultural community.

The Anglican report, *Schools and Multi-Cultural Education* (1984), emphasises that church schools can also function as important centres of reconciliation among peoples of different races and creeds.

The church school question is a central issue in the Swann Report, *Education for All* (1985). After reviewing the arguments for and against voluntary schools for other ethnic and religious groups, the majority voice of the committee stresses "misgivings about the implications and consequences of 'separate' provision of any kind". Having come to this view, the majority voice of the committee faces the consequence that:

our conclusions about the desirability of denominational voluntary aided schools for Muslims or other groups, by extension seriously call into question the long established dual system of educational provision in this country and particularly the role of the churches in the provision of education.

Six members of the committee dissented from this conclusion and formulated a different minority recommendation, supporting the provisions of the 1944 Education Act concerning voluntary schools and wishing to enable other ethnic and religious groups to benefit from these provisions.

> We believe that it is unjust at the present time not to recommend that positive assistance should be given to ethnic minority communities who wish to establish voluntary aided schools in accordance with the 1944 Education Act.

In an oral statement to the House of Commons on the afternoon of 14 March 1985, following the publication of the Swann Report, Sir Keith Joseph, Secretary of State for Education, gave an immediate assurance that the government does not "wish in any way to call in question the present dual system of county and voluntary schools". The clear division of opinion within the committee of inquiry, together with the Education Secretary's immediate response, adds a new sharpness and immediacy to the debate about the future of church schools within a multi-cultural society.

The report of the Church of England's Partners in Mission Consultation, *To a Rebellious House* (1981), questions church schools from a different basis. This report argues that the church has put too much of its resources into church schools during the past hundred years without achieving sufficient benefit in terms of mission and nurture. The report recommends that the churches should attempt to release assets currently tied up in church schools and redirect them in other educational areas.

If current criticisms of church schools carry weight, cumulatively they offer a serious challenge to the assumption underlying the 1944 Education Act that the churches have a right to promote voluntary schools within the state maintained system of education.

4 RESEARCH DESIGN

Aims

The historical review in chapter two has emphasised how the original initiative in creating the present educational system came from the churches, not from the secular authorities. This historical legacy played a crucial role in shaping the 1944 Education Act, according to which the churches continued to have a significant influence in shaping the system of state maintained education. The 1944 Education Act not only safeguarded the place of church schools, but encouraged the churches to believe that county schools were also closely involved in Christian education. The theoretical review in chapter three has emphasised how considerable changes have taken place, since the 1944 Education Act, in educational thinking on the three key religious provisions of the act, namely religious education, school worship and church schools. New educational thinking has changed the character of religious education, challenged the place of school worship and questioned the appropriateness of church schools.

Change in educational theory, however, is not the same thing as change in educational practice. It is one thing to know what is being said about the changing place of religion in education, it is another matter to discover what is happening in practice. The aim of the present research project is to describe what is happening in practice.

Against the historical and theoretical background discussed in chapters two and three, the project developed two main thrusts. One thrust wanted to look broadly at the religious provision throughout the state maintained sector. The other thrust wanted to look specifically at the character and distinctiveness of church schools. In order to provide a complete picture, both thrusts needed to involve two separate, but interrelated studies. One study involves a survey of headteachers and the other a survey of pupils.

The aim of the headteachers' survey was to collect factual information regarding the religious provision and practice of state maintained primary schools. Analysis of this factual information describes the current situation throughout county and voluntary schools and examines the manner and extent to which church schools may be distinctive in their contribution.

The aim of the pupils' survey was to look at the attitudes of fourth year junior pupils, those who have reached the last year of primary education before moving on to secondary school. The three attitudinal areas of particular concern to the project are the pupils' attitudes towards religious education, assemblies and Christianity. In order to make sense of these three attitudinal areas, the project placed them within the wider context of the child's attitudes towards school and church, together with the religious influence of the child's home. Analysis of this attitudinal information describes pupil responses throughout county and voluntary schools and examines the extent to which attendance at church schools may contribute towards the development of the child's attitudes in these areas.

The research was sponsored by the diocese of Gloucester, the Gloucestershire local education authority and the Culham College Institute, in association with the Clifton Catholic Diocesan Schools Commission. The collaborative nature of the project brought many strengths. The expertise of diocesan and local education authority staff helped to assure that the questions focused by the survey were pertinently and appropriately framed. The backing of the local education authority and the Anglican and Catholic dioceses helped to assure that the project was taken seriously throughout county, Church of England and Catholic schools. The involvement of the Culham College Institute helped to establish the research credibility of the project and made it clear to the schools that personal data would be handled with confidentiality and anonymity well outside the spheres of shire hall and diocesan offices.

Methods

The three main research methods available for collecting information from headteachers and pupils are interviews, 'open-ended' questionnaires and 'pre-coded' questionnaires. The sponsoring group considered all three methods and favoured the development of pre-coded questionnaires.

The development of pre-coded questionnaires means that every question is carefully thought out and tested beforehand, so that the respondent is given a definite range of answers from which to choose. Since the researcher can derive only a limited amount of information from the answer to each question, the skill in designing this type of questionnaire lies in the ability to devise a wide range of interrelated questions. A great deal of exact information can then be constructed from a careful analysis not only of the answers to individual questions, but of the pattern that emerges from the answers to a range of questions.

Three particular advantages of the pre-coded questionnaire over the interview helped to confirm this decision. First, there is the issue of *objectivity*. Carefully designed pre-coded questionnaires can often provide a more objective description than open-ended questionnaires or interviews. Second, there is the issue of *measurement*. We wanted to be able to measure accurately the differences in responses from different types of school. The pre-coded questionnaire is uniquely powerful in this kind of context, since it does not rely upon the interpretations of an interviewer. Third, there is the issue of *cost*. In light of the limited financial resources available to the project, we had to choose between funding a small number of interviews or a much larger number of questionnaires.

At the same time, the sponsoring group recognised that there are snags with pre-coded questionnaires. Even when the questionnaire has been well designed to achieve its goals, there can be considerable resistance from some respondents. Some people feel that questionnaires are too impersonal; others feel that questionnaires fail to give them scope to express the true range of their feelings. The presentation of the questionnaire needs to take these issues into account.

The sponsoring group was sure that, if headteachers were to be asked both to complete a questionnaire themselves and to involve their fourth year junior pupils in completing questionnaires, they should also be assured that the results of the research would become quickly available to them. As part of the design of the project, the sponsoring group committed itself to making available an interim report to the schools. This interim report was distributed by the local education authority to all the primary schools in the authority within a year of the distribution of the first questionnaires.

Gloucestershire

A major strength of focusing research of this nature on one local education authority is that the research can be undertaken thoroughly and that the researcher can personally get to know the area in considerable depth. The problem is to gauge how that particular local education authority fits into the broader picture of state maintained schools within England as a whole. In other words, how does the provision of state maintained primary schools within Gloucestershire compare with other shire counties?

The 39 local education authorities regarded by the Department of Education and Science as the English shire counties, as opposed to metropolitan counties, vary greatly in size, from the Isle of Wight with 47 primary schools to Lancashire with 640. Full details of these local education authorities are presented in tables 4.1 and 4.2. Gloucestershire is one of the smaller authorities, with 274 primary schools providing 40,190 primary school places, according to the Department of Education and Science's statistics for January 1984.

The ratio of county schools to voluntary schools also varies considerably from one local education authority to another. Throughout the shire county authorities, 62.4% of the state maintained primary schools, including middle deemed primary, are county schools. The proportion of county schools varies from 41% in Lancashire to 78% in Nottinghamshire. In Gloucestershire 54% of the state maintained primary schools are county schools.

Throughout the shire county authorities, the Catholic stake accounts / for 6.9% of the state maintained primary schools. The proportion of Catholic schools varies from 22% in Lancashire to 1% in Cambridgeshire and Norfolk. In Gloucestershire 3% of the state maintained primary schools are Catholic schools, and all of these have voluntary aided status.

At the time of the 1944 Education Act different Anglican dioceses adopted different positions on the debate between aided and controlled status. In a few areas, like Lancashire, the balance went heavily in favour of aided status; in more areas, like Leicestershire and Suffolk, the balance went heavily in favour of controlled status. Throughout the shire county authorities, Church of England controlled schools account for 19.5% of the state maintained primary schools and Church of England aided schools account for 10.6%. In Gloucestershire there are significant numbers of both Church of England controlled and Church of England aided schools: Church of England controlled schools account for 27% of the state maintained primary schools, while Church of England aided schools account for 16%.

Throughout the shire county authorities there are just 78 other voluntary schools which are neither Church of England nor Catholic, accounting for 0.6% of the state maintained primary schools. In Gloucestershire there is one voluntary controlled school in this category. This school was included in the survey, but not in the analysis reported in this book.

Gloucestershire, thus, appears to be an appropriate county in which to base this kind of research, since there are sufficient Church of England aided and Church of England controlled schools to make a sensible comparison between Church of England aided, Church of England controlled and county schools. The weakness in using Gloucestershire for such a study is that the number of Catholic schools is small. Nevertheless, it should be possible, on the basis of the present study, to make inferences about what is likely to be the situation in other shire counties. The next step in building up a detailed account of the place of religious education, assemblies and church schools in England during the 1980s is for replication studies, conducted in other local education authorities, to demonstrate objectively the extent to which the situation reported in Gloucestershire can be said to be representative of a wider picture.

Headteachers' questionnaire

The general aim of the headteachers' survey was to discover what is currently happening in the religious life and curriculum of primary schools. The information needed to be organised in such a way that it could serve two purposes: to *describe* current practice in detail and to *compare* different types of schools and different situations. From this general aim, seven main areas were defined for the focus of the study: religious education, assemblies, worship, church contact, resources, staff, and the headteachers' personal religious commitment.

Religious education Do church schools allocate more time to religious education than county schools? How closely do the different types of schools follow the county agreed syllabus or the appropriate denominational syllabus? How many schools have drawn up a detailed scheme of work for religious education? What kind of activities do fourth year junior pupils engage in during religious education and what resources are available to them? What part does the bible play in religious education? What versions of the bible are available in schools?

Assemblies How many schools are observing the letter of the law by beginning every school day 'with collective worship on the part of all pupils in attendance'? Are church schools more or less law-abiding than county schools? If schools are not holding a daily assembly for the whole school, has the pattern been replaced with other forms of assembly or are assemblies disappearing from school life? How much time is spent on school assemblies? Who is generally responsible for leading assemblies? How often do parents exercise the right to withdraw their children from assemblies and on what grounds?

Worship How explicitly Christian are assemblies? What hymn books are used in schools and what is the relationship between hymns sung in assemblies and in local churches? How frequently are prayers used in assemblies, and how often are pupils asked to say the Lord's Prayer? How often is the bible used and are psalms and canticles used? How closely do assemblies follow the pattern of the church's year, and is the situation different in church and county schools? What kind of stories are used in assemblies? What use is made of silence, drama, music or audio-visual resources? How important are radio broadcasts in determining the shape and content of school assemblies?

Church contact Do church schools have more contact with churches and clergy than county schools? How many schools arrange a school service in the local church? How many schools ever involve their pupils in a Sunday or a weekday church service? How often do the clergy visit primary schools, take assemblies or contribute to religious education? Do clergy of different denominations relate to schools differently? What contact do leaders of other world faiths have with state maintained primary schools?

Resources How much use do schools make of religious education resource centres? Are church schools more likely to use resource centres than county schools? How many headteachers feel that their schools lack certain resources, materials or help which would improve religious education or assemblies and what are their priorities for additional resources in these areas?

Staff How many schools have designated a 'consultant' for religious education, and what status does this member of staff have within the school? What proportion of the schools can draw on staff who studied religious education as a main course in their initial teacher training or as a subsidiary course? What kind of in-service training opportunities have been taken up in the area of religious education, and are teachers in church schools any more likely to attend in-service training courses in religious education than teachers in county schools?

Headteachers The focus moves from purely professional issues to more personal matters. Do younger headteachers promote a different religious perspective from older headteachers? Do church-going headteachers develop different religious emphases in their schools from non-churchgoing headteachers? Are the headteachers of church schools more likely to be practising church-goers than the headteachers of county schools?

Pupils' questionnaire

The general aim of the pupils' survey was to discover the attitudes of fourth year junior pupils. Again, the information needed to be organised in such a way that it could serve two purposes: to *describe* the attitudes held by this age group in detail and to *compare* the attitudes of different groups of pupils. Do boys and girls hold similar or different attitudes? How important is the home in shaping these attitudes? Does the school have an impact on shaping attitudes? Does it make a difference to the child's attitude whether he or she attends a church school or a county school?

The main focus of the pupils' questionnaire was on attitudes towards three areas: Christianity, religious education and assemblies. In order to make sense of these three attitudinal areas, the questionnaire also looked at the pupil's attitude towards school, church and some other areas of the curriculum.

The measurement of attitudes by means of questionnaires has a long history in social psychology. In this context, attitudes are regarded as relatively enduring, deep-seated evaluative predispositions to a positive or a negative response of an affective nature. Because attitudes are deep-seated, they are observable only through the surface behaviour which they help to characterise. The techniques of attitude scaling are designed to infer the underlying attitude from the way in which a range of observable behaviours constellate.

Different techniques of attitude scaling are associated with the names of Thurstone (1928), Likert (1932), Guttman (1944), Edwards (1957) and Osgood (1957). In earlier research projects I tested out these different techniques systematically on children between the ages of eight and sixteen and demonstrated that the techniques proposed by Likert and Osgood are the most appropriate for use among pupils of the junior age range. The present project uses a Likert scale to measure the pupils' attitudes towards Christianity and a set of Osgood semantic differential scales to measure the pupils' attitudes towards school, church and some other areas of the curriculum.

The basic idea of the Likert scaling technique is to identify empirically a set of short direct and unambiguous sentences which are indicative of the attitudinal area under review. These sentences should be evaluative in nature. The respondents are then asked to rate their level of agreement or disagreement with the individual sentences on a five-point scale, ranging from 'agree strongly', through 'agree', 'not certain' and 'disagree' to 'disagree strongly'.

In one of my earlier projects I set out to develop a Likert scale to measure the attitude of junior school pupils towards Christianity. I began by collecting 110 attitude statements about God, Jesus, the bible, prayer, church and school religion, culled mainly from children's conversations and writing. I then employed the Likert techniques of item discrimination in order to select from this bundle of statements the 24 items which cohered most satisfactorily into a reliable and valid scale (see Francis, 1976, 1978). The items selected to form this scale are presented in table 12.1. During the past decade a considerable literature has grown up using this scale in a range of different contexts, which means that the present study is able to benefit from the accumulation of previous experience.

The basic idea of the Osgood semantic differential technique, when used in attitude measurement, is to identify empirically a set of evaluative adjectives, arranged in pairs of opposites. The respondents are asked to evaluate key concepts on the adjectival grids. One of the great strengths of this technique is that the same pairs of adjectives can be used to evaluate a series of different key concepts. In this way, it is possible to compare in some detail attitudes towards different areas or issues.

In the present study, seven pairs of adjectives were chosen and a seven point semantic differential space established between the opposite poles. Once again, the precise pairs of adjectives were chosen on the basis of experience gained from previous studies. These adjectives are pleasant/unpleasant, good/bad, interesting/boring, nice/nasty, happy/sad, important/unimportant, friendly/unfriendly. Having established the basic grid of adjectives, the pupils were presented with it eight times in order to rate their attitudes towards English lessons, maths lessons, school, religious education lessons, singing or music lessons, church or other place of worship, school assemblies, physical education or games lessons. Eight presentations of the same grid are sufficient to enable us to compare the pupils' attitudes towards a range of issues, without becoming too tedious for them to complete.

Finally, to discover information about the pupils' background, multiple choice questions were developed to record sex, church attendance, attendance at Sunday school or church young people's groups, private prayer, mother's church attendance, father's church attendance and denomination. We also asked the pupils to state briefly the nature of father's job and mother's job, so that it would be possible to make some classification into different social groups.

Response

The headteachers' questionnaires were delivered to all the 274 state maintained primary schools in the Gloucestershire local education authority, accompanied by a personal letter and a pre-paid reply envelope. The local education authority religious education adviser wrote to county schools and the diocesan director of education wrote to Church of England aided and controlled schools. In the case of Catholic schools the letter came from the local education authority religious education adviser, but stressed that "the Clifton Catholic Diocesan Schools Commission has readily agreed to permit us to ask you for your assistance".

The project met with a great deal of goodwill and co-operation. The headteachers of all the Catholic and all the Church of England aided schools completed and returned their questionnaires. Just four headteachers from county schools and five headteachers from Church of England controlled schools declined to take part in this stage of the project. Overall, this gives a most impressive response rate of 96%.

The back page of the headteachers' questionnaire was left blank for the headteachers to add further comments. These comments provide important insights into the headteachers' personal reactions to such a detailed questionnaire on the religious provision of their schools. The following quotations give some indication of what the headteachers were saying about the exercise.

As a teaching head I feel the constant problem with any curriculum development is that the demands from outside school relating to administration are swamping fresh approaches. I find it tragic that there is now less and less time for undivided attention to teaching. Children's attitudes to life and people reflect this problem because they so often take second place to paper work. Questionnaire completed at midnight!!

We have given this questionnaire tremendous thought, had lots of fun in the discussion and found a few answers.

I was pleased that the opportunity was provided to answer questions in this detail. I found the questionnaire very useful as a means of self-evaluation.

When the headteachers' survey had been completed, the questionnaires for the fourth year junior pupils were delivered to all the 233 state maintained primary and junior schools within the county. Along with another covering letter, emphasising the intention of the survey of pupil attitudes, detailed instructions were sent for the administration of these questionnaires.

In this stage of the project, 82.4% of the schools invited to participate did so (table 4.3). Again this is a highly satisfactory response rate. The best response came from the county sector, where 86.5% of the schools participated; 82.9% of the Church of England aided schools and 78.1% of the Church of England controlled schools participated.

A range of reasons were given by the headteachers who did not participate in this part of the project. In the case of two small village schools, the headteachers reported that the school only contained one fourth year junior pupil and that they considered it unfair to ask just one child to complete the questionnaire. The headteachers of two urban schools said that the Christian emphasis of the questionnaire was inappropriate for their schools which had some Muslim pupils. Some headteachers considered the questionnaire to be too personal or too subjective. Some considered the questionnaire too difficult for their pupils.

The disappointing aspect of the project was the fact that only five of the eight Catholic schools permitted their pupils to take part. A month or so after the pupil questionnaires had been sent out to the schools, the honorary secretary of the Clifton Catholic Diocesan Schools Commission decided that the questionnaire was "not suitable for use in our schools" and wrote to the headteachers of the Catholic schools suggesting that they should not participate. By the time they received his letter, five of the Catholic schools had already returned their questionnaires; the other three Catholic schools did not participate in this stage of the project.

It has to be recognised that research into pupil attitudes is a controversial activity. The fact that four out of every five headteachers agreed to take part in the exercise is convincing evidence that the project was well conceived and pitched at a level appropriate for the age range of pupils concerned.

It is on the basis of the 224 questionnaires returned by the headteachers of county, Church of England controlled, Church of England aided and Catholic schools, and the 4,948 questionnaires returned by the fourth year junior pupils that the following chapters are written.

5 COUNTY SCHOOLS

Schools

County schools make the largest numerical contribution to the state maintained system of education in Gloucestershire, representing 54% of the primary schools and 62% of the primary places. County schools are generally larger than voluntary schools. The average number of pupils in the county schools is 169, compared with 119 in the voluntary schools.

Within this average, the size of the county schools varies greatly. The smallest county school has just 22 pupils on roll, while the largest has 393. Three out of every seven county schools (43%) have over 200 pupils. Only 19% of the county schools have less than 60 pupils; fewer than 4% have 30 or less. The smallest county school is a two-teacher school; the largest is a fourteen-teacher school.

Because the period for the great initiative in founding voluntary schools goes back to the middle of the nineteenth century, it is in the more recently established areas that county schools are most likely to be found. Thus, 73% of the schools serving suburban areas are county schools and so are 56% of the schools serving towns. On the other hand, only 32% of the village schools are county schools. Five of the six schools in the sample which serve educational priority areas are county schools.

The majority of the state maintained schools in Gloucestershire which cater for the primary age range combine both infant and junior provision, for five to eleven year olds: 184 of the 224 schools in the present sample are all-through primary schools. Of the 40 junior schools catering for the eight to eleven year olds, 33 are county schools.

Like many of the rural shire counties, Gloucestershire does not have much experience of catering for pupils from religious backgrounds other than Christian. Thus, 85% of the county schools say that less than 1% of their pupils come from non-Christian religious traditions; 11% of the county schools report that between 1% and 5% of their pupils belong to other world faiths, while just 3% of the county schools report that between 6% and 10% of their pupils come into this category. Only one county school reports more than 30% of its pupils belonging to other major world faiths.

In summary, county schools provide the major proportion of primary school places in Gloucestershire; only a small proportion of these places are occupied by pupils belonging to non-Christian religious traditions.

Headteachers

While there are considerably more women employed as primary teachers than men, men are much more likely to be appointed to headships. In the present sample there are three male headteachers for every female headteacher. The ratio between male and female headteachers is the same throughout the four different types of school, county, Church of England aided, Church of England controlled and Roman Catholic.

Headteachers tend to be men and women in their forties or fifties: in the present sample of county schools 40% of the headteachers are in their forties and another 37% are in their fifties. This leaves 16% of the county schools with headteachers in their thirties and the remaining 7% with headteachers in their sixties. The vast majority of headteachers working in county schools (81%) do not live within the area served by their schools. They commute to their schools from homes in other neighbourhoods.

Generally, headteachers of county schools tend to be quite clear about their preference for working in the county sector, rather than in the voluntary sector. Two-thirds (67%) of the county school headteachers say that, given the choice and all things being equal, they actually prefer working in a county school. Of the remaining third, 21% say that they have no real preference between the county and voluntary sectors. This leaves just 8% who would prefer to be in a Church of England aided school, 3% who would prefer to be in a Church of England controlled school and 1% who would prefer to work in the independent sector. No headteacher of a county school would prefer to be in a Catholic school.

Over four-fifths of the headteachers of county schools claim affiliation to one of the Christian denominations: 59% are members of the Church of England, 5% are Methodist, 9% are Baptists, 3% are members of the United Reformed Church, 3% are Catholics and a further 4% belong to other Christian groups. No headteacher of a county school calls himself or herself an atheist; 6% call themselves agnostics and 12% call themselves humanists. No headteacher of a county school is a member of another world faith.

The majority of headteachers of county schools also attend church, at least occasionally: only 13% had not attended a church service within the past year. Two in every five (42%) attend church most weeks and a further 14% attend regularly at least once a month. According to Peter

Brierley's census of church attendance conducted in 1979, *Prospect for the Eighties*, Gloucestershire emerges as one of the more religious counties in England; only Cheshire, Cumbria, East Sussex, Lancashire, Merseyside and Somerset report a higher church attendance. However, according to this survey, even in Gloucestershire only 13% of the adult population are likely to attend church on Sunday. This indicates the extent to which headteachers of county schools are considerably more committed in their religious practice than the rest of the adult population.

Perhaps partly as a consequence of their own Christian commitment, the majority of headteachers in county schools feel that religious education and assemblies should continue to play a part in school life. If the requirements of the law were to be relaxed in these areas, only one headteacher of a county school in the sample would wish to give up either assemblies or religious education.

In summary, headteachers of county schools are much more committed to church membership and church attendance than the population at large. They are also committed to maintaining religious education and assemblies in county schools.

Staff

While the survey did not include a separate questionnaire for every member of staff, it did request headteachers to collate information about the range of professional competence in religious education in the school as a whole. This means that, while it is not possible to discuss the religious affiliation and practice represented throughout the staffrooms of these schools, it is possible to discuss the professional interest and involvement in religious education as a school subject.

Of the 655 full-time staff in county schools in the survey, 39 (6%) studied religious education as a main course during initial training, while a further 75 (11%) included religious education as a subsidiary subject in their initial training. Another 14 (2%) had some other recognised qualification in religious education. Looked at from another perspective, 58% of the county schools have at last one member of staff who had undertaken some formal training to teach religious education.

To have studied religious education as part of initial training does not necessarily imply recent or up-to-date training. The survey goes on, therefore, to examine staff experience of in-service training during the past three years. In this space of time one of the 655 teachers in county schools had undertaken a short course in religious education equivalent to one or two weeks full-time study; none had undertaken a more substantial in-service programme in religious education. On the other hand, teachers from just over half of the county schools (51%) had attended a day course or series of meetings concerned with religious education during the past three years. This is a useful index of the willingness of county schools, some of which are quite small, to keep in touch with trends in religious education.

The strategy of designating a member of staff as 'consultant' for religious education helps to assure that someone has a recognised responsibility for developing and promoting the subject throughout the school. In the case of the county schools, 38% have taken steps to designate a member of staff as religious education consultant. In the majority of these cases it is not the headteachers themselves who have taken on board this responsibility, but another member of the school staff.

In summary, there is a considerable pool of professional skills in religious education among teachers in county schools, in terms of those who studied religious education during initial training or who have attended in-service training.

Religious education

One-third (32%) of the county schools in the present sample allocate specific timetable periods to religious education; in the other two-thirds religious education is taught mainly by means of an integrated approach with the general curriculum.

While it is easier to calculate the time given to religious education when it appears as a specific timetable subject, the headteachers were asked to calculate how much time the fourth year junior pupils spend on religious education, however they meet the subject. Two of the county schools stand in complete breach of the law and provide no religious education at all for their fourth year junior pupils. Just over a quarter (27%) spend less than half an hour a week on religious education. In another 44% of the county schools, religious education occupies between half an hour and one hour each week. This means that 28% give over an hour a week to religious education, but very few (2%) extend this allocation beyond one and half hours a week.

The majority of county schools hold quite lightly to the agreed syllabus. While very few (2%) claim to ignore the agreed syllabus altogether, only 3% claim to follow it very closely. Of the other 95%, one-third follow it quite closely, while two-thirds follow it only in general terms. The development of a detailed scheme of work for religious education is a way of establishing the profile and direction of the subject throughout the school and in relationship to other subjects. A detailed scheme of work for religious education exists in only 15% of the county schools.

County schools which allocate specific timetable periods to religious education tend to devote more time to the subject than schools which adopt the integrated approach: 35% of the county schools which teach religious education by separate timetable periods spend more than an hour a week on the subject, compared with 26% which rely wholly on the integrated approach. County schools which allocate specific timetable periods to religious education also tend to follow the agreed syllabus more closely than those which adopt the integrated approach: 41% of the county schools which teach religious education by separate timetable periods claim to follow the agreed syllabus closely, compared with 29% which rely wholly on the integrated approach.

The schools' attitude towards religious education can also be gauged by the kind of activities and resources which are employed. Radio broadcasts emerge as the most frequently used resource in religious education. Nearly half (47%) of the county schools say that their fourth year junior pupils often hear radio broadcasts in religious education. This compares with 23% who often use reference books, 13% who often use text books, 12% who often use bibles, 10% who often hear tapes or cassettes, 7% who often watch television, 7% who often see slides or filmstrips and 1% who often watch films. These statistics emphasise the key role which radio broadcasts play in religious education in county schools. They also emphasise the comparative lack of audio-visual resources for religious education in county schools.

Looked at from another perspective, over half the county schools (54%) never or rarely use textbooks with their fourth year junior pupils for religious education, over a third (35%) never or rarely use bibles, and over a fifth (20%) never or rarely use reference books. The proportion of county schools which never or rarely use audio-visual material for religious education among fourth year junior pupils are as follows: films (78%), television (65%), audio tapes or cassettes (47%), slides or filmstrips (46%), radio broadcasts (22%).

Next, it is worth looking in greater detail at the form in which the bible is met by pupils when it is used in their classrooms. The five versions of the bible most frequently used are, in descending order of popularity and showing the proportion of county schools in which they are used, *The New English Bible* (47%), *Good News Bible* (31%), Authorised Version (22%), Revised Standard Version (10%) and *The Jerusalem Bible* (4%). J.B. Phillips and Alan Dale paraphrases are also occasionally used by teachers in county schools, as are *The Living Bible* and *New International Version.*

While *The New English Bible* and *Good News Bible* clearly lead in their use among teachers, the Authorised Version continues to lead in terms of the number of schools which possess class sets. Thus, 32% of the county schools possess class sets of the Authorised Version, compared with 13% which possess class sets of *Good News Bible* and 15% which possess class sets of *The New English Bible*. It seems that changes in stock have not kept pace with changes in use. The overall picture is that 30% of the county schools do not possess a class set of bibles at all; 21% possess only a set of the Authorised Version and 49% possess a class set in a more modern translation.

In summary, in the majority of county schools (73%) religious education occupies less than one hour per week. The majority of county schools follow the agreed syllabus only loosely, and rely on radio broadcasts as their major resource for religious education among fourth year junior pupils. Half the county schools do not possess a set of modern bibles.

Assemblies

The letter of the law requiring an assembly for the whole school every day is being adhered to by just one in four (26%) of the county schools. This is not because the nature of the school site makes the daily assembly impossible: just 10% of the county schools argue that it would be physically difficult to assemble all the pupils everyday. Rather, educational theory and practice have moved away from the desirability of such a daily pattern.

The majority of county schools, however, do bring the whole school together for an assembly on some days of the week. Only 2% of the county schools do not hold an assembly for the whole school at least once a week, and these schools seem to have made their decision not on ideological, but on practical grounds. Thus, 11% of the county schools hold one assembly a week; 12% hold two assemblies; 20% hold three assemblies and 29% hold four assemblies a week for the whole school.

When the whole school does not meet for an assembly, this does not necessarily mean that smaller assemblies are not taking place elsewhere in the school. A variety of other patterns, including classroom assemblies for individual classes or year groups, is replacing the traditional assembly for the whole school.

Even those county schools which seem to be obeying the Education Act by holding an assembly for the whole school every day, may in fact not be fulfilling the strict letter of the law by holding their act of worship at the beginning of the school day. Only 37% of the county schools claim that assemblies necessarily take place at the beginning of the school day. Again, a variety of practices has taken over from the strict requirement set out in the 1944 Education Act.

When assemblies take place in county schools, there is now also a considerable variety in the form of leadership. The headteachers are responsible for leading at least one assembly every week in all the county schools, apart from the two schools in which assemblies are never held. Over half the headteachers of county schools (52%) are responsible for leading at least three assemblies every week. In 82% of the county schools other teachers are also responsible for leading an assembly at least once a week. In 43% of the county schools other teachers are responsible for leading two or more assemblies each week.

In many county schools classes of pupils take it in turns to prepare an assembly. Although the practice is by no means universal, the idea of allowing classes to take responsibility for leading assembly is adopted at least once a week by nearly two-thirds (64%) of the county schools.

Headteachers of county schools tend to agree that assemblies should not go on for too long. The favoured length is between 16 and 25 minutes: 43% of the headteachers say that their assemblies last between 16 and 20 minutes, while another 30% say that their assemblies last between 21 and 25 minutes. A few headteachers (14%) report that their assemblies last for less than a quarter of an hour, while another 13% report that their assemblies usually go on for more than 25 minutes.

The general tendency when primary age pupils come together for an assembly is to expect them to sit on the floor, for at least part of the time. Just 26% of the county schools provide chairs for at least some of their pupils; 8% generally expect their pupils to stand throughout the assembly.

Educational theory tends to emphasise the advantages of integrating assemblies with other aspects of the life of the school. This theory is, however, quite difficult and demanding to put into practice, since it requires considerable organisation and co-ordination. Half the county schools feel, therefore, that the majority of their assemblies remain largely unrelated to either the curriculum in general (52%) or to the religious education in particular (50%).

In making the daily collective act of worship a statutory obligation, the 1944 Education Act also safeguarded the freedom of parents to request the withdrawal of their children from this worship. In the present sample, 27% of the county schools currently have parents who assert this right.

The number of pupils withdrawn from any one county school varies between one and eleven. The most frequent reason for withdrawal, experienced by 26% of the county schools, is membership of the Jehovah's Witnesses. The next most frequent reason for withdrawal, experienced by 7% of the county schools, is membership of the Brethren. Other groups who assert the right of withdrawal from county schools in the sample are Muslims and Quakers.

Three of the county schools in the sample also report that they have members of staff who ask to be excused from assemblies. For two of these schools this involves one member of staff each; for the third school this involves three members of staff.

In summary, while the majority of county schools are technically in breach of the requirements of the 1944 Education Act regarding the daily collective act of worship, most of them maintain some regular pattern of assemblies. Headteachers continue to carry much of the responsibility for conducting these assemblies, although some share this responsibility with other teachers or with the pupils.

Worship

Headteachers were asked to judge where they would place the majority of their assemblies on a five point continuum, ranging from 'explicitly Christian and denominational', through 'explicitly Christian but not denominational', 'implicitly Christian' and 'religious, but not distinctively Christian', to 'largely secular and social'. The majority of headteachers of county schools clearly feel that it is appropriate for their school assemblies to reflect a religious ethos. Just 13% of the county schools argue that the majority of their assemblies are largely secular and social. A further 16% argue that, while being religious, the majority of their assemblies are not distinctively Christian in character. This means that assemblies in the other 71% of the county schools are regarded as Christian in one sense or another. For 41% of the county schools the major emphasis of assemblies is described as implicitly Christian, while for 28% the major emphasis is described as explicitly Christian but not denominational. Just 2% of the county schools claim that the major emphasis of their assemblies is explicitly Christian and denominational.

In contemporary educational theory the rationale for school assemblies has been considerably broadened, from imitating the churches' forms of worship, to occasions of celebration and participation. The range of experience embraced by assemblies in county schools is now very broad.

Especially where classes are given the opportunity to lead, their assemblies will sum up the whole range of project and class activities.

Today in 96% of the county schools assemblies will include, from time to time, the opportunity to listen to music, while in 94% pupils are also given the opportunity, from time to time, to provide that music by playing their own instruments. In 87% of the county schools assemblies will include, from time to time, pupil participation in drama, and in 54% pupil participation in educational dance. Similarly, 80% of the county schools sometimes use slides in assemblies, while another 80% sometimes make use of radio broadcasts. Television and video are also sometimes used in assemblies by 30% of the county schools.

While most county schools draw on this wide range of experience in assemblies from time to time, the majority still reserve this kind of experience for special occasions. Thus, only 12% of the county schools use drama at least once a week and 3% use slides at least once a week. No county schools use dance, television or video in assemblies as often as once a week. Music, on the other hand, is much more part of the day to day pattern, with 69% of the county schools using music in assemblies at least once a week and 40% inviting pupils to play their own instruments in assemblies at least once a week. Radio broadcasts, too, are part of the general scene, with nearly two-thirds (64%) of the county schools using the radio in assemblies at least once a week.

Although many headteachers of county schools (69%) would not categorise the majority of their assemblies as explicitly Christian, all the county schools in the sample still give some emphasis in assemblies to the traditional components of Christian worship. Every county school sings hymns and says prayers in assemblies, at least from time to time. Every county school uses religious stories from the Christian tradition in assemblies from time to time, and only 2% never read directly from the bible in assemblies. County schools are much more likely to draw their inspiration for assemblies from Christian traditions than from elsewhere. Thus, 79% of the county schools say that fourth year junior pupils hear in assemblies religious stories from a Christian background at least once a week, while 60% say that they hear secular stories at least once a week and only 21% say that they hear stories from other world faiths at least once a week.

Another way to assess the contact between the churches' worship and assemblies in county schools is to examine the frequency with which pupils engage in different aspects of worship. Hymns are sung by the fourth year junior pupils at least once a week in 99% of the county schools, and on as many as four or five days a week in 75%. On the other hand, the churches cannot assume that the hymns sung in assemblies necessarily have much in common with the traditional church hymn books. Indeed, only 29% of the county schools believe that there is much relationship between the hymns used in assemblies and in local churches. The singing of psalms and canticles is almost completely absent from county school assemblies.

Prayers are said by fourth year junior pupils at least once a week in 93% of the county schools, and on as many as four or five days a week in 64%. Once again, however, the link between prayers used in assemblies and prayers used in local churches may be quite tenuous. For example, while 93% of the county schools say prayers with fourth year junior pupils at least once a week, the proportion drops to 67% which use the Lord's Prayer at least once a week. Just 23% of the county schools use the Lord's Prayer among fourth year junior pupils on four or five days a week. Moreover, while a number of churches may use a modern version of the Lord's Prayer, only 7% of the county schools have departed from the traditional version. Churches cannot assume, therefore, that children will be familiar with the version of the Lord's Prayer used in their Sunday services.

While most county schools use the bible in assemblies from time to time, the churches cannot assume that assemblies are necessarily introducing children to the major biblical themes which are so fundamental to much of the churches' liturgy and hymnody. Only 33% of the county schools use the bible in assemblies at least once a week; only 3% use the bible on four or five days a week.

In summary, while county schools still generally employ hymns, prayers and bible readings as part of the repertoire for assemblies, the churches would be unwise to assume that pupils are being equipped through assemblies to feel at home in the majority of church services. The cultural assumptions of school worship and of church services are often far apart.

Church contact

In addition to fulfilling the statutory requirements of religious education and assemblies there is a range of less formal ways in which county schools can demonstrate links with the churches. For example, the majority (80%) of the county schools in the sample sometimes arrange visits to a local church.

The reasons for visiting a local church vary greatly from school to school. The most frequent reason given by county schools for visiting a local church is to look at the building. Many church buildings provide an excellent stimulus for an educational visit. While two-thirds of the county schools visit local churches specifically to look at the buildings, half of them (51%) also take the opportunity to meet and to talk with the local clergyman. Some clergy may simply introduce the children to the architecture and history of their churches; others also talk about their religious significance and use.

A closer link with local churches is established when county schools arrange a school service or take part in a Sunday service. Half (50%) of the county schools hold their own school service in a local church at least once a year. Perhaps for many county schools this may be something like the annual school carol service when parents and friends also attend. Nearly one in ten (9%) of the county schools took part in a Sunday church service during the past year.

In many cases holding a school service or attending a Sunday service does not simply mean a passive participation in worship. Many county schools enable their pupils to make an active contribution to the services they organise or attend. Thus, 27% of the county schools made a display of their work in church and 36% presented their own music, dance or drama as part of the service in which they participated.

The second main way in which contact takes place between county schools and local churches is when clergy come to school. There is quite a close relationship between many county schools and Anglican clergy in particular. Six in every seven (85%) of the county schools sometimes receive visits from Anglican clergy; 16% say that the vicar visits the school at least once a week, while another 18% say that he visits the school at least once a month. In 71% of the county schools Anglican clergy contribute to assemblies from time to time; in 11% the vicar takes an assembly at least once a week, while in another 13% he takes an assembly at least once a month. On the other hand, Anglican clergy are much less likely to contribute to religious education in county schools. Just one in five (20%) of the county schools say that Anglican clergy ever participate in religious education lessons. Nevertheless, 5% of the county schools say that the vicar takes a religious education lesson at least once a week, while another 2% say that he does so at least once a month.

Free Church ministers and Catholic priests have considerably less contact with county schools than Anglican clergy. While 85% of the county schools are visited by Anglican clergy, only 47% are visited by Free Church ministers and 10% by Catholic priests. Just 1% of the county schools say that a Free Church minister visits at least once a week; 2% say that a Catholic priest visits at least once a week. While 71% of the county schools have Anglican clergy contributing to assemblies, 47% have Free Church ministers contributing to assemblies and only 7% have Catholic priests contributing to assemblies. No county school in the sample has Catholic priests contributing to religious education and only 5% have Free Church ministers contributing to religious education.

Compared with the contact which county schools have with Christian churches and clergy, their contact with other world faiths is quite small. While 80% of the county schools have visited Christian churches within the past year, only 22% have visited non-Christian places of worship. While 71% of the county schools have invited Anglican clergy to contribute to assemblies, only 16% have invited leaders of other world faiths to do so. While 20% of the county schools have invited Anglican clergy to contribute to religious education, only 1% have invited leaders of other world faiths to do so. While 85% of the county schools receive visits from Anglican clergy, only 11% receive visits from leaders of other world faiths.

In summary, the majority of county schools continue to have significant contact with churches and clergy, especially with the Church of England and with Anglican clergy. Six out of seven county schools are visited by the vicar. Half of them arrange a school service in church at least once a year.

Resources

The establishment of resource centres played an important part in curriculum development for religious education and assemblies during the 1970s. In particular, the Church of England saw its role develop in terms of providing resource centres for the promotion of religious education and assemblies in county schools as well as in church schools. In general, the Church of England accepted the change in religious education in county schools and created resource centres equipped to promote the objective study of world religions, rather than to foster Christian commitment.

At the time of the survey, just 12% of the county schools had made use of the diocesan resource centre in Gloucester within the past year, while another 8% had made use of other resource centres to help with religious education. This still means that four out of every five of the county schools (79%) do not draw upon the facilities of any religious education resource centre.

The Christian Education Movement aims to help schools with religious education and assemblies, developing its resource material for non-confessional, multifaith religious education. Only one in twelve (8%) of the county schools pays a subscription to the Christian Education Movement and receives its material for use in religious education and assemblies.

However, many county schools agree that they lack certain resources or materials which could help to improve their religious education or assemblies. Each headteacher was presented with a checklist of potential ingredients, including resources, materials and help, for religious education and assemblies. From this list they were asked to indicate which areas, if any, they would wish to strengthen in order to improve the religious education or assemblies in their school. The list included bibles, hymn books, sets of text books, reference books, visits from the adviser, contact with local churches, co-operation from local clergy, in-service training courses, slides or filmstrips, films, television programmes, radio broadcasts, goodwill of staff, goodwill of pupils, and goodwill of parents.

From this range of options, the two which came to the top of the list of county school headteachers were slides or filmstrips and reference books. Thus, 47% said that their religious education or assemblies could be improved by the availability of more slides or filmstrips, and 44% said that they lacked sufficient reference books. The next two items on the headteachers' lists were films (37%) and television programmes (32%). At the same time, 26% said that their religious education lacked sufficient sets of text books, while 25% said that they lacked sufficient bibles; 15% reported that they lacked sufficient quantities of an appropriate hymn book.

Comparatively few county schools complained of lack of contact with local churches or lack of co-operation from local clergy. Just 13% said that more contact with local churches would be helpful, while 12% said that more co-operation from local clergy would be helpful. One in five (21%) of the county schools thought that their religious education and assemblies could be helped by more visits from the adviser.

The most significant response from this part of the questionnaire, however, is the proportion of county school headteachers who feel that more in-service training courses are needed in the areas of religious education and assemblies. Two in every five of the county school headteachers argue that their religious education and assemblies could be improved by more in-service training. It needs to be recognised, however, that to ask for more in-service training is not the same thing as to attend courses when they are provided.

Another point which comes through clearly is that county schools do not lack the goodwill needed to promote religious education and assemblies. The overall picture is that only .8% of the county schools report that they lack the goodwill of staff towards religion, 11% lack the goodwill of pupils towards religion and 14% lack the goodwill of parents towards religion.

Looked at from another perspective, just 21% of the county schools say that they lack none of these resources, materials or help, which could improve their religious education or assemblies. The impression gained is that the majority of county schools could and would use additional resources in these areas if they were easily available to them.

In summary, the majority of county schools do not make good use of the available religious education resource centres. At the same time, many county schools feel in need of better resourcing for religious education and assemblies. In particular, they point to the need for more reference books, better visual materials and appropriate in-service training courses.

Overview

The overall impression gained from this chapter is that Christianity is still far from dead in county schools in Gloucestershire. The data present a much more traditionally Christian picture than current educational theory seems to promote. The gap between contemporary educational theory and current educational practice in the county school is quite large.

The majority of county schools claim goodwill for religion on the part of parents, pupils and staff. The majority of county schools continue to have relationships with local churches and clergy. Most significant of all, the majority of the headteachers of county schools in Gloucestershire own allegiance to one of the Christian churches and more than two-fifths of them are weekly church-goers. It is probably through these headteachers that the churches continue to assert their influence over county schools. From the churches' point of view, this is both the strength and the vulnerability of their present situation, as chapter 12 demonstrates.

6 CATHOLIC SCHOOLS

Schools

Catholic schools in Gloucestershire provide a marked contrast to the county schools described in the previous chapter. In quantitative terms the Catholic sector makes a comparatively small contribution, providing 3.3% of the primary schools and 5% of the primary places. While voluntary schools as a group tend to be smaller than county schools, Catholic schools clearly go against this trend. The average number of pupils on the rolls of the Catholic schools is 197, compared with an average of 169 on the rolls of the county schools. The smallest Catholic school in the county is a three teacher school with 60 full-time pupils. The largest Catholic school has 14 classes and 423 full-time pupils, making it the largest primary school in Gloucestershire.

All the Catholic schools in the sample operate a selective admissions policy based on religious criteria. Two of the eight schools claim that their admissions policies are based entirely on religious criteria. The other six claim to take other issues into account and to admit a proportion of non-Catholic pupils. In seven of the Catholic schools there are no pupils from non-Christian religious backgrounds.

The provision of Catholic schools in a rural county is very uneven. Four of the eight schools are concentrated in the main conurbations of Gloucester, Cheltenham and Churchdown. Three of the other Catholic schools are also quite close together: one in the town of Stroud and two in villages. The eighth school is in Chipping Campden. This means that large tracts of the county are not readily served by a Catholic school.

Headteachers

The headteachers of the eight Catholic schools include six men and two women, which exactly reflects the balance of the sexes in the headships of county schools. In the Catholic schools, both the female headteachers are members of a religious order. Four of the headteachers of these eight Catholic schools are in their forties, two are in their fifties, and the remaining two refused to divulge their ages.

Generally there seems to be a very close identity between holding the

C

headship of a Catholic school and support for the Catholic church. All eight headteachers of Catholic schools in the present sample say that they are practising Catholics, attending church each Sunday. It is worth bearing in mind that in the rest of the sample of 234 schools there are only three other Catholic headteachers, all in county schools. Like their eight colleagues working in Catholic schools, the three Catholic headteachers of county schools are also weekly mass-attenders.

The majority of Catholic headteachers in Catholic schools are very clear regarding their personal commitment to the Catholic school system. Seven of the eight headteachers believe that they are in the right place teaching in a Catholic school. At the same time, it is interesting to note that none of the three Catholic headteachers in county schools is eager to leave the county sector to work in the Catholic sector.

There is also often a link between the headteacher of Catholic schools and the local Catholic church. Five of the eight headteachers of Catholic schools say that they live in the area served by their schools. This helps to consolidate the close link between Catholic schools, the local Catholic church and the Catholic families who send their children to Catholic schools.

All eight headteachers of these Catholic schools are content with the present statutory provisions for religious education and assemblies. None of them wishes to have less religious education or less worship in school.

Staff

Just as Catholic schools have attracted to their headships practising Catholics, so they have attracted teachers who have a professional interest in religious education. This may well be a reflection of the Catholic system of sponsoring colleges of teacher training. Of the 52 full-time staff in the Catholic schools in the survey, 11 (21%) studied religious education as a main course in their initial training, while a further 22 (42%) included religious education in their initial teacher training as a subsidiary subject. Yet another 12 (23%) have some other recognised qualification in religious education. This means that very few teachers in Catholic schools are not professionally qualified to teach religious education. All Catholic schools in the sample have a religious education specialist on their staff.

Not only are Catholic schools able to draw on several members of staff with specialist training in religious education, three-quarters of them contain teachers who have undertaken some in-service training in religious education within the past three years. Teachers from six of the eight Catholic schools had attended a day course or series of meetings concerned with religious education during the past three years. Another teacher had undertaken a short course in religious education, equivalent to one or two week's full-time study; none had undertaken a more substantial in-service training programme.

The professional interest of the teachers in Catholic schools in religious education is also reflected in the fact that half the Catholic schools have a staff member designated as a consultant for religious education. In the case of one of the schools this is the headteacher; in the case of the other three schools it is one of the other teachers.

Religious education

Catholic schools claim to follow a Catholic programme of religious education much more closely than county schools claim to follow the agreed syllabus. Of the eight Catholic schools in the sample, only one ignores the religious education syllabus and one other follows the syllabus only in general terms. The other six follow closely a Catholic programme of religious education. Moreover, Catholic schools are five times as likely as county schools to have developed a detailed scheme of work for religious education. Religious education is a subject which Catholic schools take seriously.

Similarly, Catholic schools allocate considerably more time to religious education than county schools. While 73% of the county schools give less than an hour a week to religious education among their fourth year junior pupils, all Catholic schools spend more than an hour a week on this subject. Three of the eight Catholic schools spend between one and one and a half hours a week on religious education; one spends between one and a half and two hours a week; the other four spend more than two hours a week on religious education.

Catholic schools are also more inclined to see that religious education takes place on a regular basis by allocating specific periods of time to the subject. While 68% of the county schools deal with religious education largely by means of an integrated approach only 37% of the Catholic schools take this approach. The other 63% of the Catholic schools deal with religious education by means of separate timetable periods.

Catholic schools are much more likely to resource their own religious education than county schools. Catholic schools do not regard radio broadcasts as satisfying their particular needs in religious education: seven of the eight Catholic schools in the sample never use radio broadcasts for religious education, while the other school does so only rarely. Similarly, five of the eight Catholic schools never watch television in religious education, while the other three do so only rarely. Catholic schools use films and slides with the same frequency as county schools: five of the eight Catholic schools use slides occasionally or often; two watch films occasionally or often. It is the audio tape or cassette which is more frequently used in Catholic schools than in county schools. Seven of the eight Catholic schools use this medium occasionally or often, compared with 42% of the county schools.

Text books, reference books and bibles also play a more central role in religious education in Catholic schools than in county schools. All the Catholic schools make regular use of text books, compared with 46% of the county schools; all the Catholic schools make regular use of reference books, compared with 79% of the county schools. Only one of the Catholic schools does not make regular use of bibles in religious education, compared with 35% of the county schools where the bible is never used or used only very rarely.

The two versions of the bible most favoured in Catholic schools are *The Jerusalem Bible* and *Good News Bible*. Teachers in six of the eight Catholic schools regularly use both *The Jerusalem Bible* and *Good News Bible*. In the other two Catholic schools the teachers regularly use either *The Jerusalem Bible* or *Good News Bible*. Neither the Authorised Version nor *The New English Bible* is used in Catholic schools.

While Catholic schools say that they use the bible quite regularly in religious education, the schools are not well equipped with sets of bibles for the pupils. Four of the Catholic schools do not possess any class sets of the bible. One possesses a set of the Revised Standard Version, while another possesses a set of *Good News Bible*. A third school has two sets, *The Jerusalem Bible* and the *Good News Bible*, while the fourth possesses four sets: the Revised Standard Version, *The Jerusalem Bible*, *Good News Bible* and the Alan Dale paraphrase.

Assemblies

No Catholic school in the sample keeps strictly to the letter of the law which requires every school day to begin with a collective act of worship. Of the eight Catholic schools, one holds assemblies for the whole school four days a week; five do so three days a week, and the remaining one does so just once a week.

When assemblies are held, in four of the Catholic schools they always take place at the beginning of the day, while in a further three this is usually the case. The other Catholic school reports that assemblies are never held at the beginning of the day, but that it seems more appropriate to hold them at a later time.

Headteachers of Catholic schools share the leadership of assemblies quite well. Five of the eight headteachers are personally responsible for taking assemblies on only one day a week; two take on this responsibility three times a week, and one claims most weeks not to be responsible for leading an assembly at all. In six of the eight Catholic schools a class is given responsibility for organising an assembly at least once a week. Other members of staff are also involved in leading assemblies in Catholic schools.

Assemblies in Catholic schools tend to be slightly shorter than in county schools. Assemblies go on for more than 20 minutes in only one of the eight Catholic schools, while this is the case in 43% of the county schools. This is consistent with Catholic school assemblies being more focused acts of worship.

As in county schools, the general assumption is that pupils attending assemblies will sit on the floor for at least part of the time. Just one of the eight Catholic schools expects pupils to stand throughout assembly, while two make chairs available for at least some of their pupils.

In Catholic schools there is a much closer relationship between assemblies and other aspects of school life than in county schools. All the Catholic schools claim that there is a close relationship between what takes place in assemblies and religious education lessons. Half of them say that this extends to a relationship with the general curriculum as well.

The parental right to withdraw their children from assemblies applies equally to voluntary schools as to county schools. The Catholic schools report, however, that no parents assert this right. Indeed, one reason parents elect to send their children to a Catholic school is because of their agreement with the religious provisions of the school. Catholic schools do not appear to admit pupils whose parents are not in agreement with the religious provision of the school.

Worship

In Catholic schools the link between assemblies and the worship of the church is much more strongly asserted than in county schools. When asked to judge where they would place the majority of their assemblies on the five point continuum, ranging from 'explicitly Christian and denominational', through 'explicitly Christian but not denominational', 'implicitly Christian' and 'religious but not distinctively Christian' to 'largely secular and social', headteachers of Catholic schools emerged in fairly clear agreement. Thus, seven of the eight Catholic schools classified the majority of their assemblies as explicitly Christian and denominational, while the remaining one classified the majority of assemblies as explicitly Christian but not denominational.

As a consequence of the Catholic schools' choice to emphasise the denominational character of school worship, assemblies in Catholic schools differ from county schools not only in content but also in style. Assemblies in Catholic schools embrace a more limited range of educational experience. Pupils attending Catholic schools are less likely to experience in their assemblies dance, drama, films, slides, radio broadcasts or music than pupils attending county schools. For example, a quarter of the Catholic schools never use drama in assemblies, or music, apart from accompanying singing; half of the Catholic schools never use films or slides in assemblies, and three-quarters never use dance or listen to radio broadcasts. Catholic schools appear to have a more restricted view of what constitutes assemblies.

At the same time, assemblies in Catholic schools make much more use of the traditional components of Christian worship and establish strong links between what takes place in school and what takes place in local churches. In five of the eight Catholic schools the pupils sing hymns and say prayers daily, while in three of them the daily pattern also includes reading from scripture. The other Catholic schools include these characteristic features of the church's worship at least once a week.

Moreover, hymns sung in Catholic school assemblies also bear a close relationship with hymns sung in Catholic churches. Seven of the eight Catholic schools believe that this relationship is deliberately close, while the other Catholic school believes that the relationship, while still real, is less close. The reason for this close relationship between the hymnody of school and church is that seven of the eight Catholic schools use a hymn book which is also used frequently in Catholic churches. The relationship between the hymnody of school and church also extends to introducing psalms and canticles into school worship. Only one of the eight Catholic schools claims never to sing psalms or canticles in assemblies, while five of them do so every week.

As part of the pattern of prayer in assemblies the Lord's Prayer is used at least once a week in all the Catholic schools and daily in five of them. It is used in the same translation as the child would encounter in the parish mass. Moreover, all the Catholic schools argue that the prayers and themes of assemblies follow closely the pattern of the church's year.

Since assemblies in Catholic schools are more inclined to be rooted in the Christian tradition, they are also less likely to include input from other sources. While all the Catholic schools employ themes from the Christian tradition every week in assemblies, only one of the eight Catholic schools uses stories from secular sources at least weekly and none uses stories from other world faiths as often as once a week. Indeed, one Catholic school says that it never uses secular stories in assemblies and three say that they never use stories from the sacred traditions of other world faiths.

Church contact

Catholic schools often have close links with the neighbouring Catholic church. Six of the eight Catholic schools have been involved in services in their local church within the past year. For four of them this has meant involvement both in Sunday services and school services; for one of them it has involved only Sunday services and for the other only school services.

The six Catholic schools which attend services in their local church also make sure that the pupils are involved in the services they attend and that they have something to contribute to those services. All of these six Catholic schools say that their pupils have prepared music, dance or drama to contribute to the services. On the other hand, Catholic schools are less good at encouraging their pupils to share their creative work with the local church. Only two Catholic schools in the sample say that they have made a display of the pupils' work in church during the past year.

The two Catholic schools which have not attended services in their local church during the past year have been involved in regular masses in the school itself. One of these schools has also made visits to the local church to look at the building, to study the purpose of the church and to talk with the priest.

All the Catholic schools in the sample keep in close contact with the Catholic priest. All eight schools report that the priest visits them at least once a week. The frequency with which priests contribute to religious education or assemblies varies from school to school. Two of the schools say that the priest never contributes to assemblies, while another two say that the priest does so at least once a week. In five of the Catholic schools the priest contributes to religious education at least once a week; in one of them he does so at least once a month and in the other two he does so less frequently.

One of the significant bridges which the Catholic clergy help to build between Catholic schools and the Catholic worshipping community is the celebration of mass in school. Three-quarters of the Catholic schools have mass celebrated in the school itself at least once a term.

While the relationship between Catholic schools and Catholic clergy is close, Catholic schools tend not to have much contact with clergy from other Christian denominations. None of the Catholic schools in the sample ever invites Anglican clergy or Free Church ministers to contribute to assemblies or to religious education lessons. Just one of the eight Catholic schools says that an Anglican clergyman sometimes visits the school.

Catholic schools have no contact with the religious buildings or the leaders of other world faiths. None of the Catholic schools has arranged visits to non-Christian places of worship; none of them has invited leaders from other world faiths to contribute to religious education or assemblies; none of them has received informal visits from those representing other world faiths.

Resources

Catholic schools are more likely to use religious education resource centres than county schools. Five of the eight Catholic schools in the sample have made use of a religious education resource centre during the past year, compared with less than one in four of the county schools. No Catholic school, however, has made use of the religious education resource centre established by the Anglican diocese. No Catholic school has taken out membership of the Christian Education Movement. The needs which Catholic schools experience for religious education resources and for resource centres seem to be met from within the Catholic community itself.

Although Catholic schools make greater use of religious education resource centres than county schools, they still plead for better resources for religious education within the schools themselves. Thus, three of the eight Catholic schools say that they lack adequate bibles, reference books and slides or filmstrips. Two of the eight Catholic schools say that they lack adequate hymn books, sets of religious education text books, appropriate television programmes and appropriate radio broadcasts.

None of the Catholic schools feels that it lacks the support it needs for religious education and assemblies from staff, pupils or parents. All the Catholic schools say that they have the goodwill of staff, pupils and parents for the religious purposes of the school. Not all the Catholic schools, however, are so totally convinced that they receive all the support and help they need from the wider Catholic community. One of the schools feels that it lacks adequate co-operation from the local Catholic clergy; two of them feel that they could benefit from more contact with specialist advisers; three of them complain that they do not receive sufficient support from the local churches. There is also the feeling among five of the eight headteachers that more could be provided by way of in-service training to improve religious education in Catholic schools.

Overview

Qualitatively speaking, Catholic schools are offering a very distinctive contribution to the overall primary provision in Gloucestershire. The aim of these schools is to offer an explicitly Christian education within a distinctively denominational environment and both staff and pupils are recruited primarily on religious criteria.

The denominational distinctiveness of Catholic schools is secured in a number of key ways. First, the headteachers of Catholic schools are themselves committed and practising Catholics. All are weekly mass-attenders; two are members of a religious order. As part of the Catholic community these headteachers are able to lead by example as well as by precept. Second, a number of staff in Catholic schools have also been recruited from the Catholic community. Those trained to teach in Catholic colleges have been equipped to understand and to promote the religious purposes of Catholic schools. Third, there is a close relationship between Catholic schools and the local Catholic church. This relationship is cemented by the role of the parish priest as a regular visitor to the school.

As a consequence of the close links between Catholic schools and the Catholic church, the religious education and worship of Catholic schools also emerge as thoroughly distinctive. Catholic schools follow a Catholic programme of religious education closely. Links are made between religious education and assemblies, between assemblies and the church's year, between school worship and parish worship. Mass is celebrated in school. The hymns sung in school are also sung in the local church. Catholic schools give a more serious allocation of time to religious education than county schools and are better resourced for teaching religious education. Catholic schools are more likely to make use of religious education resource centres.

While qualitatively speaking Catholic schools are offering a very distinctive contribution to the overall primary provision in Gloucester-shire, quantitatively speaking they hold only a very small stake in the provision of state maintained primary school places. Catholic schools have grown up where local needs, initiatives and resources have made the establishment of aided schools a real possibility. It is particularly in rural and scattered areas that the Catholic population has been numerically too small to sustain the development of a separatist school system. While the main conurbations are served by Catholic schools, there are large tracts of the county which are not. In other words, it is considerably easier for Catholic parents living in some parts of Gloucestershire to benefit from a Catholic schooling for their children than for Catholic parents living in other parts of Gloucestershire.

The unequal distribution of Catholic schools makes problems for Catholic parents moving from one part of the country to another. It also accentuates difficulties for a denomination which shares catechetical responsibility between home, church and school, when in some areas the Catholic school is part of the equation and in other areas it is not.

7 CHURCH OF ENGLAND AIDED SCHOOLS

Schools

The Church of England aided sector provides 16% of the primary schools and 12% of the primary places in Gloucestershire. Of the 41 Church of England aided schools in the sample, 29 (71%) are in villages, seven are in towns and five in suburban areas. The two smallest schools in Gloucestershire at the time of the survey were both Church of England aided schools, each with 17 full-time pupils on the roll. In fact, 17% of the Church of England aided schools had 30 or less pupils; 27% had 40 or less pupils; 42% had 60 or less pupils. The largest Church of England aided school in Gloucestershire had 310 pupils on the roll, compared with 393 in the largest county school and 423 in the largest Catholic school.

The majority of pupils who attend Church of England aided schools do so because it happens to be their neighbourhood school. No Church of England aided school in the sample claims to select its pupils mainly on religious criteria. Thus, 15% of the Church of England aided schools claim to operate exclusively as neighbourhood schools, while the other 85% say that they are mainly neighbourhood schools, but that they also admit some pupils from a wider area whose parents wish them to attend a Church of England aided school.

Because Church of England aided schools operate mainly as neighbourhood schools, the credal and racial mix of each school is a function more of its immediate environment than direct recruitment policy. Some headteachers of Church of England aided schools do, however, report that some parents from other religious traditions actually prefer their children to attend a church school, where religion is thought to be taken more seriously, than to attend a county school. In fact 24% of the Church of England aided schools claim to have on their rolls pupils from religious backgrounds other than Christian, compared with just 15% of the county schools. Two Church of England aided schools claim that over 30% of their pupils are from non-Christian religious backgrounds, while another two claim that this is the case for between 11% and 20% of their pupils.

Headteachers

The average age of headteachers of Church of England aided schools is identical to that of county schools. There is also an identical ratio between men and women holding the headships of these two types of school: 76% of the headteachers of Church of England aided schools are men, while 24% are women. On the two criteria of age and sex Church of England aided schools are offering the same opportunities for headships as county schools.

The first difference between headteachers of county schools and Church of England aided schools concerns where they choose to live. While only 19% of the headteachers of county schools live in the area served by their school, the proportion of headteachers of Church of England aided schools who live in the area served by their school rises to 33%. This could mean that Church of England aided schools are in more appropriate residential areas or that headteachers of Church of England aided schools feel a greater commitment to identifying with the local area served by their school.

The second difference between headteachers of Church of England aided schools and county schools is that headteachers of Church of England aided schools are less likely to be firmly committed to the sector in which they are working. While 67% of the headteachers of county schools say that they are in the right place in a county school, only 49% of the headteachers of Church of England aided schools say that the aided sector is the right place for them. One in every six of the headteachers of Church of England aided schools say that they would prefer not to be in a Church of England aided school, while one in three say that they really have no strong preference between a Church of England aided school or a county school. Thus, half the headteachers currently working in Church of England aided schools are doing so more by chance than choice. This compares with the fact that seven of the eight headteachers of Catholic schools were quite clear that they wanted to be working in the Catholic sector.

While half the headteachers may not have exercised a real preference for working in a Church of England aided school, the governors of these schools seem to have made a real choice in selecting headteachers who claim membership of the Church of England. Indeed, 88% of the headteachers of Church of England aided schools regard themselves as members of the Church of England. The other 12% of the headteachers are all members of one or another of the Free Churches. None of the headteachers of Church of England aided schools is a Catholic; none is a humanist, atheist or agnostic.

The greater religious involvement of headteachers of Church of England aided schools is not simply nominal; it is also expressed in practice. While 42% of the headteachers of county schools are weekly church-goers, the proportion rises to 71% of the headteachers of Church of England aided schools. A further 24% attend church at least monthly. This means that many more headteachers of Church of England aided schools are committed to the Church of England or to one of the Christian churches than are committed to working in a church school.

The personal religious disposition of the headteachers seems to assure the place of religious education and assemblies in Church of England aided schools. All except one of the headteachers in the Church of England aided sector are committed to maintaining the place of religious education and assemblies in their schools.

Staff

Just as Church of England aided schools are more likely to have a church-going headteacher than county schools, so they are more likely to have on their staff people who have some formal qualification in religious education. Of the 174 full-time staff in Church of England aided schools in the sample, 25 (14%) studied religious education as a main course in their initial training, while a further 53 (30%) included religious education as a subsidiary subject. Another 14 (8%) had some other recognised qualification in religious education. This means that 71% of the Church of England aided schools can draw on at least one member of staff who has undertaken training to teach religious education, compared with 58% of the county schools.

While more members of staff in Church of England aided schools bring with them professional training in religious education than in county schools, they have no better record for participation in in-service training courses than teachers in county schools. Thus, teachers from just under half the Church of England aided schools (46%) had attended a day course or series of meetings concerned with religious education during the past three years. One teacher had undertaken a short course in religious education equivalent to one or two weeks' full-time study; none had undertaken a more substantial in-service programme in religious education.

If the appointment of a designated consultant in religious education is an index of commitment to the subject, the record of Church of England aided schools is slightly more impressive than county schools. In the case of Church of England aided schools, 44% have designated a member of staff as religious education consultant, compared with 38% of the county schools. The small difference in overall percentages disguises a larger real difference in the sense that Church of England aided schools tend to be smaller and in general the smaller schools are less likely to see the advantages of appointing designated subject consultants. While in county schools the majority of designated consultants in religious education are not headteachers, in the case of Church of England aided schools only one designated consultant in religious education is not of headteacher status.

Religious education

In general terms, Church of England aided schools take religious education more seriously than county schools, but less seriously than Catholic schools. This is indicated, for example, by the fact that 39% of the Church of England aided schools have developed their own detailed scheme of work for religious education, compared with 15% of the county schools and 63% of the Catholic schools.

Similarly, Church of England aided schools allocate more time to religious education than county schools, but less time than Catholic schools. While 29% of the county schools give less than half an hour a week to religious education among their fourth year junior pupils, this is the case in only 2% of the Church of England aided schools. On the other hand, while all the Catholic schools give more than an hour a week to religious education among their fourth year junior pupils, only 60% of the Church of England aided schools deem the subject to be worth as much time as this. A detailed analysis of the time allocated to religious education among fourth year junior pupils by Church of England aided schools indicates that 2% of them give less than half an hour per week; 38% give between a half an hour and one hour; another 38% give between one hour and one and a half hours; 12% give between one and a half hours and two hours and 10% give more than two hours a week.

While Church of England aided schools give considerably more time and emphasis to religious education than county schools, they are not more likely to give religious education a fixed period on the timetable. In fact, 73% of the Church of England aided schools say that religious education is taught largely by means of an integrated approach, compared with 68% of the county schools. Church of England aided schools are more committed than Catholic schools to integrating religious education with the general curriculum, but they try harder than county schools not to lose sight of the distinctive religious component.

Headteachers of Church of England aided schools show a greater commitment to their religious education syllabus than headteachers of county schools, although they show less commitment than headteachers of Catholic schools. Thus, 48% of the Church of England aided schools follow their syllabus very closely or quite closely, compared with 37% of the county schools and 75% of the Catholic schools. This leaves 46% of the Church of England aided schools which follow their syllabus only in general terms and 5% who ignore their syllabus totally.

As far as resources for religious education are concerned, Church of England aided schools rely on radio broadcasts nearly as heavily as county schools. Thus, 70% of the Church of England aided schools make regular use of the radio for religious education, compared with 76% of the county schools and none of the Catholic schools. Church of England aided schools use other audio-visual material for religious education with no more frequency than county schools. Thus, 83% of the Church of England aided schools never or rarely watch films as part of their religious education lessons, 73% never or rarely use television, 58% rarely or never hear audio tapes or cassettes, 42% rarely or never show slides or filmstrips.

Similarly, Church of England aided schools are no more likely than county schools to use text books in religious education: 51% of the Church of England aided schools and 54% of the county schools never or rarely use text books for fourth year junior religious education. Where, however, Church of England aided schools are better resourced than county schools is in the area of reference books and bibles. Thus, 90% of the Church of England aided schools regularly use reference books for fourth year junior religious education, compared with 80% of the county schools; 95% of the Church of England aided schools regularly use bibles for fourth year junior religious education, compared with 65% of county schools.

Teachers in Church of England aided schools use a wider range of translations of the bible than county schools. They are also much more likely to go for a modern translation of the bible. *The New English Bible* is used in 66% of the Church of England aided schools, compared with 47% of the county schools. *Good News Bible* is used in 63% of the Church of England aided schools, compared with 31% of the county schools. Pupils in Church of England aided schools are also more likely to encounter the Revised Standard Version, *The Jerusalem Bible* and *The Living Bible*. The Authorised Version is used by teachers in the same proportion of Church of England aided schools as county schools (22%).

Class sets of the Authorised Version exist in two out of every five Church of England aided schools (39%), compared with 32% of the county schools. At the same time, Church of England aided schools are much more likely to possess sets of a modern translation of the bible. While only 13% of the county schools possess sets of *Good News Bible*, 44% of the Church of England aided schools have sets of this translation. While only 15% of the county schools possess sets of *The New English Bible*, 27% of the Church of England aided schools have sets of this translation. Another 15% of the Church of England aided schools possess class sets of the Revised Standard Version, while one or two have sets of the Alan Dale or J.B. Phillips paraphrases.

Looked at from another perspective, only 5% of the Church of England aided schools do not possess a set of bibles, compared with 30% of the county schools. This leaves 22% of the Church of England aided schools which possess sets of the Authorised Version only, while the other 73% possess sets of a modern translation of the bible.

Assemblies

In the sense of providing an assembly for the whole school every day, Church of England aided schools emerge as the most law abiding sector in Gloucestershire. Half (51%) of the Church of England aided schools provide an assembly for the whole school every day, compared with a quarter (26%) of the county schools and none of the Catholic schools. Again, 41% of the Church of England aided schools say that assemblies always take place at the beginning of the school day, while a further 56% say that this is usually the case. While half the Church of England aided schools provide the traditional pattern of an assembly for the whole school every day, the pattern of assemblies in the other half varies as widely as in county schools. In 19% of the Church of England aided schools an assembly for the whole school takes place three or four days a week and in 22% one or two days a week. This means that 7% of the Church of England aided schools do not hold an assembly for the whole school at least once a week.

Headteachers of Church of England aided schools are personally involved in leading more assemblies than headteachers of county schools. This reflects the two facts that assemblies are held more frequently in Church of England aided schools and these schools have fewer staff. Headteachers of Church of England aided schools are also less likely to involve other teachers or classes in leading assemblies. Thus, 27% of the

Church of England aided schools say that teachers are not generally involved in leading assemblies, compared with 8% of the county schools; 51% of the Church of England aided schools say that pupils are not generally involved in leading assemblies, compared with 26% of the county schools.

Like Catholic schools, Church of England aided schools make their assemblies shorter than county schools. Thus, 37% of the Church of England aided schools say that their assemblies generally last for less than 20 minutes, compared with 57% of the county schools. Church of England aided schools also try to make their assemblies more comfortable for the pupils. Thus, fewer of the Church of England aided schools expect their pupils to sit on the floor for assemblies; 41% of the Church of England aided schools provide chairs or benches, compared with 26% of the county schools.

Unlike Catholic schools, however, Church of England aided schools do not make more effort than county schools to relate assemblies to either the curriculum in general or to religious education in particular. As is the case in county schools, about half the Church of England aided schools say that some relationship exists between assemblies and religious education or the wider curriculum.

While Catholic schools do not experience parents asserting the right to withdraw their children from assemblies, Church of England aided schools, being on the whole neighbourhood schools, do have this experience. However, while 27% of the county schools have one or more pupils withdrawn from assemblies, this affects only 19% of the Church of England aided schools. The number of pupils withdrawn from assemblies in Church of England aided schools varies between one and six.

The two main reasons given for withdrawal from assemblies are the same as in county schools, namely membership of the Jehovah's Witnesses or Brethren. One pupil is withdrawn on the grounds of being a Buddhist. Church of England aided schools in the sample have no experience of teachers currently requesting to be excused from assemblies.

Worship

When asked to judge where they would place the majority of their assemblies on the five point continuum, ranging from 'explicitly Christian and denominational', through 'explicitly Christian but not denominational', 'implicitly Christian' and 'religious but not distinctively Christian' to 'largely secular and social', headteachers of Church of England aided schools demonstrate the more overtly Christian character of their schools. While 13% of the county schools argue that the majority of their assemblies are largely secular and social, no Church of England aided school feels this way. While 16% of the county schools argue that the majority of their assemblies are religious but not distinctively Christian, just 7% of the Church of England aided schools feel this way. Similarly, a higher proportion (47%) of the Church of England aided schools argue that their assemblies are explicitly Christian in character, compared with 30% of the county schools. On the other hand, only a small proportion of Church of England aided schools claim to exercise their right to make assemblies truly denominational in character. While 87% of the Catholic schools claim that their assemblies are denominational in character, only 10% of the Church of England aided schools claim that this is the case.

The range of educational experience available to the pupils through assemblies in Church of England aided schools is as wide as in county schools and wider than in Catholic schools. In 98% of the Church of England aided schools assemblies include, from time to time, listening to music, while in 95% pupils provide that music by playing their own instruments. In 90% of the Church of England aided schools assemblies include, from time to time, pupils participating in drama, while in 49% pupils participate in educational dance. Similarly, 78% of the Church of England aided schools sometimes use slides in assemblies; 85% sometimes make use of radio broadcasts; 29% sometimes use television and video.

While most Church of England aided schools draw on this wide range of experience in assemblies from time to time, like county schools the majority reserve these experiences for special occasions. Thus, only 7% use drama in assemblies at least once a week and none use dance, slides, television or video once a week. Music is much more part of the day to day pattern, with 61% of the Church of England aided schools using music in assemblies at least once a week and 46% giving pupils the opportunity to play their own instruments at least once a week. Radio broadcasts, too, are part of the general scene, with 71% of the Church of England aided schools using the radio in assemblies at least once a week.

Church of England aided schools give considerably more emphasis in assemblies to the forms of worship characteristic of the churches. Hymns, prayers and scripture readings are all used more frequently in Church of England aided schools than county schools. Thus, in 93% of the Church of England aided schools fourth year junior pupils sing hymns nearly every day, compared with 75% of the county schools. Prayers are said with fourth year junior pupils nearly every day in 76% of the Church of

England aided schools, compared with 64% of the county schools. Bible passages are read at least once a week in 71% of the Church of England aided schools, compared with 36% of the county schools.

Headteachers of Church of England aided schools also judge assemblies in their schools to be more closely related to the church's year than the headteachers of county schools. Thus, assemblies in 80% of the Church of England aided schools reflect the church's year, compared with 63% of the county schools. On the other hand, the relationship between assemblies and the church's liturgy is much less close in Church of England aided schools than Catholic schools. For example, while 87% of the Catholic schools report that there is a close relationship between hymns sung in church and school, only 31% of the Church of England aided schools and 29% of the county schools feel that this is the case. While 87% of the Catholic schools introduce their pupils to singing psalms and canticles, this is the case in only 31% of the Church of England aided schools and 26% of the county schools. While Catholic schools and Catholic churches often share in a common hymn book, the job of creating links between hymns in church and school is not made easier for Church of England schools by the reluctance of many Anglican churches to adopt a hymn book suitable for use in schools.

Church of England aided schools experience a similar problem if they try to establish a link between the version of the Lord's Prayer used in school and church, because of the diversity of practice in the Church of England. Just 17% of the Church of England aided schools have departed from the traditional version of the Lord's Prayer. By way of comparison, only 7% of the county schools have adopted a modern translation of the Lord's Prayer. This indicates that Church of England aided schools are slightly more likely to reflect liturgical changes in school practice.

Just as Church of England aided schools use scripture more frequently in assemblies, so they also use stories from a Christian background more frequently. While fourth year junior pupils in 79% of the county schools hear stories in assemblies from a Christian background at least once a week, the proportion rises to 92% of the Church of England aided schools. Similarly, while fourth year junior pupils in 60% of the county schools hear stories from a secular background at least once a week, the proportion drops to 49% of the Church of England aided schools.

On the other hand, Church of England aided schools are just as likely as county schools to use stories from other world faiths: 21% of the county schools and 24% of the Church of England aided schools report that their fourth year junior pupils are likely to hear stories from other world faiths at least once a week. While for Catholic schools a consequence of emphasising their Christian roots is to give less time to sharing traditions from other world faiths, Church of England aided schools give more emphasis to their Christian roots without giving less emphasis than county schools to sharing traditions from other world faiths.

Church contact

On the whole, Church of England aided schools have a closer relationship with the local church than county schools. Just 7% of the Church of England aided schools say that they had no contact with local churches during the past year; the other 93% make contact with local churches in a range of ways. During the past year, 85% of the Church of England aided schools arranged visits to a local church to look at the building; 66% stayed on to study the purpose of the church, and 68% talked with the clergyman. By way of comparison, 68% of the county schools visited a local church within the past year; 39% stayed on to study the purpose of the church, and 51% talked with the clergyman.

The majority of Church of England aided schools (85%) held a school service in church during the past year, while a third of them (32%) were involved in at least one Sunday service. By way of comparison, 50% of the county schools held a school service in church, while 9% were involved in Sunday service. When they take part in a church service, a good proportion of Church of England aided schools make sure that the pupils have something to contribute. Thus, 71% of the Church of England aided schools say that their pupils presented music, dance or drama in church during the past year, while 44% of them had displayed pupils' work in church. By way of comparison, 27% of the county schools had displayed pupils' work in church.

The majority of Church of England aided schools also have a close relationship with the Anglican clergy. Thus, 83% of the Church of England aided schools receive a visit from Anglican clergy at least once a week. In 68% of the Church of England aided schools Anglican clergy take assemblies at least once a week and in 54% they take religious education once a week. On the other hand, 7% of the Church of England aided schools say that Anglican clergy never come to the school. Anglican clergy celebrate communion at least once a term in just two of the 41 Church of England aided schools in the sample.

While Church of England aided schools have a closer relationship with Anglican clergy than county schools, they have a less close relationship with Free Church ministers. Thus, only 22% of the Church of England aided schools sometimes receive visits from Free Church ministers, compared with 39% of the county schools; only 19% of the Church of England aided schools involve Free Church ministers in leading assemblies, compared with 47% of the county schools. Free Church ministers sometimes take religious education in 5% of the county schools and in 5% of the Church of England aided schools.

Catholic priests have very little contact with Church of England aided schools, but slightly more than with county schools. Thus, 12% of the Church of England aided schools sometimes receive visits from a Catholic priest; 7% say that a Catholic priest sometimes contributes to assemblies and 5% say that a Catholic priest sometimes contributes to religious education.

Unlike pupils at Catholic schools, pupils at Church of England aided schools are as likely to have contact with other world faiths as pupils who attend county schools. While this contact is not great, it does indicate that Church of England aided schools are no less open to exploring other religious traditions than county schools. Thus, 22% of the Church of England aided schools have visited a non-Christian place of worship in the past year; 10% have invited leaders from other world traditions to contribute to school assemblies and 2% have invited them to contribute to religious education; 10% have received visits from leaders of other world faiths.

Resources

The diocesan religious education resource centre was used during the past year by just 12% of the county schools. Usage is not much higher among Church of England aided schools: 19% of the Church of England aided schools made use of the centre during the past year. At the same time, there is a slightly higher usage by Church of England aided schools of other religious education resource centres. While 12% of the county schools made use of other centres during the past year, the proportion rises to 17% of the Church of England aided schools. In other words, while 21% of the county schools used at least one religious education resource centre during the past year, 29% of the Church of England aided schools did so.

Church of England aided schools are no more likely to be subscribing members of the Christian Education Movement than county schools; 8% of the county schools and 10% of the Church of England aided schools belong to the Christian Education Movement. Just 29% of the Church of England aided schools are subscribing members of the National Society, contributing to and benefiting from this national body which represents the interests of Church of England schools.

Four out of five (79%) of the Church of England aided schools feel that they need extra resources, materials or help to improve their religious education and assemblies. This indicates that Church of England aided schools are no more content with their available resources in this area than county schools. Indeed the needs most frequently reported by Church of England aided schools are the same as those listed by county schools. Thus, 49% of the Church of England aided schools say that they need more reference books; 54% need more visual material in the form of slides or filmstrips; 24% need more text books. On the other hand, Church of England aided schools feel that they are better provided for than county schools in terms of bibles and hymn books. While 25% of the county schools feel that they are inadequately resourced with bibles, only 19% of the Church of England aided schools complain that this is the case. While 15% of the county schools feel that they are inadequately resourced with hymn books, only 5% of the Church of England aided schools complain that this is the case.

Perceptions of local churches and local clergy held by Church of England aided schools are similar to those held by county schools. Thus, 13% of the county schools and 12% of the Church of England aided schools feel that they lack the contact they need with local churches; 12% of the county schools and 12% of the Church of England aided schools feel that they lack the co-operation they need from local clergy. Church of England aided schools and county schools also share similar perceptions of advisory and in-service training support: 21% of the county schools and 24% of the Church of England aided schools say that they would benefit from more contact with the adviser; 37% of the Church of England aided schools and 42% of the county schools ask for more in-service training opportunities to help with religious education and assemblies.

Church of England aided schools are even more confident of the goodwill of their staff and pupils towards religion than county schools. Only one (2%) of the Church of England aided schools feels that it lacks the goodwill of staff, compared with 8% of the county schools. Only one (2%) of the Church of England aided schools feels that it lacks the goodwill of the pupils, compared with 11% of the county schools. On the other hand, Church of England aided schools and county schools share a similar perception of the situation among parents: 14% of the county schools and 12% of the Church of England aided schools feel that they lack the goodwill of parents towards religion.

Overview

While Catholic schools understand their role as serving the Catholic community, Church of England aided schools fulfil the twin functions of serving the general needs of the nation and the domestic needs of the Anglican church. Accordingly, all the Church of England aided schools in Gloucestershire see themselves primarily as neighbourhood schools, serving a local community in the same way as county schools. Nevertheless, while Church of England aided schools set out to do the same job as county schools, the data show that they do so in a distinctive way. While less overtly religious than Catholic schools, Church of England aided schools are certainly more religious than county schools.

To begin with, governors of Church of England aided schools tend to appoint a practising Christian as headteacher and to choose staff with professional interest and training in religious education. Second, Church of England aided schools are likely to take religious education more seriously than county schools and to give more time to the subject. Third, daily assemblies are likely to be a more regular feature in Church of England aided schools than county schools. Moreover, assemblies in Church of England aided schools are more likely to include hymns, prayers and bible readings and to reflect the rhythm of the church's year. Fourth, Church of England aided schools are likely to have much closer contact with the local Anglican church and with local clergy than county schools. The vicar is much more likely to visit Church of England aided schools, to take assemblies and to take religious education. Church of England aided schools are more likely to organise a school service or to contribute to a Sunday service in the local church.

It is precisely this Christian distinctiveness of Church of England aided schools which raises a key problem regarding the nature of the overall contribution made by the Church of England to the state maintained system of schools. The problem has its roots in the fact that Church of England schools try both to serve the general needs of the nation and the domestic needs of the church.

If church schools set out primarily to serve the needs of the church, it is appropriate that they should demonstrate their Christian distinctiveness. Catholic schools, for example, work in this kind of way. They exist primarily to offer parents an opportunity for educational choice and they receive their mandate to be distinctive in a Christian sense precisely because parents choose these schools on explicit religious criteria. Indeed, if church schools which claim to operate on the rationale of providing an alternative educational environment for the children of church members could not demonstrate their religious distinctiveness, it may become increasingly difficult to justify their place within a secular state maintained educational system.

On the other hand, if church schools set out primarily to serve the needs of a specific local community, in the same sense as county schools, it is considerably less easy to justify their religious distinctiveness. If parents do not have a real choice in deciding to send their children to a church school, but do so because it happens to be the neighbourhood school, it may be difficult to justify providing those pupils with an educational environment different from what they would find if their neighbourhood school was a county school. Indeed, if church schools which claim to operate on the rationale of serving the local neighbourhood demonstrate that they also provide this neighbourhood with a distinctively Christian school, it may become increasingly difficult to justify their place within a secular state maintained educational system.

What is clear from the present data is that Church of England aided schools operate primarily as neighbourhood schools, but in such a way as to promote some distinctively Christian emphases in education.

8 CHURCH OF ENGLAND CONTROLLED SCHOOLS

Schools

More Church of England schools in Gloucestershire have opted for controlled status than have kept aided status. Today the Church of England controlled sector provides 27% of the primary schools and 21% of the primary places in Gloucestershire. Like Church of England aided schools, the majority of Church of England controlled schools tend to be small. At the time of the survey, the smallest Church of England controlled school in Gloucestershire had just 19 full-time pupils At the same time, 13% of the Church of England controlled schools had 30 or less pupils; 24% had 40 or less pupils and 43% had 60 or less pupils. At the other end of the spectrum, there are some quite large Church of England controlled schools, including six catering for over 300 pupils, with the largest having 385 full-time pupils.

Like Church of England aided schools, the majority of Church of England controlled schools are in rural areas. Thus, 78% of the Church of England controlled schools are situated in village environments; 8% are in suburban areas and 14% are in towns. One Church of England controlled school is in an educational priority area.

Like county schools, Church of England controlled schools exist primarily to serve their local neighbourhood. None of the Church of England controlled schools has religious criteria in its admissions policy, although 70% of them claim that they may admit a few pupils from outside their immediate neighbourhood. The range of pupils attending Church of England controlled schools, therefore, depends largely on the environment in which these schools are located, not on religious criteria. In the event, 80% of the Church of England controlled schools have no pupils on roll from non-Christian religious backgrounds; nine Church of England controlled schools in the present sample have a small minority of pupils, between 1% and 5%, from non-Christian religious backgrounds; three claim between 6% and 10%, one claims between 11% and 20% and another claims between 21% and 30% of the pupils as coming from non-Christian religious backgrounds.

Headteachers

Headteachers of Church of England controlled schools are slightly younger than their colleagues in other schools: 32% of the headteachers in the Church of England controlled sector are in their thirties, compared with 22% in the Church of England aided sector, 16% in the county sector and none in the Catholic sector. The ratio between men and women holding headships in Church of England controlled schools is basically the same as in other schools: there are three male headteachers for every female headteacher. One in five (22%) of the headteachers of Church of England controlled schools live in the catchment area of their school; this is the same proportion as in the county sector and significantly less than in the Church of England aided sector.

Just as headteachers of Church of England aided schools are less likely to be committed to the sector in which they are working than headteachers of county schools, so headteachers of Church of England controlled schools are less likely to be committed to their sector than headteachers of Church of England aided schools. While 67% of the headteachers of county schools and 49% of the headteachers of Church of England aided schools say that they are working in their preferred type of school, only 30% of the headteachers of Church of England controlled schools say that they prefer the controlled sector. Half the headteachers in Church of England controlled schools say that they really have no strong preferences between a church school or a county school; 16% say that they took their present headship as second best to a county school, while a further 6% say that they took their present headship as second best to a Church of England aided school.

The church allegiance of headteachers in Church of England controlled schools lies midway between that of headteachers in Church of England aided schools and county schools. Thus, 71% of the headteachers in Church of England controlled schools claim to be members of the Church of England, compared with 88% in Church of England aided schools and 59% in county schools. A further 22% of the headteachers in Church of England controlled schools claim to belong to one of the Free Churches. There are no Catholic headteachers in the Church of England controlled sector. The remaining 7% of the headteachers in Church of England controlled schools call themselves agnostics. This means that one in every fourteen of the Church of England controlled schools is in the care of a headteacher who has no Christian affiliation, compared with one in five of the county schools and none of the Catholic or Church of England aided schools.

The religious practice of headteachers of Church of England controlled schools reflects greater nominal religious affiliation than in the Church of England aided sector: 51% of the headteachers of Church of England controlled schools attend church weekly, compared with 43% of the headteachers of county schools and 71% of the headteachers of Church of England aided schools. Another 13% of the headteachers of Church of England controlled schools attend church at least monthly. This leaves 10% of the headteachers of Church of England controlled schools who never go to church and 27% who go at least once a year, but not on a regular basis.

Headteachers of Church of England controlled schools emerge as slightly less certain than headteachers of Church of England aided schools about the desirability of maintaining the present system of assemblies and religious education. Nevertheless, 90% of them are happy with the present legal requirements for assemblies and 85% are happy with the present legal requirements for religious education. Just two of the present sample of headteachers of Church of England controlled schools would like to see religious education and assemblies completely abandoned.

Staff

Just as the level of church allegiance among headteachers in Church of England controlled schools lies midway between their colleagues in Church of England aided schools and county schools, so the professional interest of the teaching staff of Church of England controlled schools in religious education lies midway between the situations already described in the county sector and the Church of England aided sector. In Church of England controlled schools a higher proportion of the staff have some professional qualification in religious education than is the case in county schools, but this proportion is lower than is the case in Church of England aided schools.

Of the 288 full-time staff in Church of England controlled schools in the survey, 21 (7%) studied religious education as a main course during initial training, while a further 45 (16%) included religious education in their initial training as a subsidiary subject. Another ten (3%) had some other recognised qualification in religious education. This means that 59% of the Church of England controlled schools could draw on at least one member of staff who had undertaken some formal training to teach religious education. This is the same proportion as in county schools and considerably lower than in Church of England aided schools.

The proportion of staff in Church of England controlled schools who have undertaken in-service training in religious education is similar to that in Church of England aided schools and county schools. Thus, teachers from just under half the Church of England controlled schools (46%) had attended a day course or series of meetings concerned with religious education during the past three years. Two teachers had undertaken a short course in religious education equivalent to one or two weeks' full-time study; none had undertaken a more substantial in-service programme in religious education during the past three years.

When it comes to the appointment of a designated consultant in religious education, the record of Church of England controlled schools is less impressive than that of Church of England aided schools and on a par with county schools. This means that 38% of the Church of England controlled schools have a designated consultant for religious education. In two out of every three of the Church of England controlled schools which have a designated consultant for religious education, the person so designated is the headteacher. This contrasts interestingly with the situation in Church of England aided schools where almost all the designated consultants in religious education are the headteachers and with the situation in county schools where just one in three of the designated consultants in religious education is the headteacher. This is another indication of the way in which headteachers of Church of England controlled schools occupy middle territory in terms of their interest in religion and religious education between headteachers of Church of England aided schools and headteachers of county schools.

According to the 1944 Education Act, controlled schools can offer denominational religious education for pupils whose parents request that provision. In order to enable controlled schools to draw on staff able to provide this denominational instruction the act instituted the provision of 'reserved teachers'. Provided the teaching staff of the controlled school exceeds two, up to one fifth of the staff can be 'selected for their fitness and competence to give such religious instruction'. While 44 Church of England controlled schools in the sample employ more than two teachers, just nine of them have appointed a reserved teacher.

Religious education

Religious education in Church of England controlled schools should follow the local education authority's agreed syllabus, like county schools. In fact, headteachers of Church of England controlled schools show more commitment to the agreed syllabus than headteachers of county schools. Thus, 47% of the headteachers of Church of England controlled schools say that they follow the agreed syllabus very closely or quite closely, compared with 37% of the headteachers of county schools. Over half (52%) of the Church of England controlled schools say that they follow the agreed syllabus only in general terms and one of the controlled schools claims to disregard the syllabus altogether.

Few county schools (15%) take the place of religious education sufficiently seriously to develop a detailed scheme of work to co-ordinate the subject in the school. The higher profile of religious education in Church of England aided schools is reflected in the fact that 39% of them have developed detailed schemes of work. In Catholic schools the proportion rises to 63%. The situation in Church of England controlled schools is much closer to county schools than to Church of England aided schools, with 22% of the Church of England controlled schools developing detailed schemes of work for religious education. In three-quarters (74%) of the Church of England controlled schools religious education is taught by means of an integrated approach rather than through separate timetable periods.

Another index of the seriousness attributed to religious education is the amount of time given to the subject, whether through timetable allocation or within an integrated curriculum. Less time is given to religious education among fourth year junior pupils in Church of England controlled schools than county schools. While three-quarters (73%) of the county schools give less than one hour per week to religious education among their fourth year junior pupils, the proportion rises to 85% of the Church of England controlled schools. Looked at from another perspective, just 15% of the Church of England controlled schools give more than one hour a week to religious education, compared with 27% of the county schools, 60% of the Church of England aided schools and 100% of the Catholic schools.

Just as in county schools, when Church of England controlled schools say that their religious education is taught by an integrated approach it means that less time is actually spent on the subject than when timetable periods are specifically allocated. It also means that the syllabus is less likely to be followed. Thus, 58% of the Church of England controlled schools which teach religious education by timetable periods follow the syllabus closely, compared with 35% of those which adopt the integrated approach. Similarly, 29% of the Church of England controlled schools which teach religious education by timetable periods have devised their own detailed scheme of work for the subject, compared with 17% of those which adopt the integrated approach.

Religious education in Church of England controlled schools appears, in most ways, to be less well resourced than in county schools. Less use is made of films: 87% of the Church of England controlled schools never or rarely use films, compared with 78% of the county schools. Less use is made of television: 77% of the Church of England controlled schools never or rarely watch television, compared with 65% of the county schools. Less use is made of slides or filmstrips: 59% of the Church of England controlled schools never or rarely use slides or filmstrips, compared with 46% of the county schools. Less use is made of audio tapes or cassettes: 57% of the Church of England controlled schools never or rarely use audio tapes or cassettes, compared with 47% of the county schools. Less use is made even of radio broadcasts: 28% of the Church of England controlled schools never or rarely make use of radio broadcasts in religious education, compared with 22% of the county schools.

Text books and reference books are used with the same frequency for religious education in Church of England controlled schools and county schools. Fourth year junior pupils regularly use text books in 46% of the Church of England controlled schools and 46% of the county schools; they regularly use reference books in 79% of the Church of England controlled schools and 79% of the county schools. The one resource more frequently used in Church of England controlled schools is the bible. Fourth year junior pupils regularly use the bible in 80% of the Church of England controlled schools, compared with 65% of the county schools. This compares with 95% of the Church of England aided schools and 87% of the Catholic schools.

The versions of the bible used by teachers in Church of England controlled schools are more limited and more traditional than in Church of England aided schools. Their practice is much more closely aligned to that of teachers in county schools. The Authorised Version is used in a higher proportion of Church of England controlled schools than in county schools, while *The New English Bible* is used in a lower proportion of Church of England controlled schools than county schools. *Good News Bible* is used in 54% of the Church of England controlled schools, compared with 31% of the county schools and 63% of the Church of England aided schools.

The Authorised Version is available in class sets in 41% of the Church of England controlled schools; class sets of *Good News Bible* are available in 35%, the Revised Standard Version in 15% and *The New English Bible* in 6%. Church of England controlled schools are better resourced for bibles than county schools, but less well resourced than Church of England aided schools. Thus, 16% of the Church of England controlled schools do not possess a class set of bibles, compared with 30% of the county schools and 5% of the Church of England aided schools. Another 24% of the Church of England controlled schools possess class sets only of the Authorised Version. This means that 60% of the Church of England controlled schools possess class sets of a modern translation of the bible, compared with 49% of the county schools and 73% of the Church of England aided schools.

Assemblies

In the sense of providing an assembly for the whole school every day, Church of England controlled schools are more law abiding than county schools, but less so than Church of England aided schools. Thus, 35% of the Church of England controlled schools provide an assembly for the whole school every day, compared with 26% of the county schools and 51% of the Church of England aided schools. The majority of Church of England controlled schools say that assemblies take place at the beginning of the school day: this is always the case in 41% and usually the case in a further 56%.

While 9% of the Church of England controlled schools report that the nature of the school building makes an assembly for the whole school difficult, only 4% do not go ahead with holding an assembly for the whole school at least once a week. The pattern in the remaining 61% of the Church of England controlled schools which neither hold an assembly every day nor refrain altogether from holding assemblies for the whole school is that 10% hold one assembly, 10% hold two assemblies, 17% hold three assemblies and 24% hold four assemblies for the whole school every week.

Headteachers of Church of England controlled schools keep an even firmer hold on leading assemblies themselves than headteachers of Church of England aided schools. This does not mean that headteachers in Church of England controlled schools are personally involved in taking more assemblies each week than headteachers in Church of England aided schools, since overall fewer assemblies are held in Church of England controlled schools. It does mean, however, that other teachers and pupils in Church of England controlled schools have less experience of leading assemblies. Thus, other teachers are not usually involved in leading assemblies in 35% of the Church of England controlled schools, compared with 27% of the Church of England aided schools and 19% of the county schools. Similarly, pupils are not usually involved in leading assemblies in 56% of the Church of England controlled schools, compared with 51% of the Church of England aided schools and 36% of the county schools.

The average length of assemblies in Church of England controlled schools is longer than in Church of England aided schools, but shorter than in county schools. While only 27% of the Church of England aided schools say that their assemblies usually go on for more than 20 minutes, the proportion rises to 38% of the Church of England controlled schools and 43% of the county schools.

Like Church of England aided schools, Church of England controlled schools are more aware than county schools of pupil comfort in assemblies. Thus, 41% of the Church of England controlled schools and 41% of the Church of England aided schools provide chairs or benches, for at least some pupils, during assemblies, compared with 26% of the county schools.

The relationship between assemblies and the rest of the life of the school is much the same in Church of England controlled schools as in Church of England aided schools and county schools. In about half the Church of England controlled schools there is some relationship between assemblies and religious education or the general curriculum.

The right of parents to withdraw pupils from assemblies is just as likely to be asserted in Church of England controlled schools as in county schools and more likely than in Church of England aided schools. Thus, 27% of the Church of England controlled schools report that at least one pupil is currently withdrawn from assemblies, compared with 27% of the county schools and 19% of the Church of England aided schools. The number of pupils withdrawn from any one Church of England controlled school varies between 1 and 20. The school where 20 pupils are withdrawn is one of the few schools in the sample with a significant number of Hindu and Muslim pupils on roll. The 20 pupils withdrawn from assemblies in this school represent nearly 20% of the total school population.

The most frequent reason for withdrawal from assemblies in Church of England controlled schools is membership of the Jehovah Witnesses, experienced by 25% of the schools. The second most frequent reason is membership of other world religions, namely Muslims and Hindus, experienced by 6% of the Church of England controlled schools. Brethren also assert the right of withdrawal from assemblies in Church of England controlled schools. Church of England controlled schools in the sample have no current experience of members of staff requesting to be excused attendance at assemblies.

Worship

When asked to judge where they would place the majority of their assemblies on the five point continuum, ranging from 'explicitly Christian and denominational', through 'explicitly Christian but not denominational', 'implicitly Christian' and 'religious but not distinctively Christian' to 'largely secular and social', headteachers of Church of England controlled schools (49%) are just as likely to opt for an explicitly Christian position as headteachers of Church of England aided schools (47%). They are less likely, however, to opt for a denominational position. Thus, only 3% of the Church of England controlled schools say that these explicitly Christian assemblies are denominational in character, compared with 10% of the Church of England aided schools. At the other end of the continuum, in 6% of the Church of England controlled schools the majority of assemblies are largely secular and social, compared with none of the Church of England aided schools. The same proportion (7%) of Church of England controlled schools and Church of England aided schools describe the majority of their assemblies as religious, but not distinctively Christian. This leaves 38% of the Church of England controlled schools describing the majority of their assemblies as implicitly Christian, compared with 46% of the Church of England aided schools.

The range of educational experience available to pupils through assemblies is more restricted in Church of England controlled schools than in either Church of England aided schools or county schools. Pupils attending Church of England controlled schools are less likely to participate in dance or drama as part of their assemblies. They are less likely to see slides, television or video. They are less likely to experience silence. Thus, 79% of the Church of England controlled schools sometimes use drama, compared with 90% of the Church of England aided schools and 87% of the county schools; 32% of the Church of England controlled schools sometimes use dance, compared with 49% of the Church of England aided schools and 54% of the county schools; 68% of the Church of England controlled schools sometimes use slides, compared with 78% of the Church of England aided schools and 80% of the county schools; 69% of the Church of England controlled schools sometimes use silence, compared with 78% of the Church of England aided schools and 85% of the county schools. On the other hand, Church of England controlled schools are just as likely to use music or radio broadcasts as Church of England aided schools and county schools.

As far as the Christian character of assemblies is concerned, Church of England controlled schools occupy a middle place between Church of

D

England aided schools and county schools. The bible and the Lord's Prayer are used more frequently in Church of England controlled schools than in county schools, but less frequently than in Church of England aided schools. Thus, 31% of the Church of England controlled schools say that the Lord's Prayer is used daily among the fourth year junior pupils, compared with 23% of the county schools and 51% of the Church of England aided schools; 46% of the Church of England controlled schools say that scripture is read in assemblies at least once a week, compared with 71% of the Church of England aided schools and 36% of the county schools.

Similarly, assemblies in Church of England controlled schools are more likely to reflect the church's year than county schools, but less likely to do so than Church of England aided schools. Thus, 73% of the Church of England controlled schools say that their assemblies are closely related to the church's year, compared with 80% of the Church of England aided schools and 63% of the county schools.

On the other hand, pupils in Church of England controlled schools are no more likely to sing hymns or say prayers in assemblies than pupils in county schools. Thus, fourth year junior pupils sing hymns nearly every day in 71% of the Church of England controlled schools, compared with 75% of the county schools and 93% of the Church of England aided schools; they say prayers nearly every day in 66% of the Church of England controlled schools, compared with 64% of the county schools and 76% of the Church of England aided schools. Pupils are less likely to sing psalms or canticles in Church of England controlled schools than county schools: psalms and canticles are never sung in 90% of the Church of England controlled schools, compared with 68% of the Church of England aided schools and 74% of the county schools.

Headteachers of Church of England controlled schools are more inclined to think that hymns used in assemblies are related to hymns used in local churches than headteachers of either Church of England aided schools or county schools. Thus, 41% of the headteachers of Church of England controlled schools believe that there is a close relationship between hymns sung in assemblies and in local churches, compared with 31% of the headteachers of Church of England aided schools and 29% of the headteachers of county schools. This may simply reflect the conservatism of hymns chosen in Church of England controlled schools. This is consistent with the fact that Church of England controlled schools are even less likely to use a modern version of the Lord's Prayer than county schools.

Church of England controlled schools are less likely to use stories and traditions from other world faiths in assemblies than either Church of England aided schools or county schools: 14% of the Church of England controlled schools say that their assemblies draw on traditions from other world faiths at least once a week, compared with 24% of the Church of England aided schools and 21% of the county schools. On the other hand, Church of England controlled schools are more likely to use secular stories in assemblies than either Church of England aided schools or county schools: 66% of the Church of England controlled schools say their assemblies draw on secular stories at least once a week, compared with 49% of the Church of England aided schools and 60% of the county schools.

Church contact

Church of England controlled schools are less likely to be involved with local churches than Church of England aided schools, but more likely than county schools. Thus, 15% of the Church of England controlled schools had no contact with local churches during the last year, compared with 7% of the Church of England aided schools and 20% of the county schools.

During the past year, 74% of the Church of England controlled schools visited a local church to look at the building; 49% also stayed on to study the purpose of the church. By way of comparison, 68% of the county schools and 85% of the Church of England aided schools visited a local church within the past year; 39% of the county schools and 66% of the Church of England aided schools stayed on to study the purpose of the church. While Church of England controlled schools are more likely than county schools to have studied the purpose of the church, they are less likely to have talked with the clergy about the church. Thus, when they visited a local church, 44% of the Church of England controlled schools talked with the clergy about the church, compared with 51% of the county schools and 68% of the Church of England aided schools.

Church of England controlled schools are just as likely to hold a school service in church as Church of England aided schools (85%). On the other hand, Church of England controlled schools appear less committed to their school services than Church of England aided schools. While 71% of the Church of England aided schools actively involve their pupils in church services through the presentation of music, dance or drama, only 56% of the Church of England controlled schools make opportunities for this kind of active involvement. While 44% of the Church of England aided schools have displayed their pupils' work in church, only 31% of the

Church of England controlled schools have helped to foster links between church and school in this kind of way.

Similarly, Church of England controlled schools are less likely to take part in Sunday services than Church of England aided schools, but more likely than county schools. Thus, 22% of the Church of England controlled schools have taken part in a Sunday service during the past year, compared with 33% of the Church of England aided schools and 9% of the county schools.

Anglican clergy are less likely to keep in close touch with Church of England controlled schools than with Church of England aided schools, although they are more likely to do so than with county schools. Thus, 69% of the Church of England controlled schools receive weekly visits from the Anglican clergy, compared with 83% of the Church of England aided schools. Another 9% of the Church of England controlled schools say that the Anglican clergy visit the school at least once a month and 16% say that they visit less frequently than once a month. This means that 6% of the Church of England controlled schools are never visited by the Anglican clergy.

Anglican clergy are less likely to be involved in taking assemblies and religious education in Church of England controlled schools than in Church of England aided schools. While Anglican clergy take assemblies at least once a month in 68% of the Church of England aided schools, they do so in 54% of the Church of England controlled schools. In 13% of the Church of England controlled schools the Anglican clergy are never involved in taking assemblies. While Anglican clergy take religious education lessons at least once a month in 54% of the Church of England aided schools, they do so in 32% of the Church of England controlled schools. In 50% of the Church of England controlled schools the Anglican clergy are never involved in religious education. Anglican clergy celebrate communion at least once a term in just one of the 68 Church of England controlled schools in the sample.

The level of contact by Free Church ministers and Catholic priests with Church of England controlled schools is similar to that with Church of England aided schools. Just 21% of the Church of England controlled schools receive visits from Free Church ministers and 6% receive visits from Catholic priests. Free Church ministers are involved in assemblies in 18% of the Church of England controlled schools; Catholic priests are involved in assemblies in 4% of the Church of England controlled schools. Neither Free Church ministers nor Catholic priests are involved in religious education in the Church of England controlled schools in the sample.

Church of England controlled schools have less contact with other world religions than either Church of England aided schools or county schools. Only 10% of the Church of England controlled schools have visited a non-Christian place of worship within the past year, compared with 22% of both the county schools and the Church of England aided schools. Only 4% of the Church of England controlled schools have invited leaders of other world faiths to contribute to assemblies, compared with 10% of the Church of England aided schools and 16% of the county schools. Only 6% of the Church of England controlled schools have received visits from leaders of other world faiths, compared with 10% of the Church of England aided schools and 11% of the county schools. No Church of England controlled school in the sample has invited leaders of other world faiths to contribute to religious education lessons.

Resources

Church of England controlled schools are no more likely to use the diocesan religious education resource centre than county schools and less likely to do so than Church of England aided schools. Similarly, Church of England controlled schools are no more likely to make use of other religious education resource centres than county schools and less likely to do so than Church of England aided schools. Thus, 13% of the Church of England controlled schools used the diocesan religious education resource centre during the past year; 3% used both the diocesan centre and another centre; 6% used just another religious education resource centre. This means that during the past year 81% of the Church of England controlled schools made no use of a religious education resource centre.

Membership of the Christian Education Movement has been taken up by 15% of the Church of England controlled schools, compared with 10% of the Church of England aided schools and 8% of the county schools. While only 29% of the Church of England aided schools are subscribing members of the National Society, the proportion is considerably lower among the Church of England controlled schools. Only 12% of the Church of England controlled schools in the sample are subscribing members of the National Society.

Most Church of England controlled schools feel that they need extra resourcing with religious education and assemblies. While 78% of the Church of England aided schools and 79% of the county schools point to specific ways in which they could benefit from additional resourcing in these areas, the proportion rises to 91% among the Church of England controlled schools.

The specific needs identified by Church of England controlled schools are ranked in a similar order to those identified by county schools and Church of England aided schools. At the top of the list comes the need for more reference books (62%). Second on the list comes the need for more visual material, slides or filmstrips (43%). The provision of more text books is seen as the third priority (34%). Church of England controlled schools feel that they are less adequately resourced than Church of England aided schools in the area of bibles and hymn books. Thus, 13% of the Church of England controlled schools put in a plea for more copies of an appropriate hymn book, compared with 5% of the Church of England aided schools; 29% of the Church of England controlled schools put in a plea for new bibles, compared with 10% of the Church of England aided schools.

Generally, Church of England controlled schools feel that they are less adequately serviced by local churches, local clergy or the religious education advisory staff than Church of England aided schools. Thus, 19% of the Church of England controlled schools say that they lack sufficient contact with local churches, compared with 12% of the Church of England aided schools; 16% of the Church of England controlled schools say that they lack sufficient co-operation from local clergy, compared with 12% of the Church of England aided schools; 29% of the Church of England controlled schools say that they lack sufficient contact with the religious education adviser, compared with 24% of the Church of England aided schools.

Like county schools and Church of England aided schools, only a very small proportion of Church of England controlled schools feel that they lack the goodwill of staff, pupils or parents for religious education. Just 2% of the Church of England controlled schools feel that they lack the goodwill of staff; 9% feel that they lack the goodwill of pupils; 9% feel that they lack the goodwill of parents.

Overview

The determining difference between whether a Church of England school is currently aided or controlled was a crucial decision taken by the governing body. In the case of controlled status, the governing body decided not to maintain an on-going financial commitment to the school.

Various interesting consequences emerge from these decisions. There are more Church of England controlled schools in Gloucestershire than

Church of England aided schools: more governing bodies sought to be released from on-going financial commitment than sought to retain it. Larger Church of England schools are more likely to have opted for voluntary controlled status than aided status: larger school buildings are more expensive for the churches to maintain. Church of England schools in poorer urban areas are more likely to have opted for controlled status: the decision to keep aided status was generally a local one and depended for its success, at least initially, on local financial resources.

Because controlled schools do not involve the churches in on-going financial commitment, the Church of England does not maintain a majority voice on their governing bodies. Nevertheless, the church still appears to exercise significant influence over the appointment of headteachers. Headteachers of Church of England controlled schools are more likely to be church-going Anglicans than headteachers of county schools.

Contact between Church of England controlled schools and the local church varies greatly from place to place. In practice some Church of England controlled schools are indistinguishable from the most church-related Church of England aided schools. They have frequent contact with the local clergy and regular contact with the local church. In these cases, the church may have as much influence through controlled status as through aided status. Other Church of England controlled schools are indistinguishable from the least church-related county schools. They have minimal contact with the local clergy and practically no contact with the local church. In these cases, the church may exercise little influence through retaining its historic investment in the school.

Both these contrasting implementations of controlled status raise questions for the church. In essence, controlled schools operate as neighbourhood schools, serving the needs of specific communities, just like county schools. Through controlled schools, the Church of England exercises first and foremost its theology of service to the nation, or its general function in education. Although controlled status gives the church the right to provide denominational worship throughout the school and denominational religious education for the pupils whose parents request it, controlled schools are not ideally suited to fulfil first and foremost the Church of England's theology of nurture, or its domestic function in education.

Accordingly, controlled schools which are operated as distinctively Christian schools pose for the church the problem of justifying the use of neighbourhood schools for specific Christian purposes. How can legitimate service of the nation's educational needs also legitimate the use of controlled schools for communicating the values and belief systems of a religious group? On the other hand, controlled schools which are operated as indistinguishable from county schools pose for the church the problem of justifying involvement in the state maintained system of education to which it is not making a distinctive contribution. If Church of England controlled schools have nothing distinctive to offer to the state maintained system of education, on what grounds can the church build a case for wishing to retain these schools?

In the meantime, the theoretical uncertainty surrounding the nature and purpose of controlled schools is clearly reflected in the practical attitudes of headteachers and in the curriculum provision. Of the four types of school discussed in this study, it is the headteachers of Church of England controlled schools who are least certain about their commitment to the type of school in which they are working. They are experiencing the uncertainty of inhabiting a no-man's land between the interests of church and state.

This uncertainty is also reflected in Church of England controlled schools' attitudes towards religious education and assemblies. Less time is given to religious education in Church of England controlled schools than in any other kind of school in the sample; less imaginative use is made of curriculum resources for religious education in Church of England controlled schools than in any other kind of school in the sample; assemblies tend to be more formal and to give less opportunity for active staff and pupil involvement in Church of England controlled schools than in any other kind of school in the sample. Uncertainty about the religious identity of the controlled sector seems to be having a detrimental effect on what is available for pupils to experience in the statutory areas of religious education and school worship.

9 VILLAGE SCHOOLS

Villages

Of the 224 primary and junior schools in the present sample, 116 were described by the local education authority as village schools. Overall, the average population of these 116 communities is just over 900 people, but this average conceals quite a wide range of community sizes. The smallest village still supporting a primary school has a population of only 140; four of the communities have populations of 200 or less, while a further 43 have populations between 201 and 500. Another 33 of the communities have populations between 501 and 1,000. This leaves only 36 of the village schools in communities of over 1,000 people.

Today, village schools do not exist simply to serve the needs of the community in which they are situated. Young children are brought into village schools by bus, taxi or private car, from a number of neighbouring hamlets or villages. It cannot, therefore, be assumed that children attending village schools necessarily have specific points of contact with the community in which the school is situated, or that the school is necessarily easily accessible for children or for parents. A number of small village schools may well be serving more children from outside the village than from the village itself.

Nevertheless, the retention of the village school is an important symbol for the life of a village. At the turn of the century, a great number of Gloucestershire villages possessed their own school, church, chapel and parsonage. Now a feature of many villages is the closed chapel, the converted school and the 'old rectory'. The withdrawal of these resources from villages is rarely co-ordinated. Today half (48%) of the villages which retain their school have lost their parsonage house. Other village amenities, like shops, post offices and buses are also disappearing.

From the point of view of the religious life of the school, the changing face of the church in the countryside may have significant implications. Those villages which have lost their Anglican parsonage are unlikely to have a Free Church minister living in the community. When clergy are not resident, it is less easy for village schools to build up a close relationship with them. If church life is symbolised by a redundant chapel and an Anglican church used only once a fortnight, there may be little incentive for village schools to identify with local churches. If children are recruited into village schools from a number of neighbouring parishes, which relate to different groups of churches, it is often difficult for schools and clergy to establish the right lines of communication. All but two village schools in the present sample exist primarily to serve a specific neighbourhood. The other two village schools are Catholic schools which exist primarily to serve the Catholic community over a wider geographical area. Since the main purpose of the statistical analysis in the first half of this chapter is to characterise the religious provision of village neighbourhood schools, the two Catholic schools will be omitted.

Schools

Many village schools in Gloucestershire are small schools. At the time of survey, two village schools supported a roll of only 17 full-time pupils; nearly one in five (18%) had 30 or less pupils, while nearly three in five (59%) had 60 or less pupils. As many as 45% of the village schools had less than three full-time teachers. Following the publication of the White Paper *Better Schools* (1985) a number of local education authorities have begun to speak in terms of 60 pupils and three teachers as the minimum desirable size for a primary school. A large proportion of village schools clearly fail to meet these two criteria.

The profile of headteachers of village schools emerges as rather different from town and suburban schools. Headteachers of village schools tend to be younger: while in the county as a whole only 22% of the headteachers are under the age of forty, 31% of the headteachers of village schools are under forty. Small village schools are not infrequently used as first headships and serve as stepping stones to larger schools. Second, the headships of village schools are more likely to be held by women than the headships of town or suburban schools.

Parents who live in areas served by village schools are much more likely to find that their children are attending a Church of England school: 65% of the village schools in the sample are Church of England controlled or Church of England aided schools. This is mainly due to the way in which so many village churches took the initiative to found schools during the nineteenth century. Now the Church of England remains financially committed to 25% of the village schools in Gloucestershire through aided status, and retains its historic investment in another 40% through controlled status.

The vast majority (93%) of the headteachers of village schools claim to be members of one of the Christian churches. Only 7% of these headteachers style themselves as agnostics or humanists. Over half (51%) attend Sunday church services most weeks. From this point of view, there is likely to be considerable goodwill and sympathy towards the churches in village schools.

Statutory provision

Village schools devote more time to religious education than other schools in the county. A third of the village schools (33%) give more than an hour a week for religious education among their fourth year junior pupils, compared with a quarter (25%) of the other schools. Village schools are also more inclined to give closer attention to the appropriate syllabus of religious education: 47% of the village schools follow their syllabus closely, compared with 36% of the other schools.

What actually takes place in religious education in village schools differs in some interesting ways from other schools. The range of resources available for religious education is more restricted in village schools, for example audio-visual aids and reference books. Only 39% of the village schools use slides or filmstrips for religious education among their fourth year junior pupils, even occasionally, compared with 64% of the other schools; 78% of the village schools use reference books for religious education among their fourth year junior pupils, often or occasionally, compared with 85% of the other schools. Village schools rely much more heavily on radio broadcasts for religious education: 53% of the village schools often use the radio for religious education among their fourth year junior pupils, compared with 41% of the other schools. Village schools also make more frequent use of bibles in religious education: 27% of the village schools often use copies of the bible among their fourth year junior pupils, compared with 15% of the other schools.

A number of factors probably helps to explain these differences in religious education in village schools. Because village schools are smaller, they draw upon a more restricted range of staff skills, they work with a more limited budget and they need to develop curricula for wider age ranges.

Children attending village schools are more likely to experience a daily assembly for the whole school: 41% of the village schools hold a daily assembly for the whole school, compared with 25% of the other schools. Assemblies in village schools are also likely to be more traditional in format.

Because village schools are smaller, the atmosphere in assemblies is rather different from larger schools. Assemblies in village schools tend to be shorter: 22% of the village schools say that generally their assemblies do not last for more than 15 minutes, compared with just 5% of the other schools. The older pupils are more likely to sit on chairs or benches during assemblies in village schools: 44% of the village schools say that this happens, compared with 23% of the other schools. In village schools, assemblies are more likely to be related to other aspects of the curriculum: 54% of the village schools say that there is a close relationship between assemblies and other components of the curriculum, compared with 49% of the other schools. More significantly, 59% of the village schools say that there is a close relationship between assemblies and religious education, compared with 45% of the other schools.

The resources available for enriching assemblies are more limited in village schools, where pupils are less likely to experience music, dance, drama or slides. For example, music is used at least once a week during assemblies in 53% of the village schools, compared with 72% of the other schools. Village schools are much more reliant on radio broadcasts to help with assemblies.

The other way in which assemblies in village schools differ from town and suburban schools is that they tend to be more explicitly Christian. For example, 73% of the village schools say that there is a close relationship between assemblies and the church's year, compared with 66% of the other schools; the Lord's Prayer is used daily in 35% of the village schools, compared with 26% of the other schools.

Church contact

Children who attend village schools have considerably more contact with Anglican clergy than children who attend suburban or town schools. Over half (56%) of the village schools are visited at least once a week by the vicar, compared with a third (33%) of the other schools. Anglican clergy are also more likely to make a regular contribution to assemblies and to religious education in village schools than in suburban or town schools. Thus, the vicar takes an assembly at least once a week in 44% of the village schools, compared with 37% of the other schools; the vicar takes religious education at least once a week in 35% of the village schools, compared with 11% of the other schools.

The higher level of contact between Anglican clergy and village schools is partly a consequence of the greater concentration of Church of England schools in rural areas, and partly a consequence of the different pastoral strategy operated by rural Anglican clergy in comparison with their urban and suburban colleagues. Anglican clergy living or working in comparatively small communities often find themselves involved in many aspects of the life of those communities, including the village school, whether or not this school happens to be a church foundation.

Although children who attend village schools have more contact with Anglican clergy, they have less contact with clergy of other denominations. While 56% of the village schools are visited weekly by Anglican clergy, none is visited weekly by a Free Church minister and just 2% receive weekly visits from Catholic priests. Looked at from another perspective, 95% of the village schools never receive a visit from Catholic priests, compared with 85% of the other schools; 80% of the village schools never receive a visit from Free Church ministers, compared with 51% of the other schools.

While 80% of the village schools sometimes invite Anglican clergy to conduct assemblies, only 20% ever invite Free Church ministers and 2% invite Catholic priests to do so. This compares with 46% of the other schools in the county which invite Free Church ministers to take assemblies, at least occasionally, and 12% of the other schools which invite Catholic priests to take assemblies, at least occasionally. Free Church ministers occasionally contribute to religious education in just 4% of the village schools; Catholic priests contribute to religious education lessons in none of the village schools.

The lower level of contact between Free Church ministers and village schools may be an interesting reflection not on the denominational exclusivity of Church of England village schools, but on the general withdrawal of the Free Churches from the countryside. It is now comparatively rare for Free Church ministers to live in villages. The surviving village chapels are serviced by local preachers and by ministers who live in the towns.

The contact between village schools and the local church is by no means all one way. Not only do the clergy visit the school; the pupils also visit the church. As many as three-quarters (73%) of the village schools hold at least one school service in church each year. A fifth (22%) of the village schools actually involve their pupils in a Sunday church service from time to time. Village schools clearly continue to express a range of close relationships with the Christian churches.

School profiles

The first half of this chapter has made statistical generalisations about village schools as a group. This kind of analysis is only part of the story and actually conceals some of the wide differences between village schools. The second half of the chapter provides the opportunity to meet four village schools in depth, as a reminder that beneath statistical generalisation we are the whole time dealing with uniqueness and individuality. The framework for these school profiles is provided by the headteachers' replies to the questionnaire, but the detail is augmented by other sources of information, including school information brochures and personal visits. It is important to emphasise that, unlike the statistical analysis, these school profiles are not limited to Gloucestershire.

The four schools selected include a county school, a Church of England controlled school, a Church of England aided school and a Catholic school. These four schools are not meant to be typical of the categories from which they are drawn. While the profiles are carefully based on real situations, the names attributed to the schools are entirely fictitious.

Castle Wold County Primary School

Castle Wold school was built without church sponsorship just four years after the 1870 Education Act, to serve the small village of Castle Wold, a neighbouring village and the surrounding hamlets. The catchment area of Castle Wold school was extended when a neighbouring church school was closed some years ago.

Castle Wold school still occupies the original building. Various enlargements have taken place and the school house has been converted to provide library, office and storage space. Nevertheless, space is still rather cramped and the school uses the village hall for drama, physical education, concerts and so on. Today Castle Wold school has 50 full-time pupils and a full-time staff of three teachers, including the teaching head.

Castle Wold has a population of around 600 people. Although a village of this size no longer qualifies for a full-time parson, Castle Wold has retained its parsonage house and shares its vicar with several neighbouring communities. Because the vicar still lives in Castle Wold, he is able to contribute to the life of the community in a number of ways. He takes a special interest in the village school: he leads an assembly once a week and sometimes makes more frequent visits. He has no statutory right to do this, but the school welcomes his interest and involvement. The vicar is the only clergyman living in Castle Wold and the school has no contact with Free Church ministers or Catholic priests.

The vicar's welcome at the school is due largely to the headteacher, a woman in her mid-fifties. She lives in the village and is an active member of the local church congregation. She says that, given the choice and all things being equal, she would generally prefer to teach in a Church of

England aided school, rather than in a county school. As things are, she tries to encourage as much church involvement in her county school as possible, and the vicar's weekly assembly is one way towards achieving this.

During the past year, the headteacher has arranged for pupils to visit the local Anglican church, to look at the building and to talk with the vicar. The school also holds an occasional school service in the church. When the school does this, it makes every effort to involve the pupils fully. They present their own music and drama in the service; they take some of their art work along to make a display in the church. On the other hand, the school does not become involved in Sunday worship in the church.

Every day begins in Castle Wold County Primary School with an assembly for the whole school. Each week the vicar leads one assembly, an assistant teacher leads one assembly, the headteacher leads two assemblies and the radio takes care of the other day. The headteacher explains that the majority of the assemblies are explicitly Christian, but not denominational. A hymn is sung and prayers are said each morning. Usually the hymns are chosen from the BBC's hymn book for schools, *Come and Praise*, but sometimes hymns and songs are chosen from *Sound of Living Waters* or *Fresh Sounds*. Most days a story is told from a Christian background, although sometimes the story is totally secular. It is very rare for a story to be chosen from a non-Christian religious tradition. At least once a week a passage is read from the bible, usually *Good News Bible*, although sometimes *The New English Bible*, *The Living Bible* or *New International Version* is preferred. At least once a week pupils join in saying the Lord's Prayer, always in the traditional form.

Assemblies tend to go on for between 21 and 25 minutes. Care is taken to make sure that the pupils feel comfortable during assemblies and so chairs and benches are provided. Assemblies are formal occasions in Castle Wold school. They follow the pattern of the church's year very closely, but are not related to the general curriculum or to the religious education lessons. Only very occasionally do assemblies include anything in addition to hymns, prayers, stories and bible readings. Pupils are not generally encouraged to play their own musical instruments in assemblies or to write their own prayers.

The school information booklet explains the function of the daily assembly in the following words.

> Daily assembly plays an important part in the life of the school. Staff and children take an active part.... Stories from the bible and more recent examples are used to illustrate themes such as caring, courage, faith, etc. The

children are encouraged to be aware of the wonder of the created world and to be thankful for it. They are also encouraged to understand and respect the rights and opinions of other people and to develop concern for those less privileged than themselves. . . . Parents who wish to withdraw their children from attendance at religious worship or instruction are asked to discuss this with the headteacher.

Being a county school, religous education in Castle Wold follows the county's agreed syllabus. The headteacher says that the school follows this syllabus quite closely and has devised its own detailed scheme of work for religious education based on the syllabus. Although the headteacher is keen on the religious life of the school, neither she nor another member of staff has undertaken any in-service training in religious education during the past three years. No one among the staff has been designated to act as 'consultant' for religious education. No recent use has been made of the diocesan religious education resource centre nor of any other resource centre for religious education.

Religious education is taught in Castle Wold school primarily as a separate timetable subject, occupying between half an hour and one hour each week. The main resources available for religious education are a set of *Good News Bible* and the weekly radio broadcasts. Sometimes slides, audio cassettes and reference books are used as well. The headteacher is far from content with the range of resources available for religious education within the school and would like to be able to build up a better supply, especially of slides and reference books.

From the church's point of view, Castle Wold County Primary School seems to be serving the local church as effectively as if it were a Church of England controlled school. This is a direct consequence of the Christian commitment of the headteacher and her good working relationship with the local vicar. The church cannot assume that the same situation would arise under a new headteacher, nor can the vicar directly influence the appointment of the next headteacher, since he is not a governor of the school.

Lower Wold C of E Controlled Primary School

Lower Wold school was opened by the rector in 1844, for the children of the parish. The school was built with financial aid from the National Society to provide education in accordance with the principles of the established church. At the time of the 1944 Education Act, the managers of the school elected for aided status. During the early 1960s, major structural repairs needed by the building encouraged the managers to revise their decision. They decided to accept controlled status and to be relieved of their ongoing financial liability.

Today Lower Wold school has 42 pupils on roll. A school of this size qualifies for two full-time teachers, including the teaching head, and an additional part-time teacher for one day a week. The school building is elderly, but spacious. Although only two classes are currently needed, the building provides a third classroom, as well as the former school house which has been converted to provide ancillary accommodation. The school makes good use of the available space.

The headteacher of Lower Wold school is a man in his early fifties. He was trained at a Church of England college and regards himself as a non-practising member of the Church of England. This is his first headship. He is not particularly keen on the church school system and would prefer to be working in a county school. He is one of the few headteachers in the county who would like to see the law about religious education and assemblies changed so that they would no longer be compulsory.

The other full-time member of staff has a completely different view on church schools and on the place of religion in school life. She is a licensed reader in the Church of England and keen to cement links between church and school which the headteacher would not actively encourage.

The teaching of religious education in the school is shared between both members of staff and the local vicar. The school information brochures explains that:

> Religious education is seen as part of the integrated curriculum of the school, and as we are a church school, the vicar does take the older children for one session a week. In accordance with the 1944 Education Act, parents still have the right to withdraw their children from religious education, and where they do so, pupils would be expected to occupy these times with private study.

The older children spend between half an hour and one hour on religious education each week. The headteacher feels that neither the school staff nor the vicar pays much attention to the syllabus of religious education. No one in the school has an overall brief for co-ordinating religious education; the school has not developed its own detailed scheme of work for the subject. Apart from the vicar's visits, the main resources used in religious education are radio broadcasts. Occasionally text books and bibles are used, and on rare occasions use is made of audio cassettes. The school never uses reference books, slides, filmstrips or films in religious education. Nor is the headteacher particularly keen on building up a better range of resources for religious education. He is content not to use reference books, slides, filmstrips, films or audio cassettes. The school already possesses two sets of bibles, a set of the Authorised Version and a set of *Good News Bibles*, which the headteacher would prefer not to use. He does, however, feel that a new set of text books might make preparing religious education lessons easier.

The school information booklet says that the accent in religious education is on:

> themes of caring, helping, sharing, sacrifice, generosity, determination, honesty, etc., drawn from many sources. . . . These would concentrate on things close to children; their families, friends, other children, school, neighbours and pets.

Lower Wold school maintains the pattern of beginning every school day with an assembly. On three days a week the whole school meets for an assembly. The headteacher and the other teacher take it in turns to lead these assemblies for the whole school. On the other two days separate classroom assemblies are held for the infants and the juniors. The vicar does not help with leading assemblies, nor is it the practice of the school to invite other outside speakers.

Assemblies in Lower Wold school follow the traditional shape of a hymn, a prayer and a story. The school uses the BBC hymn book for schools, *Come and Praise*, and once a week tunes into the radio service for schools. The daily hymn is invariably accompanied by a small group of recorder players. Once a week the pupils are encouraged to prepare their own prayers for use in assembly. The Lord's Prayer is said at least three days a week; the school continues to use the traditional version of this prayer, although the village church uses the new translation from *The Alternative Service Book* at the main Sunday services. The story is usually taken from a Christian background, but not usually from the bible itself. Assemblies in Lower Wold school rarely include drama, dance, music or silence.

Although the headteacher is not personally keen on developing links between the village school and the local church, and although the school is controlled rather than aided, quite close ties continue to exist between school and church. This is largely due to the influence of the assistant teacher and the rector.

Once a term the village school prepares for an act of worship in the parish church on a Sunday, when the pupils, their parents and the local congregation join together to share in the same service. Sometimes the school prepares for a special Sunday evening service; sometimes the school shares in the Sunday morning parish communion. In either case the pupils prepare music, dance or drama and project work to share with their parents and the congregation. A lot of the preparation is done in the school, but then, during the week before the service, the children come down to the church several times to put the finishing touches to their contribution and to display their work.

The services shared by school and church are a powerful symbol in the local community of the church's involvement in the life of the school and the school's concern for the life of the church. Although most of the pupils come from other villages and from families who are not regular church-goers, their parents seem to welcome this arrangement. It is, however, an arrangement secured not because the church originally built the school, nor because the school continues to have controlled status, nor even because the foundation governors appointed a practising churchman as headteacher, but mainly because the right relationships exist between the rector and the assistant teacher.

Upper Wold C of E Aided Primary School

Architecturally, Upper Wold school symbolises the historic link between village church and village school. Under the influence of the Tractarian movement, an extravagant and beautiful complex of church, vicarage and school was built around 1850, a half a mile or so out of the village.

At the time of the 1944 Education Act, the managers of Upper Wold school elected for aided status and they have been able to afford to retain that status. Today Upper Wold school has 83 full-time pupils, divided into three classes. There are three full-time teachers and two part-time teachers. In order to accommodate three classes, the Victorian building has been augmented by two additional classrooms.

Although architecturally the school clearly proclaims its historic link with the church, the school brochure is much more reticent about this link. The cover of the school brochure simply reads 'Upper Wold C of E School'. Nowhere in the brochure is the school described as being 'voluntary aided', nor is any attempt made to explain the history of the school or its contemporary institutional links with the church. No mention is made of denominational worship, denominational religious education, or contact with the rector.

There are just three specific mentions made of religion in the school brochure. The first mention occurs in a statement about the overall aims and objectives of the school.

> The curricular programme is concerned with the development of the 'whole' child, namely, intellectual, spiritual, moral, emotional, social and physical.

The second mention is in one of the specific aims of the school.

> To foster the children's understanding of the Christian religion.

The third mention concerns the right of exemption from religious education.

Parents who wish to exercise their right to withdraw their child from worship or RE under Section 25 of the 1944 Education Act are asked to consult the headteacher.

The church-related character of the school is much more in evidence than the school brochure would lead us to expect. The headteacher of Upper Wold school, a man in his fifties, says that he was attracted to the post specifically because it is a church school. He is a member of the Church of England and a regular church-goer. He believes in church schools and is clear that he would rather teach in a Church of England aided school than in any other type of school. The headteacher's personal commitment to the Christian faith plays a large part in shaping the religious life of Upper Wold school.

The rector also has a significant role in the life of Upper Wold school. To begin with he is chairman of the governors. Then he makes full use of the privileges of aided status. He is a regular visitor to the school, he conducts an assembly every week and he takes the top class for religious education each week.

Both the rector and the headteacher take the place of religious education in the school very seriously. Religious education is dealt with as separate timetable periods for the top class; between one and a half and two hours are devoted to the subject every week. As a Church of England aided school, the headteacher says that the school follows the diocesan syllabus very closely. In addition to following the diocesan syllabus closely, Upper Wold school has also drawn up its own detailed scheme of work for religious education.

Religious education in the top class often uses copies of the bible. The school possesses two class sets of bibles, the Authorised Version and *Good News Bible*. It is *Good News Bible* which is most frequently used. Religious education also makes regular use of slides or filmstrips, reference books and radio broadcasts. The school has built up its own set of resources for religious education and the headteacher feels that the school is now well stocked. There are no specific resources which he feels the school lacks in this area. On the other hand, neither the headteacher nor any other member of staff has made use of a religious education resource centre during the past year.

Each day in Upper Wold school begins with an assembly. Once a week the assembly is conducted by the rector and once a week by the deputy head or the assistant teacher. The headteacher is responsible for leading assembly on two other days each week. Once a week the assembly is directed by the radio broadcasts. The majority of assemblies are explicitly Christian and never entirely secular. They usually last between 16 and 20 minutes. The daily pattern for assemblies includes hymns, prayers and the Lord's Prayer. On most days a passage is read from the bible or a story is told from a Christian background. Occasionally the story is secular rather than religious, but stories are used from non-Christian religious traditions only rarely. The children are not generally encouraged to shape an assembly themselves. Once a term the instrumentalists are given a chance to share their music and two or three times a term individual children write their own prayers and read them out in front of the school.

Daily assemblies are seen very much as a discrete part of the school day. The themes chosen for assemblies closely reflect the church's year. They do not attempt to integrate with either the curriculum in general or the religious education programme.

While the local rector plays a prominent role in the life of the school, other denominations do not. The school is never visited by Free Church ministers or Catholic priests. Free Church ministers and Catholic priests are never invited to contribute to assemblies or to religious education.

In some ways the school's proximity to the church enables the pupils to make frequent use of the church building as a resource. Within the past year the top class has studied the architecture of the church and made a study of the purpose of the church. The rector has shown the pupils round the church and talked to them about his work. Once a year the school holds a service in the church. In other ways, however, the school fails to make use of its proximity to the church. The children's work is never taken into the church and when there is a school service it tends to be something arranged for the children rather than by them. The school never becomes involved in the Sunday worship of the church.

Aided status seems to have been important in shaping the religious life of Upper Wold school. Aided status enables the rector to visit the school, to conduct assemblies and to take religious education classes. Aided status attracted the present headteacher as a practising church-goer who wanted his Christian commitment to be reflected in his professional work. On the other hand, while aided status is affecting the life of the school, the school does not appear to be having much effect on the life of the local church. If the local church wished, so much more could be done to build bridges between church and school.

Wold Abbey Catholic Primary School

St Teresa's Catholic Primary School at Wold Abbey is an aided school established to serve a large and scattered Catholic parish. While the school exists primarily to serve Catholic families, the school's information booklet explains that:

> Non-Catholic children are admitted after discussion with, and at the discretion of, the headmaster and chairman of governors.

The chairman of the governors is a Catholic priest. The headteacher is also a practising Catholic, a man in his forties who attends mass weekly. The headteacher is committed to the Catholic school system.

Today St Teresa's school has just 60 pupils, which makes it one of the smallest Catholic schools in the country. There is a full-time staff of three, including a teaching head, and one part-time remedial teacher. The school is divided into three classes: infants, lower juniors and upper juniors.

The Catholic faith plays an important part in the life of the school. All children are expected to participate fully in the religious life and ceremonies of the school, even the non-Catholics. The school information booklet makes it plain to parents that:

> The religious and moral development is in accordance with the rites and beliefs of the Roman Catholic church. The children are encouraged to see the school as part of the parish community. Through daily contact with the parish priest or his curate, the children are kept in close contact with all parish activities. The week begins with Holy Mass on Monday morning, and ends with Benediction on Friday afternoon. Due to the shortage of staff it is not possible to allow non-Catholic children to absent from religious classes or ceremonies. The moral virtues of honesty, truthfulness and charity are stressed at all times. No direct lessons in sex education are given but any questions the children might ask are answered in a straightforward manner.

Religious education is taught as separate timetable periods. The top class devotes more than two hours to religious education each week. The school follows a Catholic programme of religious education closely and has developed its own detailed scheme of work for the subject. Some religious education is taught by a Catholic priest who comes into the school twice a week. At the same time all three full-time members of staff are qualified to teach religious education.

The three main resources used in teaching religious education in St Teresa's school are text books, reference books and the local church. The school does not possess a class set of bibles and never uses slides, filmstrips, audio cassettes, films, radio or television for religious education among the top class. The headteacher feels that his school is properly and adequately resourced for religious education. The pupils have frequent contact with the local Catholic church. While many county or Church of England village schools go to the local church to study the building or to look at the architecture, the children of St Teresa's go to their church to worship. They take part in weekday services and Sunday services, as well as arranging their own school services. When the pupils take part in a service, they present their own music, but they do not display their work.

In addition to attending mass on Monday, benediction on Friday and classroom prayers, St Teresa's school meets just once a week for an assembly for the whole school. This assembly is always conducted by the headteacher and lasts between 16 and 20 minutes. Assemblies follow very closely the structure of the church's year and also have a close relationship with what is going on in religious education. On the other hand, assemblies are not related to the general curriculum.

The headteacher sees the aim of the weekly assembly to be explicitly Christian and denominational. Each week this act of worship includes hymns, prayers, a passage from the bible and a religious story from a Christian background. Each week the pupils sing psalms or canticles and say the Lord's Prayer. The hymns are usually chosen from *Celebration Hymnal*. The choice of *Celebration Hymnal* means that the school uses the same book as the local church, thus creating a firm link between the hymns sung in school and church. The pupils prepare for their weekly assemblies in two main ways. Some children write their own prayers, while the instrumentalists practise the tunes to accompany the hymns.

St Teresa's school has a strongly denominational environment. Although non-Catholic children are admitted, they are expected to behave as if they were Catholics. Clergy from other denominations are not invited to play a part in the life of St Teresa's school. Practising Christian parents from other denominations who elect to send their children to this school need to accept that their own denominational traditions will not be respected. On the other hand, they know that the religious formation of their children, within a Catholic context, is taken most seriously.

10 TOWN SCHOOLS

Towns

Of the 224 primary and junior schools in the present sample, 11 are town schools in the centre of Cheltenham or Gloucester and a further 47 are town schools in one of the smaller towns. These other towns range in population size from 1,717 to 21,000. In closer analysis, 17 town schools are located in communities of 5,000 or less, while a further 22 are located in communities between 5,000 and 10,000. This leaves eight town schools in communities of between 10,000 and 21,000.

Just as village schools tend to serve a wider neighbourhood than the village itself, many schools in small towns also serve the neighbouring area. However, while it cannot be assumed that all pupils attending schools in small towns live in the town itself, it is likely that the school is easily accessible for many of the pupils and their parents. It is easier for schools in small towns to assume a closer relationship between the pupils and the immediate environment than for village schools.

Town schools, even in small towns, have easier access than village schools to a range of amenities. From the point of view of the religious life of the school, this may include easier access to churches and to clergy. The chapels built by the Free Churches in the eighteenth and nineteenth centuries are more likely to have survived in small towns than in villages. Today Free Church ministers are housed in centres of population and serve a wide network of village chapels. The reorganisation of rural ministry in the Anglican church, while withdrawing clergy from many villages, has tended to retain a parsonage house in small towns. In the present sample of 47 small towns, only one no longer has a resident Anglican clergyman; this small town has an estimated population of about 2,000. Church life may be more vibrant and the churches may seem to be playing a more significant part in the life of small towns than in the life of small villages.

All but four town schools in the present sample exist primarily to serve the local neighbourhood. The other four town schools are Catholic schools, which exist primarily to serve the Catholic community over a wider geographical area. Since the main purpose of the statistical analysis in the first half of this chapter is to characterise the religious provision of town neighbourhood schools, the four Catholic schools will be omitted.

Schools

Unlike village schools, all the town schools in Gloucestershire at the time of the survey had more than 60 pupils and at least three full-time members of staff. The smallest town school had 73 pupils; the largest had 393. Two-thirds (65%) of the town schools had over 200 pupils, while one-sixth (17%) had over 300 pupils. The small school controversy which affects the future of so many village schools is not such a problem for town schools.

Headteachers of town schools tend to be older than headteachers of village schools. While 37% of the headteachers of village schools are fifty or over, the proportion in this age group rises to 46% of the headteachers of town schools. Women are less likely to hold the headships of town schools catering for junior aged pupils than of village schools. Headteachers of town schools are more likely to live in the area served by their school than headteachers of village schools. While 22% of the headteachers of village schools live in the area served by their school, the proportion rises to 30% of the headteachers of town schools.

Parents who live in areas served by town schools are less likely to find that their children are attending a Church of England school than parents who live in areas served by village schools. While 65% of the village schools are Church of England schools, the proportion drops to 43% of the town schools; 30% of the town schools are Church of England controlled and 13% are Church of England aided.

Although there are fewer church schools in towns than in villages, the vast majority (89%) of the headteachers of town schools claim membership of one or other of the Christian churches. Only 11% of these headteachers style themselves as agnostics or humanists. Indeed, headteachers of town schools are even more inclined to be regular church-goers than headteachers of village schools; 57% of the headteachers of town schools and 51% of the headteachers of village schools say that they attend church most Sundays.

Town schools are more likely than village schools to be able to draw on the skills of staff who have undertaken professional initial training in religious education or have attended recent in-service training in religious education. For example, 37% of the town schools have a member of staff who studied religious education as a main course during initial training, compared with 19% of the village schools; 57% of the town schools have a member of staff who has attended an in-service day course or series of meetings on religious education during the past three years, compared with 39% of the village schools. Similarly, 50% of the town schools have a member of staff designated to act as 'consultant' for religious education, compared with 32% of the village schools. These differences reflect the wider range of staff and professional resources available to larger schools.

Statutory provision

Town schools devote less time to religious education than village schools. Only 24% of the town schools give more than an hour a week to religious education among their fourth year junior pupils, compared with 33% of the village schools. On the other hand, town schools are just as likely as village schools to say that they give close attention to the appropriate syllabus of religious education and they are more inclined to develop their own detailed scheme of work for the subject. Thus, 44% of the town schools and 47% of the village schools say that they follow the syllabus closely; 30% of the town schools have developed their own detailed scheme of work for religious education, compared with 21% of the village schools.

Town schools are considerably better resourced for religious education than village schools. Thus, 61% of the town schools use slides or filmstrips, at least occasionally, for religious education among their fourth year junior pupils, compared with 39% of the village schools; 54% of the town schools use sound cassettes or tapes at least occasionally, compared with 41% of the village schools; 28% of the town schools use films at least occasionally, compared with 12% of the village schools; 67% of the town schools use text books at least occasionally, compared with 48% of the village schools; 87% of the town schools use reference books at least occasionally, compared with 78% of the village schools. Possibly as a consequence of this wider range of resources, town schools are less reliant on radio broadcasts for help with religious education: 39% of the town schools often use radio broadcasts for religious education among their fourth year junior pupils, compared with 53% of the village schools.

Town schools also use the bible less frequently in religious education than village schools. Thus, 19% of the town schools say that they often use copies of the bible for religious education among their fourth year junior pupils, compared with 27% of the village schools.

Children attending town schools are less likely to experience a daily assembly for the whole school than children attending village schools. Thus, only 18% of the town schools hold a daily assembly for the whole school, compared with 41% of the village schools.

Assemblies in town schools are likely to embrace more variety and a wider range of educational experiences than village schools. In town schools the headteacher is more likely to share the responsibility for conducting assemblies with other members of staff and with the pupils. Other teachers are involved in leading assemblies at least once a week in 91% of the town schools, compared with 67% of the village schools; pupils are involved in leading assemblies at least once a week in 78% of the town schools, compared with 38% of the village schools.

Town schools make more use of music, dance and drama in assemblies than village schools. Pupils listen to music in assemblies at least once a week in 79% of the town schools, compared with 53% of the village schools. Dance is used from time to time in assemblies in 59% of the town schools, compared with 32% of the village schools. Drama is used at least once a week in assemblies in 17% of the town schools, compared with 3% of the village schools. Town schools are also less reliant on the radio for help with assemblies. The fourth year junior pupils listen to radio broadcasts once a week in assemblies in 57% of the town schools, compared with 78% of the village schools.

While assemblies in town schools draw on a wider range of educational experience than assemblies in village schools, they are less likely to be related to other aspects of life in the school. Only 46% of the town schools say there is a close relationship between assemblies and other components of the curriculum, compared with 54% of the village schools; only 37% of the town schools say that there is a close relationship between assemblies and religious education, compared with 59% of the village schools.

Pupils are less likely to meet a regular pattern of explicit Christian practice in assemblies held in town schools. Fourth year junior pupils sing hymns almost daily in 70% of the town schools, compared with 79% of the village schools; they say prayers almost daily in 54% of the town schools, compared with 69% of the village schools; they recite the Lord's Prayer almost daily in 24% of the town schools, compared with 35% of the village schools. Fourth year junior pupils hear passages read from the bible in assemblies at least once a week in 37% of the town schools, compared with 48% of the village schools; they hear stories from a Christian background at least once a week in 74% of the town schools, compared with 85% of the village schools.

Church contact

Children who attend town schools have less contact with Anglican clergy than children who attend village schools. Anglican clergy make a weekly visit to 35% of the town schools, compared with 56% of the village schools; they take a weekly assembly in 32% of the town schools, compared with 44% of the village schools; they contribute to a weekly religious education lesson in 6% of the town schools, compared with 35% of the village schools.

While children who attend town schools have less contact with Anglican clergy than children who attend village schools, they have more contact with Free Church ministers. Free Church ministers visit 52% of the town schools, at least occasionally, compared with 20% of the village schools; they contribute to assemblies in 48% of the town schools, at least occasionally, compared with 20% of the village schools. On the other hand, Free Church ministers only rarely contribute to religious education in town schools. Just 6% of the town schools sometimes have Free Church ministers assist with religious education, compared with 30% where Church of England clergy sometimes assist with religious education.

Catholic priests are more likely to have contact with town schools than with village schools, although even in towns the level of contact is small. Just two of the town schools receive weekly visits from a Catholic priest and a further 13% receive occasional visits; two of the town schools make provision for a Catholic priest to conduct weekly religious education lessons and one other does so occasionally. Catholic priests sometimes contribute to assemblies in 13% of the town schools, compared with just 2% of the village schools.

Town schools are just as likely as village schools to go to a local church to hold a school service: three-quarters (74%) of the town schools and three-quarters (73%) of the village schools hold a school service in church at least once a year. Moveover, town schools are almost as likely as village schools to become involved with a Sunday service in a local church: 18% of the town schools and 22% of the village schools have done this during the past year.

Perhaps because clergy are less likely to visit town schools than village schools, town schools are more likely to visit local churches to talk with the clergy. Thus, 78% of the town schools visited a local church during the past year in order to look at the building, compared with 69% of the village schools. For 57% of the town schools this visit included an opportunity to talk with the clergy, compared with 47% of the village schools. Town schools, like village schools, clearly continue to express a range of close relationships with the Christian churches.

School profiles

The first half of this chapter has made statistical generalisations about town schools as a group. Now, following the pattern of the previous chapter, it is time to look in depth and detail at a few specific examples of town schools. The framework for these school profiles is provided by the headteachers' replies to the questionnaire, but the detail is augmented by other sources of information, including school information brochures and personal visits. Unlike the statistical analysis, these school profiles are not limited to Gloucestershire.

Again I have selected an example of a county school, a Church of England controlled school, a Church of England aided school and a Catholic school. While these profiles are carefully based on real situations, the names attributed to the schools are entirely fictitious. The four examples chosen are not intended to be typical of the categories from which they are drawn, but to emphasise the uniqueness and individuality which can be so easily lost beneath statistical generalisations.

Churnbury County Junior School

Churnbury is a large market town, served by both a county school and a Church of England aided school. Both schools operate primarily as neighbourhood schools, for different parts of the town.

Churnbury County Junior School traces its history back to the late 1870s when the first Churnbury board school was opened, as an all age school with separate departments for boys and girls. Prior to the first board school, the educational needs of the town were served by the British school and the National school. When the board school opened, the British school was closed and the children were transferred to the new school. Since the 1870s the school has moved site twice.

Today Churnbury County Junior School has nearly 300 pupils, organised into ten classes. The buildings are spacious, providing a television room, remedial room, resources room, library, staff room and various smaller rooms, as well as the ten main classrooms. The school is proud of its history and its tradition. The school information booklet explains that:

> Children have to learn good behaviour, manners and co-operation and that they not only have rights but also responsibilities. We expect children to take a pride in their school . . . and to maintain the reputation the school has for its happy atmosphere, disciplined behaviour and hard work.

The headteacher of Churnbury County Junior School is a man in his forties. He describes himself as a member of the Church of England, but not a particularly active member. He attends church two or three times a year, but not more regularly.

The school information booklet explains that religious education takes place in the school because the law demands that it should.

> By law every school must hold assemblies and include religious education as part of its curriculum. In a county school such as this all assemblies and religious education carried out is undenominational. Parents may ask for their children to be excused religious education lessons and attendance at assemblies on religious grounds.

In fact only one child is withdrawn from assemblies and religious education throughout the whole school. The parents of this child are members of the Jehovah Witnesses.

One timetable period a week is allocated to religious education among the fourth year junior pupils in the school. The school information booklet explains the aim of religious education as follows.

> Through religious education lessons we hope children will develop more awareness of themselves and a sensitivity to the needs of others, acquire a set of moral values and judgements which will hopefully motivate self discipline and acceptable behaviour. The bible and the Christian faith will form the basis of many lessons but we hope to provide the children with some knowledge of other major world religions.

The school has appointed a teacher with responsibility for co-ordinating religious education throughout the various classes and has also developed guidelines for the subject. These guidelines follow the county's agreed syllabus only in general terms. The teacher given responsibility for religious education has no formal training or qualifications in the subject, but does represent the school on appropriate in-service courses.

The headteacher does not feel that the school is adequately resourced for religious education. He says that the situation could be improved by more reference books, text books and audio-visual resources. The only set of bibles in the school is the Authorised Version, but the headteacher does not wish to acquire a more modern translation. The school has made no use of any religious education resource centre within the past year.

The whole school meets for an assembly once a week. On other days assemblies are held for individual classes or year groups. The school has opted for this pattern partly because it is a tight fit to assemble the whole school in the hall and partly for the sake of variety. The school information booket explains that:

> The pattern of the assembly changes every day to avoid it becoming a repetitive routine. Music and drama play an active part in many assemblies and the subject matter is drawn from an endless variety of themes.

This means that a number of the teachers are involved in conducting assemblies, as well as the headteacher. Each of the ten classes takes an assembly once a term.

The headteacher feels that assemblies should be religious, but not distinctively Christian. He would like assemblies to include four main features on most days of the week: listening to good music, spending some time in complete silence, hearing a secular story and singing a hymn. Once a week they should include a religious story, probably from a Christian background, and prayers, including the Lord's Prayer in the traditional translation.

As a rule assemblies in Churnbury County Junior School are not closely related to what is going on in religious education or in other aspects of the curriculum. They generally last for more than 25 minutes and the pupils are expected to sit on the floor for all or part of the time.

The headteacher is dissatisfied with the present school hymn book, *The Daily Service*. He is hoping to replace it as soon as finance will allow. Meanwhile, the teachers write out hymns on large sheets of paper and hang them in the school hall. These are usually copied from *Come and Praise*, *Someone's Singing Lord*, *Morning has Broken* and *With Cheerful Voice*.

Churnbury County Junior School has little contact with local churches. Although from time to time a class may decide to visit one of the local churches to meet with the clergy, the school never arranges a school service or participates in the Sunday worship of a local church. The headteacher says that clergy from none of the churches in town, Anglican, Catholic or Free Church, make informal visits to the school. On his side, he never invites them to contribute to assemblies. On the other hand, the school does have an arrangement with the local Catholic church, whereby the priest is able to come into school twice a week to take a Catholic group for special classes. Generally, however, it is left to the Church of England school on the other side of town to build up relationships with the clergy and the churches.

Churnbury C of E Aided Primary School

Churnbury Church of England Aided Primary School has a long history, going back to the beginning of the eighteenth century, when two separate schools were formed in Churnbury. These schools were amalgamated in the 1870s to form a new school, endowed with an educational trust by a local citizen. After the 1944 Education Act, the school became recognised as a Church of England aided school. In recent years the old school building has been enlarged and improved to provide good and flexible educational facilities. Today the school has over 300 pupils and ten class teachers.

Churnbury Church of England Aided Primary School is proud of its long history and its links with the church. The school information booklet draws attention to both.

Being 'aided' . . . the spiritual as well as the mental and physical development of the children is our concern.

Many generations have been to school here and all present members are expected to do their utmost to maintain the school's good name.

Pupils are encouraged to identify with the ethos of the school by wearing the school uniform.

The headteacher of Churnbury Church of England Aided Primary School is a man in his fifties. He is a committed and practising member of the Church of England who firmly believes in the church school system and who deliberately chose to apply for a headship in a large Church of England aided school. Having been appointed to his present school, he moved to Churnbury and put his roots down in the community. He is now an active member of the parish church to which his school is linked.

The vicar of Churnbury is chairman of the governors and plays an important part in the life of the school. Both the vicar and his curate are frequent visitors to the school and they share responsibility for conducting an assembly once a week. While they are not responsible for a regular teaching spot in the school, there are a number of opportunities open to them to work with the teaching staff and pupils.

The contact between church and school is quite close. Within the past year the fourth year junior pupils have conducted a project on the history of the church. They have looked at the building and studied the vestments. They have talked with the curate about the life and worship of the church. They have also taken part in a weekday service arranged for the school. The curate worked closely with the school to prepare for this service and there was plenty of opportunity for the pupils to make their own contribution to the worship. On the other hand, there has been no direct contact between the school and the Sunday services of the church.

Not only does the parish church play an important part in the life of the school, other denominations are made very welcome as well. Since there is no Catholic school in Churnbury, the local Catholic priest is invited to take a couple of classes each week for the Catholic pupils just as in Churnbury County Junior School. In the Church of England school, however, the Catholic priest is also invited to contribute to school assemblies from time to time. The relationship with the Free Churches is less close, but closer than with Churnbury County Junior School. Free Church ministers are not invited to contribute to religious education, but they sometimes visit the school and lead occasional assemblies.

Churnbury Church of England Aided Primary School likes to think that it takes the place of religious education and assemblies very seriously. In the school brochure the headteacher writes as follows.

> Religious education is at the heart of the school. Every day includes a corporate act of worship and this coming together is a most important element in the life of the school. The great church festivals are recognised. Being a Church of England voluntary aided school, there are close links with the parish church of Churnbury. The vicar and his staff visit the school regularly to help with religious education. . . . Parents may exclude their children from religious education after consultation with the headmaster.

At the time of the survey, six pupils were withdrawn from assembly, on the grounds of membership either of the Jehovah Witnesses or of the Brethren.

In the top classes religious education is a timetable subject, which means in practice that between one and a half hours and two hours are devoted to the subject each week. What actually happens in these periods is not quite so well co-ordinated as it might be. According to the headteacher, the diocesan syllabus is followed only in general terms; the school has not designated a member of staff to act as 'consultant' for religious education, nor has it developed its own detailed scheme of work. On the other hand, the school is able to draw on a number of staff who studied religious education during initial teacher training as a main or subsidiary subject. Staff from the school have also attended in-service training courses in religious education within the past three years. The headteacher feels that the school is quite well resourced for religious education. During their religious education lessons, the fourth year junior pupils make use of bibles, text books, reference books, audio cassettes, radio broadcasts and slides. The school possesses class sets of two modern translations of the bible, *The New English Bible* and *Good News Bible*.

When asked to suggest ways in which provision for religious education in the school could be improved, the headteacher mentioned two areas.

E

The first is to do with visual resources: he would like to be able to spend more on slides, filmstrips, films and videos. The second is to do with keeping up to date with ideas and materials: he would like his staff to be more closely involved in in-service training in religious education. The school is a subscribing member of the National Society and receives the journal *Together*, published by the General Synod Board of Education; it does not subscribe to the Christian Education Movement.

The daily assembly for the whole school sets out to be explicitly Christian, but not specifically denominational. As a rule assemblies last between 20 and 25 minutes. The vicar is responsible for one assembly a week and the headteacher for two. Other members of staff and the pupils share the leadership on the other days. Each day the pupils sing hymns, say prayers and join in saying the Lord's Prayer. At least once a week they sing a canticle or psalm and hear a reading from the bible. The stories come from a Christian background; occasionally a secular story is used, but only rarely does assembly include stories from other world faiths.

The school uses a range of hymn books, including *Come and Praise*, *The Junior Hymn Book*, *Someone's Singing Lord* and *New Orbit*. There is a close relationship between hymns sung in school and the parish church. The headteacher also tries to make sure that there are links between prayers used in school and church. For example, both the traditional version of the Lord's Prayer and the version used in new Anglican liturgy are used in school.

Although the religious ethos of Churnbury Church of England Aided Primary School is so different from Churnbury County Junior School at the other end of town, both schools regard themselves first and foremost as neighbourhood schools, serving different areas of the town. A few children are admitted to the Church of England school from outside its neighbourhood on religious grounds, but the school does not regard this as its main function. Whether children receive a church-related primary education in Churnbury is seen more appropriately to depend on the part of the town in which their parents live rather than on their parents' conscious decision.

The headteacher does not wish for the admissions policy of his church school to be changed, but he is acutely aware of the difficulties involved in running a church-related school for families who do not belong to a church. On the back page of his questionnaire he writes:

> Only about 5% of children and their families have regular contact with church life in the parish. Most parents are indifferent to religious education but want their children to have it! Parents attend school services more to support their children than to take part in a corporate act of worship.

All Saints' C of E Controlled Primary School

All Saints' Church of England Controlled Primary School is at the centre of a large town. The school has undergone a number of changes during its long life before occupying its present buildings in the early 1970s. Today there are just over 170 pupils and seven full-time teachers. The primary function of All Saints' school is to serve a particular part of town. In recent years it has also developed a specialist function, catering for children with learning difficulties. The governors see this as part of the church's response to changing educational needs and as part of the church's service to the local community.

The vicar of All Saints' church is chairman of the governors. He does not, however, play a very active role in the life of the school. He visits the school just once or twice a term and takes one assembly each term. He takes no part in the religious education of the school.

On the other hand, All Saints' school remains keen to keep its links with the local church. Classes visit the church, to look at the building and to study the purpose of the church. They have met the vicar in church to talk with him about his work. The school uses the church for occasional school services and contributes something, from time to time, to Sunday worship. The school information booklet explains to parents that:

The school enjoys a close relationship with the church .... The children are occasionally invited to provide items for family services on Sundays, and take part in church fetes. The school sometimes uses the church for carol services or concerts and also for end of term services.

While All Saints' school is keen to exercise its links with the Anglican church, it has not developed contacts with other denominations. Neither Free Church ministers nor Catholic priests are invited to play a part in the life of the school. Although there are now some pupils who come from religious backgrounds other than Christian, the school does not involve leaders from other world faiths.

The headteacher of All Saints' school is a man in his forties, a practising member of the Church of England who attends church most Sundays. He is not, however, particularly committed to the church school system. His current post in a Church of England controlled school is more a matter of chance than deliberate choice. He does not live within the neighbourhood served by the school, nor is he a regular member of All Saints' church congregation.

Religious education is given in All Saints' school according to the agreed syllabus; the headteacher says that this syllabus is followed quite closely, but not very closely. The deputy head has been appointed to act as 'consultant' for religious education, but as yet the school has not developed its own scheme of work for the subject. The school has been represented on a recent in-service training course in religious education. Although All Saints' is a controlled school with a teaching staff of more than two, the governors have not appointed a reserved teacher. No opportunities are given for Anglican parents to seek denominational instruction for their children.

Religious education appears as a separate timetable period for the fourth year junior class and occupies between half an hour and one hour each week. The most frequently used resource for religious education among this age group are radio programmes. They also use bibles and reference books. The only class set of bibles is the Authorised Version. The headteacher is content with the resources available for religious education and has no particular wish to strengthen them.

The school information booklet explains that much importance is given to morning assemblies. The whole school meets for an assembly on two days a week. On the other three days the infants and juniors meet separately. All the classes take it in turns to lead an assembly for the whole school each week. The headteacher is personally responsible for leading at least three assemblies each week and other teachers are involved as well. This means that there is quite a variety in morning assemblies. Sometimes they are closely related to the church's year; sometimes they emerge from class project work and are closely related to the general curriculum.

The majority of assemblies are implicitly Christian, but not explicitly Christian or denominational. The children sing a hymn every day and spend a short time in silence, but they are not asked to join in prayers every day. The school uses a wide range of stories in assemblies, drawn from secular sources and from other world faiths, as well as from Christian sources. The Lord's Prayer and bible readings are used from time to time, but not as frequently as once a week. The school draws its hymns from a variety of sources, including *Come and Praise*, *Morning has Broken*, *Carol Gaily Carol* and *Hymns Ancient and Modern*, but there is no particularly close link between the hymns sung in school and All Saints' church.

All Saints' school, therefore, seems a good example of a Church of England controlled school where the church's emphasis is on service to the community, rather than on maintaining a distinctive denominational presence. If church-going Anglican parents were specifically seeking a church-related primary education for their children, All Saints' would not be the school for them. On the other hand, because of its church foundation, All Saints' school is able to bring non-churchgoing pupils and their parents into closer contact with the local church than they would otherwise experience.

Sacred Heart Catholic Primary School

Sacred Heart Catholic Primary School is situated in a town of under 10,000 inhabitants. It traces its origin to the mid 1870s, when the Catholic parish opened an all age school. The school moved into its present purpose-built plant in the late 1960s. Today there are about 230 pupils, divided into eight classes.

The school information booklet makes it clear that Sacred Heart school exists primarily to serve the Catholic parish. The admissions policy:

> will endeavour to accommodate all Catholic applicants providing they do not live within the agreed catchment area of another Catholic school. The governors will consider applications from pupils who are not Catholic but who wish to share in the Christian atmosphere and religious education of the school, only if space is available.

Catholic parents who consider sending their child to the school are invited to contact the headteacher directly; parents of children other than Catholics are advised to see the chairman of the governors to discuss the matter. It is made plain that non-Catholics are accepted:

> only if they are willing for their children to take a full part in the religious instruction given in the school. . . . Religious teaching is part of the everyday school life and may be part of any lesson. It is necessary that religion is a way of life.

The chairman of the governors of Sacred Heart school is a Catholic priest. He is a frequent visitor to the school; he contributes to assemblies once a week and to religious education at least once a month. During the past year the pupils have been to church to take part in a weekday service, to take part in a Sunday service and to hold their own school service. They have made a display of their work in church and they have offered their music and work as part of the service.

The headteacher of Sacred Heart school is a man in his fifties, a practising Catholic who attends mass weekly. He is committed to the Catholic school system and is clear that he is best able to fulfil his vocation as a Catholic teacher by working in a Catholic school. He lives in the parish which his school serves and worships in the parish church

Sunday by Sunday. This brings him into contact with pupils and their families in church as well as in school.

On average the fourth year junior pupils spend over two hours on religious education each week. The school has also developed its own detailed scheme of work for religious education, based on a Catholic programme. The headteacher has taken personal responsibility to act as 'consultant' for religious education throughout the school. The school information booklet explains the aims of religious education in the following terms:

> Religious ideas are to help the child to form a spiritual and physical relationship with God. At first this will be very simple, but with time should lead to a fuller understanding which will be the unshakable foundation upon which the quickened spirituality of adolescence can build with the utmost security. Parents take a full part in religious activities through invitation.

The main resources used for religious education among the fourth year junior pupils are text books and reference books. The school possesses a set of *Good News Bible* which are sometimes used in class work. Reviewing the resources available in the school for religious education, there are a number of areas which the headteacher would like to strengthen. In particular, he would like to be able to invest in a wider range of reference books and in a new set of text books. He would also like to build up a larger supply of audio-visual materials. He is conscious of the important contribution which radio and television can make to religious education and wishes that there were more programmes suitable for Catholic schools.

The eight teachers are well qualified for undertaking the religious education of the school. Three studied religious education as a main course in their initial teacher training and most of the others studied religious education as a subsidiary course. They have kept up to date by attending in-service training courses.

The whole school meets three days a week for an assembly. These assemblies are generally in the hands of the headteacher. They last for between 15 and 20 minutes; the children are expected to stand throughout. The class teachers are responsible for leading class worship on the other days of the week. Once a month mass is celebrated in school.

The headteacher believes that the aim of school assemblies is to provide Christian denominational worship. This means that the pupils sing hymns, say prayers, hear passages read from the bible and join in the Lord's Prayer on a daily basis. Canticles or psalms are also used several days a week. Quite often the school contributes to the atmosphere of worship by the careful use of music, slides or silence. The headteacher tries to build a close relationship between the children's experience of worship in school and the local Catholic church. For example, he says that they sing the same hymns in church and school. To achieve this, they have a supply of three hymn books in school, *The Parish Hymnbook*, *Praise the Lord* and *Celebration Hymnal*.

The Sacred Heart Catholic Primary School, thus, provides a very distinctive educational experience for young Catholics and for the children of non-Catholic parents who wish their children to be educated in a Christian environment and are happy for that environment to be explicitly Catholic.

11 SUBURBAN SCHOOLS

Suburbs

Of the 224 primary and junior schools in the present sample, 50 are suburban schools. These schools include the new suburban areas around Cheltenham and Gloucester, some well established suburban communities and some recently expanded villages.

In some suburban areas the primary school provides an important focus for community which may otherwise be lacking. The majority of children from the same neighbourhood are recruited into the same school, and through the school parents meet with each other in ways which would not otherwise happen. Unlike many village schools, suburban schools can often assume a common geographical background among their pupils and ease of access to the school for both pupils and parents.

The religious amenities available in suburbia vary greatly from one area to another, depending upon historic resources and church initiatives. Generally, however, church resources are more restricted in suburbia than in historic small towns. Suburban areas are less likely to support a range of Free Churches or to possess a medieval parish church. The Anglican clergy living in suburban areas are likely to have a larger population among whom to minister and their parishioners are less likely to have historic roots in the life of the local churches. All of these factors have implications for the religious life of suburban schools.

All but two suburban schools in the present sample exist primarily to serve a local neighbourhood. The other two suburban schools are Catholic schools, which exist to service the Catholic community over a wider geographical area. Since the main purpose of the statistical analysis in the first half of this chapter is to characterise the religious provision of suburban neighbourhood schools, the two Catholic schools will be omitted.

Schools

None of the suburban primary schools in Gloucestershire has fewer than 100 pupils or fewer than four teachers. At the time of the survey, the smallest suburban school had 105 pupils; the largest had 373. Three-fifths

(60%) of the suburban schools had over 200 pupils, while one-fifth (19%) had over 300 pupils.

At this point, it is important to recollect that the present study is concerned only with those schools which include fourth year junior pupils. This means that infant schools are omitted from the analysis. It is particularly in suburban areas that primary provision is divided into separate infant and junior schools. Of the 39 neighbourhood junior schools in the present study, 22 are suburban schools. In other words, 46% of the schools in suburban areas offering provision for fourth year junior pupils are junior schools, catering for eight to eleven year olds, rather than primary schools, catering for five to eleven year olds. This compares with 28% of the town schools and less than 2% of the village schools.

Headteachers of suburban schools tend to be older than headteachers of village schools and town schools. Thus, 56% of the headteachers of suburban schools are over fifty years of age, compared with 46% of the headteachers of town schools and 37% of the headteachers of village schools. Women are less likely to hold the headships of suburban schools catering for junior aged pupils than of town or village schools. Thus, only 10% of the headteachers of suburban schools catering for junior aged pupils are women, compared with 15% of the town schools and 41% of the village schools. The opportunity for women teachers to acquire headships in town and suburban areas is concentrated largely in the infant schools. If the infant schools are included in the analysis as well, 42% of the village headships, 38% of the suburban headships and 33% of the town headships are held by women. What is significant from this analysis is the conclusion that junior aged pupils are much less likely to experience the leadership of a female headteacher in suburban or town schools than in village schools.

Headteachers of suburban schools are less likely to live in the area served by their school than headteachers of town or village schools. Only 15% of the headteachers of suburban schools live within the area served by their school, compared with 22% of the headteachers of village schools and 30% of the headteachers of town schools.

Parents who live in areas served by suburban schools are less likely to find that their children are attending a Church of England school than parents who live in areas served by village schools or by town schools. While 65% of the village schools are Church of England schools, the proportion drops to 43% of the town schools and to 25% of the suburban schools; 10% of the suburban schools are Church of England aided and 15% are Church of England controlled. The church's institutional presence in the state maintained system of education is weakest in those new or expanded areas of residential development.

The religious affiliation of headteachers of suburban schools is less strong than headteachers of town or village schools. Nevertheless, headteachers of suburban schools are still much more likely to be actively involved with one of the Christian churches than the Gloucestershire population as a whole. Thus, 17% of the headteachers of suburban schools style themselves as agnostics or humanists, compared with 11% of the headteachers of town schools and 7% of the headteachers of village schools; 44% of the headteachers of suburban schools say that they attend Sunday church services most weeks, compared with 51% of the headteachers of village schools and 57% of the headteachers of town schools.

The professional skills available for teaching religious education in suburban schools are very similar to those available in town schools. Thus, 40% of the suburban schools and 37% of the town schools have at least one member of staff who studied religious education as a main course during initial teacher training; 40% of the suburban schools and 43% of the town schools have a member of staff who has attended an in-service day course or series of meetings in religious education during the past three years; 48% of the suburban schools and 50% of the town schools have a member of staff designated to act as 'consultant' for religious education.

Statutory provision

Suburban schools allocate the same amount of time to religous education as town schools. A quarter (25%) of the suburban schools and a quarter (24%) of the town schools give more than an hour a week to religious education among their fourth year junior pupils, compared with a third (33%) of the village schools. On the other hand, suburban schools are considerably less likely to give close attention to the appropriate syllabus of religious education: 27% of the suburban schools say that they follow the syllabus closely, compared with 44% of the town schools and 47% of the village schools. Suburban schools are also less likely to have developed their own detailed scheme of work for religious education: just 15% of the suburban schools have developed their own detailed scheme of work for religious education, compared with 21% of the village schools and 30% of the town schools.

Suburban schools make less use of resources in religious education than town schools. The difference is particularly noticeable when it comes to the use of text books. Only 29% of the suburban schools use text books, at least occasionally, for religious education among their fourth year junior pupils, compared with 67% of the town schools. They are also less likely to make use of films, sound cassettes, tapes and reference books.

Religious education in suburban schools is less likely to use the bible than town schools: 65% of the suburban schools use copies of the bible, at least occasionally, for religious education among their fourth year junior pupils, compared with 78% of the town schools and 79% of the village schools. Religious education in suburban schools is also less likely to use the resource of local churches. While fourth year junior pupils visit a local church, at least occasionally, as part of their religious education curriculum in the case of 78% of the town schools and 74% of the village schools, the proportion drops to 54% of the suburban schools.

Children attending suburban schools are more likely to experience a daily assembly for the whole school than children attending town schools, but less likely to do so than children attending village schools. Thus, 35% of the suburban schools hold a daily assembly for the whole school, compared with 18% of the town schools and 41% of the village schools.

Assemblies in suburban schools tend to be more formal and less educationally varied and imaginative than assemblies in town schools. The headteachers of suburban schools are more inclined to keep control of the assemblies in their own hands than the headteachers of town schools. In 23% of the suburban schools the pupils do not experience during a normal week an assembly led by another teacher, compared with just 9% of the town schools; in 31% of the suburban schools the pupils do not experience during a normal week an assembly led by other children, compared with 22% of the town schools.

Pupils attending suburban schools are just as likely as pupils attending village schools to have a regular diet of story, bible, hymns and prayers in assemblies. Thus, fourth year junior pupils sing hymns almost every day in 79% of the suburban schools, say prayers almost daily in 75%, hear the bible read at least once a week in 50% and hear religious stories of a Christian background at least once a week in 96%. The difference is that, in suburban schools, this diet is more often extended to include secular stories and religious stories from other world faiths. Thus, fourth year junior pupils hear secular stories once a week in assemblies in 69% of the suburban schools, compared with 57% of the village schools; they hear religious stories of other world faiths at least once a week in 25% of the suburban schools, compared with 20% of the village schools. While suburban schools are just as likely to use hymns and prayers in assemblies as village schools, they are inclined to see this religious practice in less explicitly Christian terms. For example, the Lord's Prayer is used less frequently in suburban schools than in village schools: the Lord's Prayer is used almost daily among fourth year junior pupils in 29% of the suburban schools, compared with 35% of the village schools. Similarly, only 62% of the suburban schools feel that their assemblies follow the shape of the church's year, compared with 73% of the village schools.

Church contact

Children who attend suburban schools have less overall contact with Anglican clergy than children who attend town or village schools. Weekly visits are made by Anglican clergy to 31% of the suburban schools, compared with 35% of the town schools and 56% of the village schools; Anglican clergy take a weekly assembly in 21% of the suburban schools, compared with 32% of the town schools and 44% of the village schools. Anglican clergy contribute to religious education lessons in 27% of the suburban schools, compared with 30% of the town schools and 49% of the village schools.

Free Church ministers have less contact with suburban schools than with town schools, but more than with village schools. Free Church ministers visit 44% of the suburban schools, at least occasionally, compared with 52% of the town schools and 20% of the village schools. Free Church ministers contribute to assemblies, at least occasionally, in 44% of the suburban schools, compared with 48% of the town schools and 20% of the village schools. Free Church ministers contribute to religious education in none of the suburban schools. This pattern is consistent with the way in which Free Church ministers are more likely to be resident in suburban areas than in villages, but less likely to be resident in suburban areas than in well established towns.

Catholic priests visit 12% of the suburban schools, at least occasionally, compared with 17% of the town schools and 5% of the village schools. Catholic priests contribute to assemblies, at least occasionally, in 10% of the suburban schools, compared with 13% of the town schools and 2% of the village schools. None of the suburban schools ever invites Catholic priests to contribute to religious education.

While the clergy have less contact with suburban schools than town schools, suburban schools are just as likely as town schools to visit local churches in order to meet with the clergy there. Thus, 77% of the suburban schools and 77% of the town schools arranged a visit to a local church within the past year to look at the building; for 57% of the suburban schools and 57% of the town schools this visit included an opportunity to talk with the clergy.

A significant way in which contact between church and school differs in suburban areas from towns and villages concerns the schools' involvement in church services. Suburban schools are much less likely to arrange their own school service or to support Sunday services in a local church. While three-quarters (74%) of the town schools and three-quarters (73%) of the village schools arrange a school service at least once a year, less than half (46%) of the suburban schools do so. While 22% of the village schools and 18% of the town schools take part in a Sunday church service at least once a year, only 6% of the suburban schools do so. Suburban schools clearly have a weaker relationship with local churches than either village or town schools.

School profiles

The first half of this chapter has made statistical generalisations about suburban schools as a group. Now, following the pattern of the previous two chapters, it is time to look in depth and detail at a few specific examples of suburban schools. The framework for these school profiles is provided by the headteachers' replies to the questionnaire, but the detail is augmented by other sources of information, including school information brochures and personal visits. Unlike the statistical analysis, these school profiles are not limited to Gloucestershire.

Again I have selected an example of a county school, a Church of England controlled school, a Church of England aided school and a Catholic school. While these profiles are carefully based on real situations, the names attributed to the schools are entirely fictitious. The four examples chosen are not intended to be typical of the categories from which they are drawn, but to emphasise the uniqueness and individuality which can be so easily lost beneath statistical generalisations.

Whitehall Road County Primary School

Whitehall Road County Primary School is on the edge of a major conurbation. It is a large school, catering for over 320 pupils, with 11 full-time class teachers. The school information booklet makes it very clear on the front cover that Whitehall Road County Primary School is 'co-educational and non-denominational'.

The headteacher is a man in his forties. He is a member of the Church of England and attends church services at the major Christian festivals, but not regularly week by week. He is working in the county sector as a matter of choice.

Religious education does not play a particularly important part in the life of Whitehall Road County Primary School. While the school information booklet gives a whole section and a large heading to 'religious education', what in fact it has to say tells nothing about the school's approach to the subject. The section reads:

> Parents who wish to withdraw their children from attendance at religious worship or instruction are asked to discuss this with the headteacher. Children excused from classroom RE usually read or are provided with some other work in the classroom.

Parents are not told anything about the subject from which they may wish to withdraw their children.

Overall responsibility for religious education is in the hands of one of the assistant teachers. The headteacher regards him as an appropriate person for this responsibility because he is a Methodist local preacher. He has attended no in-service training programme in religious education within the past three years, nor has he made any use of religious education resource centres. He has not developed a detailed scheme of work for religious education. His main achievement to date is to have persuaded the school to take out a subscription to the Christian Education Movement. The school follows the county's agreed syllabus only in general terms.

The fourth year junior pupils spend one period a week on religious education, which occupies their time for between half an hour and one hour. They rarely use audio-visual materials; occasionally they use reference books and work from the bible. The school does not possess a class set of bibles. The headteacher is not concerned to develop the school's resources for religious education. What he believes the school needs most to help with religious education is a good series of television programmes which the pupils could settle down to watch.

The whole school meets for an assembly just once a week, when the headteacher is generally in charge. On the other four days the class teachers are expected to conduct assemblies for their individual classes. What actually takes place in class assemblies varies from teacher to teacher. The Methodist local preacher tends to hold a fairly formal assembly in his classroom each morning; some teachers may well overlook this observance. Assemblies are understood in Whitehall Road school as mainly social, rather than religious occasions. The school information booklet explains that:

The assemblies are related to the child's experience of everyday life. Living and working together within the school community; consideration of others, caring and honesty are of prime importance. School assemblies play an important part in the development of the community spirit. We aim to engender a feeling of self-esteem in the child.

The headteacher regards some of the assemblies for which he is personally responsible to be implicitly Christian, some to be religious but not distinctively Christian, and others to be largely secular or social. He does not set out to conduct explicitly Christian assemblies. The pupils sing hymns and say prayers, but they do not generally say the Lord's Prayer or hear passages read from the bible when the headteacher is responsible for assemblies.

The headteacher says that classroom assemblies are often closely related to what is going on in the general curriculum, but that it is not possible for assemblies conducted for the whole school to be related to the general curriculum in this way. Similarly, he does not feel that the weekly assembly for the whole school can be more than slightly related to the religious education curriculum. He has no idea whether the hymns sung in assemblies have any relationship with those sung in local churches. The school does not possess a set of hymn books for all the pupils, but uses an overhead projector to project the words onto the wall.

Although Whitehall Road is a county primary school, the vicar takes an interest in what is going on in the school; he visits the school at least once a month and takes an assembly once a term. The school has no contact with Free Church ministers or Catholic priests.

Not only does the local vicar visit the school, the school also takes some interest in the local Anglican church. Within the last year the school has arranged a visit to look at the church building and to talk with the vicar about the church and about his work. Afterwards the children did some project work on the church. Sadly they were not invited to take the project work back to the church to share what they had done with the vicar and his congregation. The school does not have a tradition of using the local church for a school service.

Whitehall Road County Primary School is, thus, a relatively secular school. The headteacher does not set out to influence the life of the school in a particularly Christian direction. However, there are still clear signs of contact with the churches and with the Christian tradition. Two people in particular are responsible for keeping these contacts alive: the local vicar continues to visit the school and to show that he is interested in it; the teacher who is a Methodist local preacher allows his Christian commitment to influence what takes place in his classroom.

St Ursula's C of E Controlled Primary School

St Ursula's Church of England Controlled Primary School serves a neighbourhood similar to Whitehall Road County Primary School. Today St Ursula's school has about 280 pupils and a staff of nine full-time teachers.

The links between St Ursula's school and the local church are not strong. The vicar has a place on the governing body of the school, but he does not act as chairman. The vicar visits the school from time to time, but takes little active part in the life of the school. Just occasionally he is invited to take an assembly, but not as often as once a term; he never teaches religious education. As a controlled school, St Ursula's has the right to provide Anglican teaching for those children whose parents request it, but the school does not exercise this right.

There has been a long tradition for St Ursula's school to hold an annual school service in church. This tradition is still maintained, but appears to generate little enthusiasm. It is a service in which the pupils take only a passive role. Apart from the school service, last year the school had little contact with the church. None of the classes visited the church to look at the building, to study its purpose or to talk with the vicar.

There are no contacts between St Ursula's school and any other Christian denominations. The headteacher says that neither Catholic priests nor Free Church ministers make informal visits to the school. For his part, he never invites them to take assemblies or to contribute to religious education.

The headteacher of St Ursula's school is a practising member of the Church of England. He is a man in his fifties who goes to church most Sundays. He does not, however, live near the school and does not worship in St Ursula's church. He feels that a Church of England controlled school is the right place for him. He believes in a Christian presence in education, but does not believe that the church should dictate what goes on in his school. For that reason he would not wish to teach in a Church of England aided school.

The headteacher's views on a Christian presence in education are clearly reflected in the pattern of assemblies held in St Ursula's school. He believes that assemblies should be explicitly Christian occasions; he believes that in a church school at least half of the assemblies should be denominational acts of worship.

In practice, the whole of St Ursula's school meets for an assembly once a week. The infants meet by themselves for assemblies twice a week and the juniors also meet by themselves for assemblies twice a week. This means that the school hall is used for an assembly at the beginning of every school day and that every child participates in three assemblies each week. In a normal week the headteacher takes all five assemblies himself. Occasionally other teachers are invited to lead assemblies, but not on a regular basis.

The assemblies taken by the headteacher generally follow a fairly traditional pattern. Most days he uses a story from a Christian background, a reading from the bible and Christian prayers. The pupils join in singing a hymn and saying the Lord's Prayer. Once a term or so the pupils write their own prayers.

St Ursula's school does not tune into the radio service for schools. Perhaps as a consequence of this, St Ursula's school does not use the BBC hymn book, *Come and Praise*. They use the more traditional school hymn book, *With Cheerful Voice*, which was first published in 1966. The headteacher feels that there is a very close relationship between the hymns he chooses for assemblies and those sung in his own church. He is content with the present hymn book and has no intention of replacing it with a more modern one. He also makes sure that assemblies follow the pattern of the church's year.

The school information booklet carefully draws parents' attention to their right to withdraw their children from religious worship or instruction. Just two of the 280 or so pupils have been withdrawn by their parents.

Religious education appears as a separate timetable subject for the older classes. The fourth year juniors spend between one hour and one and a half hours on the subject each week. The school information booklet explains the aims of religious education in the school in the following terms.

Religious ideas are largely related to the child's experience of everyday life centred round the themes of caring, thought for others, honesty, etc. In our work as a church school, the life and teachings of Christ and other biblical stories also feature strongly in our studies together with lessons on people past and present, whose lives are an example for us to follow.

In fact, a lot of the religious education among the fourth year junior pupils is bible-based. The school possesses class sets of the Authorised Version and *Good News Bible*, and these are frequently used. The fourth year junior pupils also use reference books quite frequently in religious education, but the school does not possess text books for the subject. Neither radio nor television plays a part in their religious education programme.

There are three areas of resources which the headteacher would like to strengthen for religious education. He would like more bibles and more reference books. He is not concerned to build up the school's supply of audio-visual resources, but he would use television more if there were suitable programmes.

Overall responsibility for religious education is in the hands of one of the assistant teachers. This teacher has attended a day course on religious education within the past three years, but does not make use of religious education resource centres. The school does not support the Christian Education Movement, but is a subscribing member of the National Society. Although the school has given responsibility for religious education to one specific member of staff, it has not as yet developed a scheme of work to co-ordinate religious education throughout the school. The headteacher feels that the county's agreed syllabus is followed quite closely.

The main influence determining the religious life of St Ursula's Church of England Controlled School, therefore, is the headteacher rather than the local church. From the local church's point of view, the school's links with the church are more in name than in practice. Nevertheless, it is precisely from the school's church foundation that the headteacher feels he draws his mandate to give such prominence to Christian worship and bible teaching. Under a different headteacher the religious character of St Ursula's school might be radically changed.

St George's C of E Aided Primary School

St George's church was built in the 1870s to serve an expanding area. St George's school was built next to the church as part of its foundation and endowment. Together, the old school building and the church constitute an impressive monument to the Victorian church's twin concerns with worship and education. Today St George's school is housed in a new building, but still retains close contact with the church. There are about 175 pupils and six full-time teachers.

Aided status is important to the character of St George's school. The school information booklet draws parents' attention to the implications of aided status for the composition of the governing body.

> It might interest you to know that . . . in our case the foundation governors are appointed by the Diocesan Education Committee in consultation with the St George's Parochial Church Council.

The rector serves as an ex-officio foundation governor and is chairman.

The school information booklet also draws parents' attention to the implications of aided status for the aims of the school curriculum.

> St George's is a Church of England, voluntary aided school and, as such, seeks to provide an education for the pupils based upon the principles of the Christian faith. Such provision, which is essentially the governors' responsibility, is made in partnership with the local education authority and aims to prepare the pupils for subsequent phases in their education and to equip them for adulthood in an ever-changing world.

St George's school has a good reputation locally and consequently finds that many more applications for places are made than there are places available. The governors have drawn up a careful statement of their policy for admissions, giving priority first to siblings and then to 'children, at least one parent of whom is a member of St George's congregation and who lives in the neighbourhood'. The headteacher explains that in practice church families have priority and as a general rule are never turned away. Nevertheless, he feels that the school is a neighbourhood school, rather than one which selects mainly on religious criteria.

Against this background concerning the admissions policy, it is interesting to look in detail at what the fourth year junior pupils say about their own religious affiliation and practice. From the 27 fourth year junior pupils who completed a questionnaire, eight said that they did not belong to a church, two said that they were Catholics and went to church once or twice a year; one said he was a Baptist who went to church weekly. The other 16 described themselves as members of the Church of England; of these, only four were weekly or even monthly church-goers. While St George's school has an admissions policy favouring church-going Anglicans, the majority of its pupils are not church-goers.

Although in practice the majority of the pupils are not church-goers, St George's school sets out to provide a Christian curriculum. One of the aims in the school information booklet is that pupils should learn:

> to begin to understand what it means to be committed to religion and, in particular, what it means to be a Christian. As a church school we seek to provide a religious education firmly based on the principles of the Christian faith.

The school information booklet explains to parents their right to withdraw their children from religious education and from school worship, but clearly does not expect them to exercise this right.

We consider it reasonable to assume that parents who send their children here are sympathetic to the Christian ethos of the school. If, however, parents wish to withdraw their children from attendance at religious worship or religious education, they are asked to discuss this with the headmaster.

Currently none of the pupils is withdrawn from assemblies or religious education.

The fourth year junior pupils spend between one hour and one and a half hours each week on religious education. A lot of their work is bible-based, when they use *Good News Bible*. They also make frequent use of text books and reference books. They have access to audio-visual materials, like slides and sound cassettes. The school makes use of the local religious education resource centre. The headteacher is not, however, content with the level of resources for religious education and he would like to be able to strengthen the school's stock of reference books, slides, films and so on.

There is a daily pattern of worship in the school every morning. The whole school comes together for an assembly twice a week; on the other three days the five and six year olds worship separately. The school information booklet points out that the daily assembly serves both religious and secular functions.

Every day we have a school assembly. This is an opportunity for the whole school to be together for a short act of worship. In addition, school notices, information and awards are given out at this time.

The majority of the assemblies set out to be explicitly Christian and denominational in character. Hymns and prayers play a daily part in the pupils' lives. The headteacher is personally responsible for at least three assemblies each week and he says that he takes care to build bridges between school worship and worship in St George's church. Prayers from *The Alternative Service Book* are used every week as part of the school worship. The Lord's Prayer is also used in the form found in *The Alternative Service Book*. There is a very close relationship between assemblies and the church's year. On the other hand, there is not much relationship between the hymns sung in school and those used in church. St George's school has adopted the BBC hymn book, *Come and Praise*; St George's church uses a much more traditional hymn book.

The headteacher, a man in his fifties, lives in the parish and is a regular worshipper at St George's church. He deliberately chose to work in a Church of Engand aided school and believes in the close relationship between church and school.

The rector of St George's church is a frequent visitor to the school. He leads an assembly every week, but does not participate in the religious education programme. The previous rector used to conduct a monthly communion service for the school. Under the present rector this practice has been discontinued. The school also welcomes a local Free Church minister to take an assembly once a term or so. The school has no contact with a local Catholic priest.

The school uses St George's church to hold school services and also sometimes takes part in Sunday worship in the church. The school tries hard to make the pupils feel at home in church. They use the church to display their class work and, when they participate in a service, they are given an active part to play.

St George's Church of England Aided Primary School, therefore, seems to make full use of its aided status to promote a distinctive church-related education. The admissions policy enables the school to give priority to church-going parents, but emphasises service to the parish rather than to a wider area. This means that the school is seen theologically as part of the church's outreach into the parish, rather than just providing nurture for church-going children. Being in a suburban neighbourhood, it is presumably not difficult for parents living in St George's parish who do not want a church-related education for their children to opt for another nearby school.

St Anne's Catholic Primary School

St Anne's Catholic Primary School was built in the mid 1970s to serve the needs of a growing suburban Catholic parish. The original plans underestimated the demand for places and two further classrooms were added by the end of the 1970s. Today there are about 165 pupils and six class teachers. The school information booklet describes the purpose of this school in the following terms.

> The school exists to provide a Catholic education for the children of St Anne's parish, and it is the governors' policy to admit as many children of the parish as can be properly accommodated.

The Catholic parish priest is chairman of the governors. There is also a second Catholic priest serving on the governing body. The governing body was keen to appoint a practising Catholic to the post of headteacher and selected a man in his forties who attends mass weekly. The school also employs a nun as deputy headteacher. The Catholic ethos of the school seems well assured.

The headteacher, however, is far from content with the way in which the school is working. He feels that the governors do not really understand the role of the Catholic school in today's society. In short, the parish priest wants the school run one way and the headteacher wants to run it another way. Consequently, instead of church and school working closely hand in hand, they are often working at cross purposes. At times things get so uncomfortable that the headteacher thinks he would prefer to leave the Catholic sector for a job in a county school.

The headteacher feels that the problem is not just limited to his own school and parish. What is needed, he argues, is much more help from Catholic advisory staff in the areas of religious education and school worship, working both with clergy and teachers. He feels that there should also be more in-service training opportunities for clergy and headteachers to help Catholic schools and parishes work more closely together.

The school information booklet says surprisingly little about the Catholic foundation or character of the school. Although the Catholic priest is named as chairman of the governors, no mention is made of his contribution to the religious life of the school. Comparatively little attention is drawn to the denominational nature of the religious education or school worship. Overall, the emphasis is placed on the integration of religion with secular learning, rather than on explicit denominational activity. For example, when the headteacher sets out to describe the aims of religious education in the school information booklet he argues that:

> As a Catholic school we seek to provide an atmosphere in which the religious and secular aspects of learning may flourish together.

Similarly, the school information booklet emphasises the secular and social aspects of assemblies rather than their explicitly religious aspects.

> In their daily assemblies the children learn to share concern for the well-being of others and, we hope, learn to share that sense of community which is so important a part of Christian experience.

The school information booklet explains that in religious education, "the children follow an approved syllabus", but the headteacher confesses that this syllabus is not always followed closely. The school has not developed its own detailed scheme of work for religious education, although it has designated one of the assistant teachers to act as 'consultant' for religious education.

Religious education appears as separate timetable periods for the fourth year junior pupils. They spend between one hour and one and a half hours a week on the subject. The headteacher does not feel that the school is particularly well resourced for religious education. He says that the school lacks sufficient bibles, text books, reference books, slides, filmstrips and so on.

The whole school meets for an assembly four days a week. Some of these assemblies are led by the headteacher; others are led by assistant teachers or by the children themselves. As a rule, the daily assembly is a very short affair, lasting less than 15 minutes. Most days the assembly includes hymns, prayers and the Lord's Prayer. The children who are learning to play a musical instrument provide the accompaniment for the hymns. Quite often music sets the atmosphere as the pupils come into assemblies.

Assemblies reflect the church's year very closely. The hymns and prayers used in assemblies bear a close relationship with those used in church. The school uses a Catholic hymn book. There is also a close relationship between assemblies and the curriculum for religious education. At least once a month mass is celebrated in school.

Because the school values its accent on community, parents are often invited to attend assemblies. This is particularly so when the school is celebrating a Christian festival or when the children have prepared to lead the assembly themselves. The headteacher writes in the school information booklet:

> Parents are particularly welcome when they come to share in our religious celebrations. Mass is said in school on holy days and on various other days during the term. Your child may also want to invite you to school on the days when his/her class are taking assembly.

The headteacher says that every week there are some parents who accept this invitation.

As a Catholic school, St Anne's recognises that it has a role in helping to prepare pupils for membership of the Catholic community. The school information booklet explains that:

> Children are encouraged to appreciate the value of daily prayer and of regular attendance at mass and are prepared for receipt of the sacraments at appropriate stages in their development.

It is precisely this function which is made so difficult by the lack of understanding and co-operation between the headteacher and the parish priest.

On closer inspection St Anne's Catholic Primary School does not seem to be realising the close links with the local Catholic church which its institutional foundation might imply. The parish has worked hard to raise the money to build its new school and has been successful in recruiting a good number of Catholic pupils into its classroom. It has not, however, been successful in encouraging the headteacher and the parish priest to agree on a method of working and, without this, the potential of the school remains unfulfilled.

12 CHURCH RELATED EDUCATION

Measuring differences

The previous seven chapters have analysed the ways in which state maintained primary schools vary in their religious character and provision. The present chapter employs more sophisticated statistical procedures to identify the deeper structure underlying the religious differences between schools and to assess the relative influence of various factors which may account for these differences.

It has become clear from the preceding chapters that some schools understand themselves to be working in a much closer partnership with the churches than others. Some act as if they consider it appropriate for state maintained schools to function as an extension of the Christian churches, while others do not.

At first glance, however, it is not easy to specify the range of characteristics which most clearly distinguishes schools which pursue a church-related approach to education from those which do not. For example, is a daily assembly for the whole school a clear indication of a church-related approach, or can it simply mean that the school sees social and educational advantages in a daily assembly, and not necessarily explicit religious significance? Does the regular singing of hymns in assemblies indicate a clear church-related intention, or can it simply mean that hymn singing has musical and social meaning rather than explicit religious connotations? Is the imaginative use of resources in religious education indicative of a close relationship with the churches, or can it simply mean that religious education is taken seriously in the school on educational grounds, rather than on religious grounds?

In order to answer this kind of question and to form a clear idea how schools which follow a church-related approach to education differ from those which do not, the information gathered by the headteachers' questionnaires was subjected to a series of factor analyses and other exploratory correlational techniques. The idea of these techniques is to identify the various patterns implicit in the questionnaire data and to summarise the main trends underlying these patterns. The end result of this process was to identify twenty-two pieces of information which most clearly differentiate between schools which adopt a church-related approach and those which do not.

The twenty-two pieces of information which produce this scale of church-related education are listed in table 12.1, together with their statistical properties. These statistics show that, within the available indicators in the questionnaire, contact with clergy emerges as the most central feature distinguishing the schools which adopt a church-related approach to education.

This scale demonstrates that schools which encourage contact with clergy also emphasise other aspects of the religious life of the school differently from schools which do not encourage contact with clergy. Schools which encourage contact with clergy also have more contact with local churches; they hold more explicitly Christian assemblies and relate these assemblies more explicitly to the life of the church; they give more emphasis to the church-related aspects of religious education.

According to this scale, the most church-related schools receive regular visits from clergy. They invite clergy to contribute to assemblies and religious education. They arrange for pupils to visit and study the local church and to talk with the clergy during this visit. They hold a school service in church from time to time and encourage the pupils to contribute to a weekday or Sunday service. When the pupils attend a church service, these schools prepare well in advance so that the pupils can display their work in the church and have something to contribute to the service itself, in the form of music, dance or drama. Assemblies set out to be explicitly Christian acts of worship and reflect closely the shape of the church's year. They regularly make use of readings from the bible and stories from a Christian background. The pupils regularly recite the Lord's Prayer and are given the opportunity to write and use their own prayers. The hymns sung in assemblies bear a close relationship with those used in local churches and the pupils also sometimes sing the psalms and canticles used in church. Religious education makes regular use of the bible and studies church-related topics. These schools are likely to possess class sets of one or more modern translation of the bible.

According to this scale, the least church-related schools do not receive visits from clergy, nor invite clergy to contribute to religious education or assemblies. They do not make use of the local church as a resource in religious education. They do not arrange for the pupils to visit the local church to look at the building, to meet the clergy or to study the purpose of the church. They neither hold a school service in church, nor involve the pupils in a weekday or Sunday service. Assemblies do not set out to be explicitly or implicitly Christian in character. They do not have a close relationship with the shape of the church's year. While the pupils sing hymns, these hymns do not reflect the usage in local churches. The pupils do not join in saying the Lord's Prayer. They do not sing psalms or canticles. Passages are not read from the bible and stories are chosen from secular rather than Christian backgrounds. The pupils are not encouraged to write their own prayers to use in assemblies. Religious education does not make much use of the bible, nor study church-related topics. These schools are unlikely to possess class sets of a modern translation of the bible.

While the items attracted into this scale draw a clear profile of the distinguishing characteristics of church-related schools, it is equally important to learn from some of the items which do not form part of this cluster. The number of days the whole school meets for an assembly every week is not indicative of the extent to which the school adopts a church-related approach; it is the content, not the frequency of assemblies which counts. The number of days on which the pupils sing hymns each week is not indicative of the extent to which the school adopts a church-related approach; it is the relationship between hymns sung in school and church which counts. The fact that prayers are used in assemblies does not distinguish between church-related and non-churchrelated approaches; it is the specific use of the Lord's Prayer which counts. The range of resources used in religious education does not distinguish between church-related and non-churchrelated approaches, but the use of the bible in religious education does distinguish between the two approaches. The possession of a set of bibles in school does not distinguish between church-related and non-churchrelated approaches, but the possession of a set of bibles in a modern translation does distinguish between the two approaches.

Having identified the indicators which help to distinguish schools which adopt a church-related approach to education from those which do not, it is now possible to add up these pieces of information and create a score for each individual school on a scale of church-related education.

Accounting for differences

Having calculated each school's unique score on the scale of church-related education, it is now possible to explore in greater detail the factors which influence where individual schools are placed on this continuum, from being very church-related at one end to being completely non-churchrelated at the other end. Two key factors emerge as crucial in influencing the church-related character of individual schools. These are the nature of the foundation of the school and the personal religious disposition of the headteacher. The importance of these factors is summarised in table 12.2.

As far as the foundation of the school is concerned, the mean scores on the scale of church-related education confirm the impressions given by chapters five through eight. Catholic schools are clearly the most church-related and county schools the least church-related. Church of England controlled schools show more signs of being church-related than county schools, but less signs than Church of England aided schools. In their turn, Church of England aided schools show less signs of being church-related than Catholic schools.

As far as the personal religious disposition of the headteachers is concerned, three issues raised in the questionnaire show clear relationships with the level of church-relatedness demonstrated by their schools. First, the headteachers were asked to state the kind of school they would prefer to be working in. Their personal preference is clearly mirrored in the extent to which their present schools demonstrate a church-related policy. Headteachers who say that they prefer to be in the county sector show least signs of church-relatedness in their schools, while those who say that they prefer to be in the Catholic sector show most signs of church-relatedness in their schools. Those who say that they prefer to be in the Church of England aided sector show more signs of church-relatedness in their schools than those who say that they prefer to be in the Church of England controlled sector. Those who say that they have no particular preference between the church or county sectors are working in schools where the church-related profile is similar to that of Church of England controlled schools.

Second, the headteachers' denominational affiliation is a clear predictor of the church-relatedness of their present schools. Humanist or agnostic headteachers show the least signs of church-relatedness in their schools, while Catholic headteachers show the most signs of church-relatedness in their schools. Headteachers who are members of the Church of England show less signs of church-relatedness in their schools than the Catholics, but more than the members of the Free Churches.

Third, the headteachers' personal pattern of church attendance is a clear predictor of the church-relatedness of their present schools. Headteachers who never go to church or go only once a year show fewer signs of church-relatedness in their schools than those who go to church for the major festivals. In their turn, headteachers who go to church only for the major festivals show fewer signs of church-relatedness in their schools than those who go to church at least once a month.

Differences in neighbourhood schools·

In the above analysis, Catholic schools and Catholic headteachers have both emerged as the most distinctively church-related. This is consistent with the fact that most of the Catholic headteachers work in Catholic schools and that Catholic schools clearly operate a church-related admissions policy. On the other hand, Church of England aided, Church of England controlled and county schools all operate primarily to serve specific neighbourhoods, rather than specific religious communities. The rest of this chapter, therefore, proposes to concentrate on trying to understand the relative significance of the foundation, the location and the headteachers' personal religious practices in determining the level of church-relatedness displayed by neighbourhood schools. In other words, Catholic schools are excluded from the following analyses.

The statistical procedure employed to explore the church-relatedness of neighbourhood schools is path analysis. The results of this analysis are shown in path model 1. This path model sets out to answer a series of interrelated questions.

First, how do the headteachers' personal religious practices interact with the foundation of the schools? For example, is the apparent relationship between headteachers' personal religious practices and the church-relatedness of the school really an artifact of the way in which church schools tend to appoint church-going headteachers? Or do the headteachers' personal religious practices really have an influence on the church-relatedness of schools, irrespective of the nature of the foundation?

Second, does the foundation have an impact on the schools' church-relatedness independent of the headteachers' own personal religiosity? For example, do church schools where there is a headteacher who attends church weekly show any more signs of being church-related than county schools where the headteacher also attends church weekly?

Third, does the location of the school affects it church-relatedness, irrespective of the foundation and the headteachers' personal religiosity? For example, according to chapter eleven, suburban schools emerged as less church-related than village or town schools. Can this be accounted for entirely by the fact that there are fewer church schools in suburban areas and that headteachers of suburban schools are less likely to be church-goers, or is there an additional factor which can be described as the suburban environment itself?

Fourth, is the age or sex of headteachers influential in determining the church-relatedness of their schools? For example, are schools with women

Path Model 1

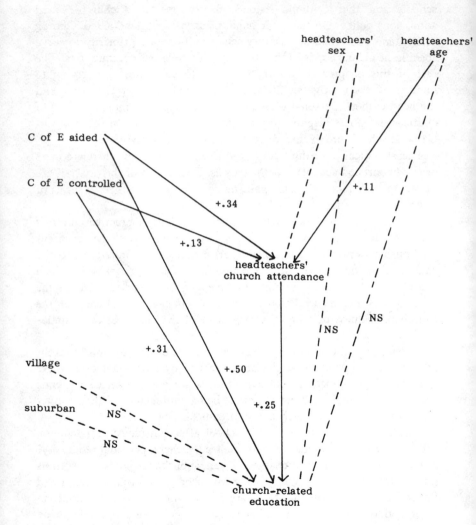

headteachers likely to be more or less church-related? Are schools with younger headteachers likely to be more or less church-related?

Path models show the hypothesised direction of relationships in terms of straight lines and arrowheads. The strength and direction of these relationships are indicated by the path coefficients or standardised regression weights and the preceding signs. The convention in path models is to locate the outcome variable, in this case the score of church-related education, at the bottom of the page, while the variables which are likely to influence this outcome are listed from the top of the page in the order in which they are entered into the equation.

According to this convention, sex and age appear at the top of the page because they are logically prior to the other factors. The foundation of the school appears next since we are interested in discovering the extent to which church schools are likely to choose church-going headteachers. Church of England aided and Church of England controlled schools are entered into the equation as 'dummy variables', with county schools serving as the reference point. Similarly, village and suburban schools are entered into the equation as 'dummy variables', with town schools serving as the reference point.

This convention means that all the arrowheads logically point down the page. Where downward progressing arrows are now drawn into the diagram, it means that statistically significant relationships do not exist. The fact that the possibility of these relationships has been taken into account in computing the equations is demonstrated in path model 12.1 by dotted lines.

The interpretation of the path diagram begins by looking at the first equation leading to headteachers' church attendance. The arrow between age and church attendance means that older headteachers are significantly more inclined to attend church than younger headteachers. On the other hand, no line emerges between sex and church attendance. This is a very interesting point since, in the population as a whole, women are much more inclined to be church-goers than men. The path model indicates that men headteachers have the same pattern of church attendance as women headteachers. In other words, in terms of their pattern of church attendance, men headteachers are likely to be more different from the population at large than women headteachers.

The arrows from Church of England aided and Church of England controlled to church attendance mean that headteachers of Church of England schools are significantly more inclined to attend church than headteachers of county schools. Comparison of the two coefficients shows that headteachers of Church of England aided schools are more inclined to be frequent church attenders than headteachers of Church of England controlled schools.

The second equation now includes the headteachers' pattern of church attendance as a predictor of the church-relatedness of schools, along with their sex and age, foundation of the school and geographical location (see table 12.3). The arrow between church attendance and church-related education means that schools where headteachers attend church regularly also display more signs of church-related education. The absence of an arrow between sex and church-related education means that the church-relatedness of schools does not depend on whether the headteacher is a man or a woman.

The absence of an arrow between age and church-related education means that the influence of the headteachers' age on the church-relatedness of schools is mediated entirely through the headteachers' pattern of church attendance. Older headteachers are more inclined to attend church and church-going headteachers are more inclined to influence schools in a church-related way, but the headteachers' age does not have an additional direct influence on the church-relatedness of schools.

The arrows from Church of England aided and Church of England controlled to church-related education mean that the foundation has a direct influence on the church-relatedness of schools in addition to the influence exerted by headteachers. Comparison of the two coefficients shows that aided status has a greater influence on the church-relatedness of schools than controlled status. Moreover, Church of England aided status and Church of England controlled status exert both an indirect influence on the church-relatedness of schools by favouring the appointment of church-going headteachers and a direct influence as well.

The absence of arrows leading from villages and suburbs means that location does not have an impact on the church-relatedness of schools, after the foundation and the religious practices of headteachers have been taken into account. In other words, the fact identified by chapter eleven that suburban schools tend to be less church-related than town schools can be explained by the lower proportion of church schools in suburban areas and the appointment of fewer church-going headteachers to suburban schools.

Two particular pointers emerge from this path model which deserve closer scrutiny. The first indicates that headteachers' personal religious practices have a significant influence on the extent to which schools display characteristics of a church-related approach to education. The second indicates that younger headteachers are less likely to show signs of religious commitment than more senior headteachers and that this is directly reflected in their schools displaying fewer characteristics of church-related education. The practical significance of these two pointers will now be examined in greater detail.

Headteachers' religious practice

In order to look more closely at the relationship between the headteachers' personal religious practices and the church-related characteristics of their schools, it is necessary to deal with county and church schools separately for two reasons. Church schools tend to appoint more church-going headteachers and the clergy have a more direct relationship with church schools, irrespective of the religious disposition of the headteachers. While it would also be interesting to look at the differences between controlled and aided schools, the size of the sample does not really permit this kind of detailed analysis. The following analyses are, therefore, based on 107 county schools and 108 church schools. The cross tabulations reported are based on two groups of headteachers: those who attend church less frequently than the major festivals and those who attend church at least monthly. For convenience in the following discussion, these two groups will be styled the non-churchgoers and the regular church-goers.

The impact of the headteachers' personal religious practices on the church related character of county schools is considerable and affects nearly all the indicators identified by the scale of church-related education.

The headteachers' personal religious practices influence the amount of contact clergy have with county schools. Where the headteacher is a regular church-goer, 74% of the county schools are visited by clergy at least once a term; 70% invite clergy to lead assemblies at least once a term; 16% invite clergy to contribute to religious education at least once a term. Where the headteacher is not a church-goer, 54% of the county schools are visited by clergy at least once a term; 54% invite clergy to lead assemblies at least once a term; 7% invite clergy to contribute to religious education at least once a term.

Similarly, the headteachers' personal religious practices influence the amount of contact county schools have with local churches. Where the headteacher is a regular church-goer, 72% of the county schools visited a local church within the past year to look at the buildings; 58% arranged to meet the clergy in church and 41% studied the purpose of the church. Where the headteacher is not a church-goer, 64% of the county schools

F

visited a local church within the past year to look at the buildings; 43% arranged to meet the clergy in church and 32% studied the purpose of the church.

Where the headteacher is a regular church-goer, 56% of the county schools held a school service in church during the past year and 12% took part in a Sunday service. Where the headteacher is not a church-goer, 39% of the county schools held a school service during the past year and 7% took part in a Sunday service. Where the headteacher is a regular church-goer, 28% of the county schools arranged a display of the pupils' work in a local church during the past year and 44% gave the pupils an opportunity to present music, dance or drama in the church. Where the headteacher is not a church-goer, 21% of the county schools arranged a display of the pupils' work in a local church during the past year and 18% gave the pupils an opportunity to present music, dance or drama in church.

County schools where the headteacher is a regular church-goer are much more likely to experience church-related assemblies. Thus, 37% of the regular church-goers describe the majority of their assemblies as explicitly Christian, compared with 18% of the non-churchgoers. Where the headteacher is a regular church-goer, the fourth year junior pupils hear the bible read in assemblies at least once a week in 47% of the county schools, compared with 7% where the headteacher is not a church-goer. Where the headteacher is a regular church-goer, the fourth year junior pupils hear religious stories from a Christian background in assemblies at least once a week in 84% of the county schools, compared with 64% where the headteacher is not a church-goer. There is a close relationship between assemblies and the church's year in 65% of the county schools where the headteacher is a regular church-goer, compared with 43% where the headteacher is not a church-goer.

Where the headteacher is a regular church-goer, 60% of the county schools possess a set of a modern translation of the bible, compared with 29% where the headteacher is not a church-goer. The fourth year junior pupils often use copies of the bible in religious education in 21% of the county schools where the headteacher is a regular church-goer and in none of the county schools where the headteacher is not a church-goer.

The impact of the headteachers' personal religious practices on the church-related nature of church schools is less considerable than in the case of county schools, but still very real.

In the case of church schools, the headteacher's personal religious commitment does not influence whether or not the school visits the local church to study the buildings; nor does it influence whether or not the school holds a school service in church. On the other hand, the headteacher's personal religious commitment does influence the extent to which the pupils become actively involved in these occasions. While 65% of the church schools where the headteacher is a regular church-goer give the pupils an opportunity to share their music, dance or drama in church, only 45% where the headteacher is not a church-goer do so. While 37% of the church schools where the headteacher is a regular church-goer make a display of the pupils' work in church, only 18% where the headteacher is not a regular church-goer do so. Headteachers who do not attend church themselves are less likely to involve their church schools in Sunday church services: 27% of the regular church-goers have involved their church school in a Sunday church service within the past year, compared with 18% of the non-churchgoing headteachers.

In the case of church schools, the headteacher's personal religious commitment does not influence whether or not the school possesses a set of modern bibles. It does, however, influence whether or not these bibles are used. The fourth year junior pupils often use copies of the bible in religious education in 38% of the church schools where the headteacher is a regular church-goer, but in none of the church schools where the headteacher is not a church-goer. The fourth year junior pupils hear passages from the bible read in assemblies at least once a week in 62% of the church schools where the headteacher is a regular church-goer, but in only 36% where the headteacher is not a church-goer.

There is also a range of other ways in which the headteachers' personal religious practices influence assemblies in church schools. Thus, 54% of the regular church-going headteachers describe the majority of their assemblies as explicitly Christian, compared with 36% of the non-churchgoers; 42% of the regular church-going headteachers say that there is a close relationship between hymns sung in assemblies and in the local church, compared with 18% of the non-churchgoers.

The frequency and degree of contact which the clergy have with church schools is also related to the religious commitment of the headteachers. Where the headteacher is a regular church-goer, 89% of the church schools are visited by the clergy at least once a term; 80% have clergy leading assemblies at least once a term; 56% have clergy contributing to religious education at least once a term. Where the headteacher is not a church-goer, 73% of the church schools are visited by the clergy at least once a term; 63% have clergy leading assemblies at least once a term; 36% have clergy contributing to religious education at least once a term.

Headteachers' age

The path model suggests that younger headteachers are less likely to be practising church-goers than more senior headteachers. In order to understand what this means in practice, the religious behaviour of the headteachers of county and Church of England schools was analysed according to age categories. From this analysis it emerges that at least monthly church attendance is practised by 58% of the headteachers under the age of forty, 68% of the headteachers in their forties or fifties and 77% of those in their sixties.

This relationship between church attendance and age can be explained in two ways: either headteachers tend to increase their church attendance as they grow older, or the younger generation of headteachers is less religious than their predecessors. While both trends may in fact contribute to the differences found in the data, the general trend in society towards lower levels of church attendance favours the theory that the present generation of headteachers may be less religious than their predecessors. At the same time, it needs to be emphasised that even the younger headteachers are much more likely to attend church regularly than the adult population as a whole.

The path model goes on to suggest that there is no direct influence between headteachers' age and the church-related character of schools, but that there is an indirect influence mediated via the impact of age on church attendance and the impact of church attendance on the church-related character of schools. Cross tabulation between headteachers' ages and the items identified by the scale of church-related education confirms that there is a relationship between the church-related character of schools and headteachers' ages. The real difference emerges between headteachers who are now in their thirties and the rest.

The majority of headteachers over the age of forty will have completed their initial teacher training before the end of the 1960s when new thinking began to emerge in educational philosophy and religious education. The headteachers who are not yet in their forties will have had greater chance of exposure to this new thinking. For convenience in the following discussion, those under the age of forty will be styled the 'younger headteachers', while those over the age of forty will be styled the 'older headteachers'.

It is particularly in county schools that the younger headteachers are moving away from the characteristics of church-related education. For example, 38% of the younger headteachers in county schools describe the majority of their assemblies as largely secular and social, compared with only 9% of the older headteachers. Fourth year junior pupils hear passages read from the bible in assemblies at least once a week in 12% of the county schools where the headteacher is under forty, compared with 40% where the headteacher is over forty. Fourth year junior pupils hear religious stories of a Christian background at least once a week in 69% of the county schools where the headteacher is under forty, compared with 80% where the headteacher is over forty. There is a close relationship between assemblies and the church's year in 37% of the county schools where the headteacher is under forty, but in 67% where the headteacher is over forty.

Similarly, the bible is less likely to be used in religious education in county schools where the headteacher is under forty. Thus, the fourth year junior pupils rarely or never use the bible in religious education in 63% of the county schools in the charge of a younger headteacher, compared with 30% in the charge of an older headteacher.

While clergy are just as likely to make informal visits to county schools where the headteacher is under forty, the younger headteachers are less likely to invite clergy to take part in assemblies or religious education. Thus, clergy are invited to take assemblies at least once a term in 56% of the county schools where the headteacher is under the age of forty, compared with 66% where the headteacher is over the age of forty.

The younger headteachers in county schools are less likely to make use of the local church as an educational resource. Thus, only 50% of the county schools where the headteacher is under forty arranged for pupils to visit a local church within the past year to look at the building, compared with 71% where the headteacher is over forty; 31% of the county schools where the headteacher is under forty arranged for pupils to meet and talk with the clergy in the local church, compared with 55% where the headteacher is over forty; 44% of the county schools where the headteacher is under forty held a school service within the past year, compared with 51% where the headteacher is over forty.

In the case of church schools, the relationship between headteachers' age and the church-related character of schools is less clear, but still evident in some specific ways. For example, only 40% of the younger headteachers of church schools describe the majority of their assemblies as explicitly Christian, compared with 51% of the older headteachers; only 43% of the younger headteachers of church schools arranged for their pupils to visit the local church to meet with the clergy during the past year, compared with 58% of the older headteachers.

Implications

These detailed statistical analyses of factors which influence the church-related character of neighbourhood schools have some clear and important implications for the Church of England's assessment of its partnership in the state maintained system of education. In particular, ten points demonstrated by this analysis are worth highlighting.

First, the church still has considerable influence to determine the church-related character of neighbourhood schools. It can do so both directly through its involvement in aided and controlled schools, and indirectly through the Christian commitment of headteachers. These two channels of influence constitute a powerful presence in the state maintained system of schools. Christian people may rejoice that the church's influence can still be so strong in a secular educational system. Secular educationalists may be suspicious of such pervasive religious influence.

Second, church schools are distinctive in the sense of displaying more characteristics of church-related education than county schools. Controlled schools are significantly more church-related than county schools; aided schools are significantly more church-related than controlled schools. Christian people may be pleased that the church is still able to utilise aided and controlled status to promote neighbourhood schools which are more church-related than county schools. Secular educationalists may accuse the church of using its theology of service to the nation to cloak confessional aims in education.

Third, headteachers hold a key position in determining the church-related character of neighbourhood schools. Primary headteachers are much more church-going than the population at large and they use their Christian commitment to influence the church-relatedness of their schools, irrespective of whether the pupils come from religious or secular backgrounds. Christian people may be happy to know that the headships of many church and county schools are held by their fellow believers who are in a key position to influence the religious development of children. Secular educationalists may raise questions about the right of headteachers to allow their personal beliefs to influence their professional practice in a state maintained system of schools.

Fourth, church schools, both aided and controlled, are more likely to appoint church-goers to the position of headships than county schools. Those in favour of church schools may applaud this as good stewardship of the church's investment in the state maintained system of education. Those not in favour of church schools may see this as further evidence of the inequality and professional divisiveness fostered by voluntary schools.

Fifth, the religious foundation of a school has a direct impact on the church-related character of the school in addition to the indirect influence exerted through the tendency to appoint church-going headteachers. At the time of the 1944 Education Act, the Free Churches tended to argue that church influence was best brought to bear on state maintained schools through the training of Christian teachers rather than through the maintenance of voluntary schools. The present study shows that, from the church's point of view, while Christian teachers are important, the foundation of the school is also important in promoting church-related education.

Sixth, aided status is a more significant influence than controlled status in promoting the church-related character of a school. At the time of the 1944 Education Act, the Church of England adopted two different views on the relative advantages of aided and controlled status. Some voices argued that aided status was essential for preserving the church-related character of church schools; other voices argued that, provided the teachers were Christian men and women, aided status offered no positive advantages over controlled status. The present study shows that, while controlled status is able to promote greater church-relatedness than county schools, aided status is considerably more powerful in achieving this end than controlled status.

Seventh, the lower level of church-relatedness in suburban schools, compared with town and village schools, can be explained in terms of the lower proportion of church schools in suburban areas and the appointment of more secular headteachers to the headships of suburban schools. This is a reflection on the church's historic inability to extend its educational influence into the more recent areas of development. Having failed to take the initiative to build new church schools in suburban areas, the church now witnesses the accelerated secularisation of educational provision in these areas.

Eighth, church aided schools differ in their church-relatedness from county schools, both in the Christian commitment of the headteachers and in the range of church-related phenomena in the life of the school. At the same time, these schools set out to serve a neighbourhood function in the same way as county schools. The church needs to ask whether it still ought to have the right to determine so radically the church-related character of some neighbourhood schools.

Ninth, some county schools are far removed from offering the same kind of church-related education as aided schools. The headteacher may not be a practising church-goer and the range of church-related contacts offered by the school may be minimal. Nevertheless, some of the pupils attending such secular neighbourhood schools may be practising church-goers from practising church-going families. The church needs to ask whether it should be content to direct the children of its practising members to predominantly secular schools.

Tenth, the younger headteachers are less likely to be regular church-goers than the more senior headteachers. They are also less likely to promote church-related education in their schools. If this trend between headteacher's age and the church-related character of schools persists, it is likely that the Christian character of schools will decrease as the older headteachers are replaced by a younger, more secular generation of headteachers. This could have important implications for the churches, especially given the conclusion of related research studies that there is already a growing gap between the churches and successive generations of young people. Secular educationalists may rejoice that the changes which have occurred in educational theory over the past two decades are now being reflected in school practice. The churches, however, need to be alert to the possibility of accelerated secularisation within state maintained schools, even in the shire counties. If the churches need to recognise that the secular educational system is unlikely to continue to make a significant contribution to church-related education, they need also to redirect their work among children in ways appropriate within an increasingly secular society.

13 MEETING THE PUPILS

Chapters five through twelve have looked in detail at the church-related character of primary schools. The present chapter turns attention from the schools to the pupils themselves, in order to examine the religious background and attitudes of those who attend the schools. What experience do these pupils have of church, outside the church-related curriculum of the school? How many of them are regular church-goers and how many attend Sunday schools or church-related groups for children and young people? How many of them come from homes where one or both parents are church-goers? What assumptions can schools make about the religious atmosphere of their pupils' homes?

What attitudes do the pupils hold towards God, Jesus, the bible, prayer, the church and religion in their school? Do they hold positive attitudes towards these areas and regard them with enthusiasm, or do they hold negative attitudes and regard them with disdain? How important are home, church and environment in shaping these attitudes? All these influences need to be taken into account before it is possible to assess whether or not the school itself plays a part in shaping the pupils' attitude towards Christianity.

These are the kind of questions which it is possible to answer on the basis of the survey conducted among the fourth year junior pupils. This survey produced 4,948 completed questionnaires from 96 county, 57 Church of England controlled, 34 Church of England aided, five Catholic and one other voluntary school.

The number of pupils from each school varies between one and 109: 3,129 pupils were in county schools, 972 in Church of England controlled, 683 in Church of England aided and 118 in Catholic schools. The very small number of pupils from Catholic schools is accounted for by the fact that three of the eight Catholic schools in Gloucestershire which cater for fourth year junior pupils refused to take part in the survey. There are slightly more boys (51%) in the sample than girls (49%).

Religious background

According to Peter Brierley's study, *Prospect for the 80s* (1980), church attendance in Gloucestershire is above the national average, with 13% of the adult population attending church on Sunday. Peter Brierley's survey also reveals that the proportion of young people under the age of 15 who attend church is higher than this. The results of the present survey are consistent with Peter Brierley's findings, since 16% of the fourth year junior pupils say that they attend church most Sundays.

Two-thirds of the children who attend church most Sundays also have contact with Sunday schools or other church provision for young people. Another 4% have weekly contact with a Sunday school or other church group for young people, but do not attend church services most Sundays. This means that one in five of the 11 year olds in Gloucestershire claims to be in regular weekly contact with one of the Christian churches.

Looked at from another perspective, however, one third (30%) of the 11 year olds in Gloucestershire never go to church on a Sunday and two-thirds (65%) never go to a Sunday school or church group for young people. This leaves 17% who go to Sunday church services at least once or twice a year, 28% who go more than twice a year but not as often as once a month and 8% who go at least monthly but not weekly. Thus, while only 16% of the pupils attend church regularly most Sundays, another 53% have some experience of Sunday church services.

Sunday schools and church groups for young people are much less likely to have occasional attenders than church services. Just 19% of the sample have some contact with a Sunday school or church group for young people, although they do not attend weekly. This means that three-quarters (77%) never have contact with a Sunday school or church group for young people.

Fourth year junior pupils are more likely to attend church than their parents. While 16% of the pupils attend church most Sundays, just 5% say that both parents attend church most Sundays; a further 6% say that mother attends church most Sundays, while father does not and 2% say that father attends church most Sundays while mother does not. In other words, 11% of the mothers and 7% of the fathers attend church most Sundays.

Looked at from another perspective, two-fifths (41%) of the mothers never attend church, 15% go once or twice a year, 26% go more than twice a year but not as often as once a month, 7% go monthly and 11% go weekly. Over half (54%) of the fathers never attend church, 14% go once or twice a year, 20% go more than twice a year but not as often as once a month, 4% go monthly and 7% go weekly.

Nearly a third (32%) of the pupils have no denominational allegiance and do not feel that they belong to any particular Christian church. The largest denominational group, to which nearly half (47%) of the pupils belong, is the Church of England. The next largest group, to which only 6% of the pupils belong, is the Baptist church. Then in third place come the Catholic and Methodist churches, which each claim 5% of the pupils. Next in sequence come the United Reformed Church with 2% and the Pentecostal churches with 1%. Other denominational groups are identified by only small numbers of pupils. These include five Brethren, four Orthodox, four House Church, eight Salvation Army, two Society of Friends, two Seventh Day Adventists, five Christadelphians, 11 Jehovah Witnesses and four Mormons. Another 13 pupils describe themselves as belonging to an evangelical church, five to a mission church and three simply say 'chapel' without specifying a denomination. The other world faiths are represented by 21 Muslims and one Hindu.

In interpreting this pattern of denominational and religious membership, two points should be kept in mind. The Catholic presence is under-represented because of the refusal of three of the eight Catholic schools to participate in the study. The other world faiths are also under-represented because two of the schools which have a significant proportion of pupils from non-Christian religious backgrounds also refused to participate in the study on the grounds that the survey was taking too much interest in Christianity.

While church attendance gives an indication of the public place of religion in the pupils' lives, personal prayer gives an indication of the private place of religion in their lives. For this reason the questionnaire also collected information about children's pattern of prayer at home, as distinct from saying prayers in school assemblies or when they attend church. Slightly more children pray every day than attend church every Sunday. Nearly one in five (19%) of the pupils say that they pray daily. Another 7% pray at least once a week and 4% pray at least once a month. A large number of pupils (42%) say that, while they do not pray as often as once a month, they do pray sometimes. This leaves more than a quarter (28%) who never pray.

Pupil attitudes

The 24 item Likert scale of attitude towards Christianity provides a great deal of detailed information about the pupils' attitudes towards God, Jesus, the bible, church, prayer and religion in school. The overall attitude held by these pupils can be illustrated by reference to the proportion of pupils who agree with certain individual items.

Just over two-thirds of the 11 year olds in Gloucestershire believe that

God and Jesus have a positive influence in people's lives: 69% believe that God helps people and 63% believe that Jesus helps people today. There is less certainty, however, about the reality of God's influence on their own lives. While 69% believe God helps other people, the proportion drops to 54% who believe that God helps them and 51% who say that God is very real to them. While 63% of the children believe that Jesus helps other people, the proportion drops to 53% who believe that Jesus helps them and 52% who feel that Jesus is close to them.

Three out of five (60%) of the children think that praying is a good thing and 58% believe that God listens to prayers. However, the proportion drops to two in five (39%) who feel that prayer is actually helpful to them. Another third (36%) are not sure whether prayer helps them or not and a quarter (25%) are clear that prayer is no help to them at all.

More of the 11 year olds hold positive attitudes towards the bible, church and school religion than hold negative attitudes in these areas. While 32% argue that church services are boring, 46% say that they are not boring. While 23% argue that the bible is boring, 54% say that it is not boring. While 26% dislike school lessons about God, 45% like them.

As well as giving insights into the proportions of pupils who agree or disagree with specific statements, the idea of the Likert scale is that the 24 individual items cohere to produce an overall scale score. All the items are listed in table 13.1, together with their statistical properties. Because each item is scored on a five point scale, ranging from 'agree strongly', through 'agree', 'not certain' and 'disagree' to 'disagree strongly', a 24 item Likert scale produces a range of scores between 24 and 120. The average score in the present sample is around 85 points, which is towards the favourable end of the continuum. This shows that there is more goodwill towards Christianity among the pupils than hostility.

As well as completing the Likert scale of attitude towards Christianity, the pupils also completed the eight semantic differential scales described in chapter four. These eight semantic differential scales place the pupils' attitude towards Christianity in a wider context by measuring their attitudes towards English lessons, maths lessons, school, religious education, music lessons, church, assemblies and games lessons.

The pairs of adjectives employed to create these semantic differential scales are listed in table 13.2, together with their statistical properties. These statistics demonstrate that it is meaningful to compare the pupils' scores recorded on different scales. Because each pair of adjectives is scored on a seven point grid, semantic differential scales composed of seven pairs of adjectives produce a range of scores between 7 and 49.

According to the scores on these semantic differential attitude scales, of the five school subjects listed, the pupils' most positive attitude is shown towards games lessons with a score of 44.8. Then in second place comes maths (38.3), in third place English (37.2), in fourth place music (37.1) and in bottom place religious education (36.0). While church also has a low score (36.1), alongside religious education, school assemblies are regarded more positively (37.3), alongside English and music lessons.

Sex differences

Many studies in the psychology of religion show that girls and women of all ages tend to be more religious than boys and men (Batson and Ventis, 1982). Eleven year olds in Gloucestershire are no exception to this trend. Thus, 20% of the girls attend church weekly, compared with 13% of the boys; 20% of the girls have weekly contact with a Sunday school or church group for young people, compared with 11% of the boys; 24% of the girls pray at home every day, compared with 14% of the boys. Looked at from another perspective, 36% of the boys never go to church, compared with 23% of the girls; 74% of the boys never have contact with a Sunday school or church group for young people, compared with 57% of the girls; 37% of the boys never pray, compared with 18% of the girls.

The boys are less inclined to feel that they belong to a Christian denomination than the girls: 37% of the boys say that they have no denominational link, compared with 26% of the girls. The Baptist and Catholic churches have roughly the same proportion of boys and girls claiming membership, while the Church of England and the Methodist church have significantly more girls than boys.

The difference in church attendance between boys and girls cannot be explained in terms of different levels of parental example and support. The same proportion of boys and girls (7%) say that their father attends church weekly and only slightly more of the girls (12%) say that their mother attends church weekly than the boys (11%).

Sex differences in religious behaviour are also reflected in differences in attitudes. According to table 13.3, girls record more favourable attitudes than boys on the scales of attitude towards Christianity, church, religious education and assemblies. At the same time, girls record more favourable attitudes to school, English and music lessons. On the other hand, boys record more favourable attitudes towards games lessons and there are no sex differences in attitude towards maths.

The more positive attitude towards Christianity held by the girls is demonstrated by their answers to the individual items of the Likert attitude scale. For example, more than a third (35%) of the boys find it hard to believe in God, compared with less than a quarter (24%) of the girls. Less than half (47%) of the boys feel Jesus is close to them, compared with 57% of the girls. Less than half (48%) of the boys believe that God helps them, compared with 61% of the girls. While 54% of the boys believe that God listens to prayer, the proportion rises to 64% of the girls; 35% of the boys find prayer helpful, compared with 46% of the girls.

Similarly, boys are less inclined to enjoy church, religious education and the bible. Thus, 39% of the boys find church services boring, compared with 24% of the girls; 28% of the boys say the bible is boring, compared with 18% of the girls; only 40% of the boys like their religious education lessons, compared with 50% of the girls.

By drawing attention to the significant differences in the responses of boys and girls, this analysis emphasises the importance of taking sex differences into account before examining the potential influence of different types of schools on pupil attitudes towards Christianity.

Home differences

A number of studies in the social psychology of religion draws attention to the importance of socio-economic status in understanding differences in religious behaviour and attitudes (Argyle and Beit-Hallahmi, 1975). In empirical research socio-economic status is often determined on the basis of grading different forms of employment.

There are several occupational classification systems in current use, but the most frequently used scale is the five point categorisation proposed by the government Office of Population, Censuses and Surveys. This scale is a classification of occupations (or to be more precise 'unit groups' of occupations) according to "the general standing within the community of the occupations concerned".

According to this classification system, professionals like doctors, accountants, solicitors and clergymen are assigned to social class one. Semi-professionals, like teachers, social workers, journalists and entertainers, are assigned to social class two. Social class three includes bus drivers, clerks, secretaries and electricians, and is generally subdivided into manual and non-manual occupations. Social class four includes postmen, machine operators, bricklayers and bus conductors. Social class five includes unskilled manual labourers, porters and messengers.

Pupils were asked to describe their mothers' and fathers' jobs and on the basis of this information each parent was assigned a socio-economic grade. While there are many problems in assessing the validity of this procedure, it is sufficiently valid to highlight the importance of social class in determining the child's religiosity and the religious influence of the home.

Children from professional homes are much more likely to have parents who go to church regularly. Thus, 26% of the fathers in class one occupations attend church weekly, compared with 13% in class two, 10% in class three non-manual and 4% in manual occupations. Similarly, 31% of the mothers married to men in class one occupations attend church weekly, compared with 19% in class two, 15% in class three non-manual and 8% in manual occupations.

The relationship between socio-economic status and parental church attendance is also closely mirrored in the children's church attendance. Thus, 36% of the children from class one homes attend church each Sunday, compared with 25% in class two, 21% in class three non-manual, 14% in class three manual, 13% in class four and 6% in class five.

The relationship between socio-economic background and the child's attitudes is not direct, but mediated through the influence of parental church attendance. Children whose parents go to church are likely to show a much more positive attitude towards Christianity than children whose parents do not go to church (see table 13.4).

The clear relationship between parental church attendance and pupil attitude towards Christianity is demonstrated by their answers to the individual items of the Likert attitude scale. For example, 38% of the pupils whose parents never attend church find it hard to believe in God, compared with 17% whose mother or father attends church each week. While 85% of the pupils whose parents attend church each week believe that Jesus helps people, the proportion falls to 52% whose parents never attend church. While 82% of the pupils whose parents attend church each week believe that God helps them to live a better life, the proportion falls to 48% whose parents never attend church. While 84% of the pupils whose parents attend church each week believe that God listens to prayers, the proportion falls to 49% whose parents never attend church.

Similarly, two-thirds (64%) of the pupils whose parents attend church each week say that prayer helps them, compared with less than a third (28%) whose parents never attend church. More than three-fifths (61%) of the pupils whose parents attend church each week like their religious education lessons at school, compared with less than two-fifths (38%) whose parents never attend church.

By drawing attention to the significant influence of the home on the pupils' responses, this analysis emphasises the importance of taking socio-economic status and parental church attendance into account before examining the potential influence of different types of schools on pupil attitudes towards Christianity.

Church-going differences

Studies in the psychology of religious development draw attention to the close relationship between parental church attendance and child church attendance and between church attendance and religious attitudes (Strommen, 1971). The present data enable both relationships to be examined.

Parental church attendance has a very strong influence on the child's church attendance. Three-quarters (76%) of the pupils whose mothers attend church weekly also go to church weekly. Less than one-quarter (24%) of the pupils whose mothers attend church monthly go to church weekly. Only 5% of the pupils whose mothers never attend church go to church weekly. Looked at from another perspective, nearly two-thirds (63%) of the pupils whose mothers never attend church never go to church themselves.

Four-fifths (79%) of the pupils whose fathers attend church weekly, also go to church weekly. Just over a quarter (27%) of the pupils whose fathers attend church monthly go to church weekly. Only 8% of the pupils whose fathers never attend church go to church weekly. Looked at from another perspective, half (51%) of the pupils whose fathers never attend church never go to church themselves.

Parental church attendance also has a strong influence on the child's pattern of praying, although the influence is less strong than on the child's church attendance. Thus, 45% of the pupils whose mothers go to church weekly pray daily, compared with 29% whose mothers go to church monthly and 12% whose mothers never attend church. Two-fifths (41%) of the pupils whose mothers never attend church never pray. Similarly, 53% of the pupils whose fathers go to church weekly, pray daily, compared with 32% whose fathers go to church monthly and 13% whose fathers never attend church. Two-fifths (39%) of the pupils whose fathers never attend church never pray.

In turn, the pupils' church attendance has a strong influence on their attitude towards Christianity. Children who go to church are likely to show a much more positive attitude towards Christianity than children who do not go to church. Table 13.5 examines this relationship for boys and girls separately.

The importance of the relationship between church attendance and attitude towards Christianity is demonstrated by reference to some of the items of the Likert attitude scale. For example, 36% of the girls who never attend church find it hard to believe in God, compared with 13% who attend church weekly; 39% of the girls who never attend church dismiss church services as boring, compared with 10% who attend church weekly. Four-fifths (81%) of the girls who attend church weekly believe that God listens to prayers, compared with half (50%) who never attend church.

Similarly, two-thirds (65%) of the girls who attend church weekly feel that prayer helps them a lot, compared with less than one-third (30%) who never attend church. Three-quarters (76%) of the girls who attend church weekly say that Jesus helps them, compared with less than half (46%) who never attend church. Religious education is enjoyed by 67% of the girls who attend church weekly and 39% who never attend church.

The relationship between church attendance and attitude towards Christianity is even more pronounced among the boys. For example, 47% of the boys who never attend church find it hard to believe in God, compared with 18% who attend church weekly; 56% of the boys who never attend church dismiss church services as boring, compared with 16% who attend church weekly. Nearly four-fifths (78%) of the boys who attend church weekly believe that God listens to prayers, compared with two-fifths (41%) who never attend church.

Similarly, three-fifths (63%) of the boys who attend church weekly feel that prayer helps them a lot, compared with one-fifth (22%) who never attend church. Three-quarters (75%) of the boys who attend church weekly know that Jesus helps them, compared with less than two-fifths (37%) who never attend church. Religious education is enjoyed by 57% of the boys who attend church weekly and 30% who never attend church.

By drawing attention to the significant relationship between church attendance and the pupils' responses, this analysis emphasises the importance of taking church attendance into account before examining the potential influence of different types of schools on pupil attitudes towards Christianity.

Environmental differences

Studies in the geography of religion draw attention to the variation in levels of religiosity from one kind of environment to another (Gay, 1971). The present data demonstrate how parental church attendance varies between the three different environments of villages, towns and suburbs.

Parents who live in villages are less likely to attend church weekly than those who live in towns or suburbs. This is consistent with the way in which many village churches no longer sustain a weekly pattern of services. On the other hand, parents who live in villages are more likely to make some contact with the church than those who live in towns or suburbs. This is consistent with the way in which some church festivals, like harvest festival and carol services, play a more significant part in village life. Parents who live in suburbs are just as likely to be weekly church-goers as those who live in towns. On the other hand, a larger proportion of suburban parents never make contact with the church.

Thus, 5% of the fathers who live in villages go to church each week, compared with 7% in towns and suburbs; 47% of the fathers who live in villages never go to church, compared with 55% in towns and 61% in suburbs. Similarly, 10% of the mothers who live in villages go to church each week, compared with 11% in towns and suburbs; 28% of the mothers who live in villages never go to church, compared with 42% in towns and 48% in suburbs.

The proportion of children who have contact with church also follows the same geographical pattern: 36% of the children who live in suburbs never go to church, compared with 30% in towns and 19% in villages. At the other end of the scale, 26% of the children who live in villages go to church at least once a month, and so do 23% in towns and 22% in suburbs.

Table 13.6 shows that there are no differences in the attitudes of pupils in villages, towns and suburbs towards maths and English. Children in village schools have a slightly less positive attitude towards games lessons than pupils in towns and suburbs. On other issues, however, pupils in village schools have a more positive attitude, especially in comparison with pupils in suburban schools. They have a more positive attitude towards school, church, assemblies, religious education and Christianity.

The relationship between geographical environment and pupil attitude towards Christianity is demonstrated by their answers to the individual items of the Likert attitude scale. For example, 44% of the pupils in village schools agree that the church is important, compared with 38% in suburbs and 39% in towns. Only 16% of the pupils in village schools feel that going to church is a waste of time, compared with 22% in suburbs and 21% in towns; 29% of the pupils in village schools dismiss church services as boring, compared with 34% in suburbs and 32% in towns. Similarly, 61% of the pupils in village schools believe that God listens to prayers, compared with 55% in suburbs and 59% in towns; 58% of the pupils in village schools believe that God helps them, compared with 51% in suburbs and 55% in towns.

By drawing attention to the significant relationship between geographical environment and the pupils' responses, this analysis emphasises the importance of taking the location of the school into account when examining the potential influence of different types of schools on pupil attitudes towards Christianity.

14 SCHOOL INFLUENCE

The previous chapter has provided an introduction to the religious attitudes and practices of the 11 year old children in Gloucestershire, whom the state maintained system of education exists to serve. Although the churches continue to make an important contribution towards shaping the state maintained system of education, the majority of the pupils are not closely associated with the churches. Just 16% of the 11 year olds attend church most Sundays. On the other hand, more pupils show goodwill towards the church than hostility against it.

The previous chapter has also demonstrated some of the important factors which are related to the pupils' religious attitudes and practices. Sex differences are important: girls are more religious than boys. Home differences are important: children from the higher socio-economic backgrounds are more religious than those from the lower socio-economic backgrounds. Parental differences are important: children whose parents attend church are more religious than children whose parents do not attend church. Church-going differences are important: children who attend church hold more positive attitudes towards Christianity than those who do not. Environmental differences are important: children who live in villages hold more positive attitudes towards Christianity than those who live in towns or suburbs.

Against this background, the present chapter addresses the key question whether the pupils' attitudes towards Christianity are related to the type of school they attend. In other words, do pupils who attend church schools hold different attitudes towards Christianity from those who attend county schools? This question can be asked in two ways.

First, this chapter examines the question of school *differences*. This is a relatively simple issue, concerned to assess the overall responses of pupils in different types of schools. It is an important issue, however, because the overall responses of the pupils contribute towards establishing the religious ethos of the school and characterising the environment in which and from which the pupils learn.

Second, this chapter examines the question of school *influence*. This is a considerably more complex issue, concerned to separate out the various factors which appear to influence the pupils' attitude towards Christianity and to ask whether the type of school attended has an additional influence, after other influences have been taken into account.

School differences

There are no differences in the proportion of parents who go to church weekly among children attending county, Church of England aided or Church of England controlled schools. In the case of all three types of school, about 7% of the fathers and 11% of the mothers attend church weekly. Where the difference does occur, however, is in relationship to the proportion of parents who attend church at least from time to time. While in county schools 59% of the fathers never attend church, the proportion drops to 53% in Church of England controlled and 44% in Church of England aided schools. While in county schools 46% of the mothers never attend church, the proportion drops to 35% in Church of England controlled and 29% in Church of England aided. Parents who might not otherwise attend church may well be supporting the church-related aspects of their children's education at church schools.

Similarly, children at Church of England controlled schools are no more likely to go to church weekly than children at county schools: 14% of the pupils at Church of England controlled schools and 15% of the pupils at county schools go to church weekly. The proportion rises to 19% of the pupils at Church of England aided schools. On the other hand, children who attend Church of England schools are more likely to go to church from time to time. While in county schools 34% of the pupils never attend church, the proportion drops to 26% in Church of England controlled schools and 19% in Church of England aided schools. Church of England schools do, therefore, appear to build some bridges between their pupils and church.

While Church of England controlled schools appear to recruit some pupils into occasional church attendance, they do not influence their habits of prayer at home. Thus, 19% of the pupils in county schools and 15% in Church of England controlled schools pray daily; 30% in county schools and 31% in Church of England controlled schools never pray. In Church of England aided schools 18% pray daily and 22% never pray.

Although Church of England schools generally operate as neighbourhood schools, like county schools, the children who attend Church of England schools have a slightly different perception of their own denominational identity. While 38% of the pupils in county schools claim no denominational label, the proportion drops to 26% in Church of

England controlled schools and 17% in Church of England aided schools. On the other hand, while 39% of the pupils in county schools call themselves Church of England, the proportion rises to 60% in Church of England controlled schools and 70% in Church of England aided schools. Again this can be accounted for in terms of the church-related contact of Church of England schools.

The religious profile of pupils in Catholic schools is quite different from other schools. Thus, 57% of the pupils in Catholic schools attend church weekly and only 5% never go to church on Sunday; 49% say their prayers daily and only 4% never do so. Similarly, 36% of the pupils in Catholic schools are supported by fathers who go to church weekly and 54% are supported by mothers who go to church weekly. Four-fifths (79%) of the pupils in Catholic schools are members of the Catholic church. Most of the others are members of the Church of England.

Table 14.1 examines the way in which the mean attitude scores differ between the four types of school. The three most highly significant differences concern attitudes towards Christianity, religious education and church. In all three cases the mean score is much higher in Catholic schools. This indicates that children attending Catholic schools are working alongside other pupils who are generally much more supportive of the church and Christianity. In other words, the Christian atmosphere of Catholic schools is more positive in terms of pupil attitudes. Differences between the other three types of school are considerably less marked.

Two-thirds of the pupils in Catholic schools (65%) say that prayer helps them a lot, compared with two-fifths in county schools (38%), Church of England controlled schools (36%) and Church of England aided schools (42%). Similarly, 81% of the pupils in Catholic schools believe that God listens to prayers, compared with 56% in county schools, 60% in Church of England controlled schools and 64% in Church of England aided schools. The church is considered to be important by 72% of the pupils in Catholic schools, compared with 38% in county schools, 41% in Church of England controlled schools and 45% in Church of England aided schools. Church services are dismissed as boring by only 16% of the pupils in Catholic schools, compared with 33% in county schools, 33% in Church of England controlled schools and 28% in Church of England aided schools. Similarly, 58% of the pupils in Catholic schools like their religious education lessons, compared with 45% in county schools, 44% in the Church of England controlled schools and 47% in Church of England aided schools.

Educating Catholics

The previous section indicates that pupils educated in Catholic schools record a more positive attitude towards Christianity than pupils educated in other types of school. Because Catholic schools operate an admissions policy intended to recruit Catholic pupils, it is not clear whether this difference in pupil attitude is due to the influence of the school or to differences in pupil intake.

A way to explore this problem further is to compare the two groups of Catholic pupils in Gloucestershire, those who attend Catholic schools and those who do not. Four-fifths of the fourth year junior pupils attending Catholic schools in the sample are themselves Catholics. The five Catholic schools which participated in this part of the project provided 91 questionnaires completed by Catholic pupils. There are also 148 completed questionnaires from Catholic pupils in non-Catholic schools.

Table 14.2 compares the mean attitude scale scores of these two groups of Catholic pupils. Those attending Catholic schools show no differences in their attitudes towards English, maths, music, games, assemblies or school itself. They do, however, record a significantly more positive attitude towards the church, religious education and Christianity.

For example, while 76% of the Catholic pupils in non-Catholic schools believe that God listens to prayers, the proportion rises to 84% in Catholic schools. While 59% of the Catholic pupils in non-Catholic schools feel that prayer helps them a lot, the proportion rises to 68% in Catholic schools. While 66% of Catholic pupils in non-Catholic schools feel that Jesus is close to them, the proportion rises to 79% in Catholic schools.

Similarly, 77% of the Catholic pupils in Catholic schools say that God is very real to them, compared with 68% in non-Catholic schools; 85% of the Catholic pupils in Catholic schools feel that Jesus helps them, compared with 73% in non-Catholic schools; 95% of the Catholic pupils in Catholic schools say that they want to love Jesus, compared with 75% in non-Catholic schools. Four-fifths (81%) of the Catholic pupils in Catholic schools say that the church is important to them, compared with three-fifths (63%) in non-Catholic schools.

These statistics highlight the differences between Catholic pupils in Catholic schools and in non-Catholic schools. However, since these statistics are not able to take into account differences in the pupils' home background, parental religious influence, church attendance and so on, it would be premature to attribute the differences between the two groups of pupils to the influence of the Catholic school system.

School influence

So far it has been demonstrated that the pupils' attitude towards Christianity is related to a range of different factors, including sex, socio-economic background, parental church attendance, religious practice, geographical environment and the type of school attended. Because these different factors are so closely interrelated one with another, it is not yet clear how much influence, if any, can be attributed to the schools themselves. For example, are the much higher scores on the scale of attitude towards Christianity among pupils in Catholic schools a consequence of the school or different home influences? Similarly, can the slightly higher scores on the same scale among pupils in Church of England aided schools be attributed to school influence or not?

Path analysis answers these questions by controlling for the influences of sex, home and church before testing for the significance of the influence of school. The results of this path analysis are displayed in path model 2 and table 14.3.

The first factors to be taken into account by the path model are the socio-economic status of mothers' and fathers' employment. These are seen to have a strong influence on parental church attendance. Men in professional employment married to women also in professional employment are the most likely to attend church, while men in unskilled manual jobs married to women in unskilled manual jobs are least likely to attend church. Similarly, women in professional employment married to men also in professional employment are the most likely to attend church, while women in unskilled manual jobs married to men in unskilled manual jobs are least likely to attend church.

Parental church attendance is also related to the type of school their children attend, after controlling for social class differences. Parents whose children attend Catholic schools are considerably more likely to go to church than parents whose children attend other types of school. This is consistent with Catholic schools recruiting pupils from church-going backgrounds. Parents whose children attend Church of England aided schools are also more likely to attend church than parents whose pupils attend Church of England controlled or county schools, but considerably less likely to do so than parents whose children attend Catholic schools. Unlike Catholic schools, Church of England aided schools in the sample do not recruit specifically on religious criteria, but they are likely to bring non-churchgoing parents into more frequent contact with the church.

After controlling for socio-economic differences and school differences, geographical environment also emerges as a factor which

Path Model 2

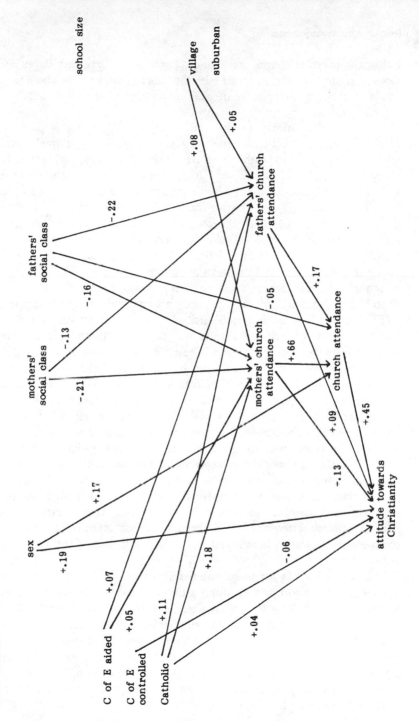

influences parental church attendance. Parents who live in villages are more likely to have some contact with the church than parents who live in towns or suburbs, irrespective of whether their child attends a church or county school.

The main determinant of the child's church attendance is parental church attendance. Children most likely to attend church weekly are those whose mother and father both attend church weekly. Girls are more likely to attend church than boys. Fathers' socio-economic status also has a small direct impact on the child's pattern of church attendance, in addition to the indirect impact mediated through parental church attendance. After parental church attendance has been taken into account, neither the type of school which the child attends, nor the geographical environment in which the child lives has any further direct power to predict the child's pattern of church attendance. The influence of school type and geographical environment on the child's pattern of church attendance is mediated indirectly via parental church attendance.

The main influences on pupils' attitude towards Christianity are their own pattern of church attendance and their sex. Girls have a more positive attitude than boys; church-going pupils have a more positive attitude than those who do not attend church. Parental church attendance also has a part to play, even after taking the child's pattern of church attendance into account. This means, for example, that children who attend church with their parents have a more positive attitude towards Christianity than children who attend church without their parents.

While religious practice and attitude towards religion may be interactive, the path model deliberately specifies the direction of practice influencing attitude, in order to be able to control for the influence of church attendance before testing for the influence of school. Thus, the final equation controls for the influence of sex, church attendance, parental church attendance and, through church attendance, parental socio-economic status, before testing for the influence of the school on pupil attitudes.

The first school factor to be entered into the equation is school size. School size has no impact on pupil attitude towards Christianity. After additionally controlling for school size, the three types of church school are entered into the equation for comparison against county schools. Then, after controlling for type of school, the geographical area is entered so that village and suburban environments can be compared with towns. Geographical area has no impact on pupil attitude towards Christianity, but some school types do have a significant impact on pupil attitude towards Christianity.

First, Church of England aided schools have no additional influence on pupil attitude towards Christianity after sex, parental socio-economic status, parental church attendance, pupil church attendance and school size have been taken into account. In other words, pupils attending Church of England aided schools show no difference in their attitude towards Christianity from pupils of comparable sex, age, religious behaviour, socio-economic background and levels of parental church attendance, educated in county schools.

Second, Church of England controlled schools have a negative influence on pupil attitude towards Christianity, after sex, parental socio-economic status, parental church attendance, pupil church attendance and size of school have been taken into account. In other words, pupils educated in Church of England controlled schools record a less favourable attitude towards Christianity than pupils of comparable sex, age, religious behaviour, socio-economic background and levels of parental church attendance, educated in county schools.

Third, Catholic schools have a positive influence on pupil attitude towards Christianity, after sex, parental socio-economic status, parental church attendance, pupil church attendance and size of school have been taken into account. In other words, pupils educated in Catholic schools record a more favourable attitude towards Christianity than pupils of comparable sex, age, religious behaviour, socio-economic background and levels of parental church attendance, educated in county schools.

Similar path models were constructed to explore the influence of school size, school type and school location on the eight semantic differential attitude scales. None of these factors influences attitudes towards English and maths. Children who attend large schools have a less positive attitude towards the school itself and a more positive attitude towards games. Children who attend suburban schools have a less positive attitude towards school, religious education, assemblies and music lessons. Children who attend Church of England controlled schools have a less positive attitude towards school, religious education, assemblies and the church. Children who attend Catholic schools have a less positive attitude towards music lessons. Church of England aided schools have no impact on any of these attitudinal areas, either positively or negatively.

These conclusions regarding the influence of church schools on pupil attitude towards Christianity are worth comparing with the conclusions of my three related studies conducted in East Anglia during 1974, 1978 and 1982. Each of these three studies involved around 2,300 pupils from 15 county schools, ten Church of England aided schools and five Catholic schools. Church of England controlled schools were not included in these studies. All three East Anglian studies point to the positive influence of Catholic schools on pupil attitude towards Christianity and the negative influence of Church of England aided schools on pupil attitude towards Christianity. My report of this research, published in the *British Educational Research Journal* (1986), concludes:

> Pupils educated in Roman Catholic schools tend to record a more favourable attitude towards Christianity than pupils, of comparable sex, age, IQ and religious behaviour from comparable social class homes with comparable levels of parental church attendance, educated in county schools. This means that they are more likely to hold a positive image of Jesus and God and to feel that they enjoy church, the bible, prayer and the religious education and worship in which they engage at school. The development of these attitudes seems highly consistent with the stated aims of Roman Catholic schools. At least at this level, Roman Catholic voluntary aided primary schools seem to be achieving something which the Roman Catholic church might find it less easy to achieve without its system of voluntary aided schools.
>
> Pupils educated in Church of England schools tend to record a less favourable attitude towards Christianity than pupils, of comparable sex, age, IQ and religious behaviour from comparable social class homes with comparable levels of parental church attendance, educated in county schools. This means that they are less likely to hold a positive image of Jesus and God and to feel that they enjoy church, the bible, prayer and the religious education and worship in which they engage at school. Since the stated aims of the Church of England's continued involvement in the state maintained sector of education do not necessarily concentrate on emphasising the religious distinctiveness of church schools, these findings are not necessarily a criticism of the success of Church of England voluntary aided schools. However, irrespective of the educational philosophy underlying the Church of England's involvement in church schools, I suspect that these findings might leave a theological problem for the Church of England to account for operating schools which actually lead to *less* favourable pupil attitudes towards Christianity than county schools.

At least in the present study in Gloucestershire, only Church of England controlled schools and not Church of England aided schools emerge as having a negative impact on pupil attitude towards Christianity.

15 CONCLUSION

This study sets out to examine the partnership between church and state in the provision of state maintained primary education, from historical, theoretical and empirical perspectives.

The historical perspective, discussed in chapter two, argues that at the time of the 1944 Education Act the partnership between church and state was considered to be a thoroughly two-way process. The churches shared with the state the responsibility for providing secular education for the nation's children through church schools. The state shared with the churches the responsibility for the Christian education of the young through statutory religious education and school worship. The twin assumptions on which this partnership was built were that England remained a Christian country and that religion and education were compatible and complementary activities.

The theoretical perspective, discussed in chapter three, argues that the assumptions on which the partnership between church and state was built in 1944 have been seriously challenged. Five key challenges are highlighted. Educational philosophers no longer necessarily accept the authority of the churches to contribute to educational debate. British society is no longer necessarily a Christian community. The aims of religious education in county schools have been redefined so as to draw a sharp distinction between the churches' function and the schools' function. The place of worship in the county school has been questioned. A number of caveats have been placed against the existence of church schools within the state maintained system. As a consequence of these challenges, the nature of the partnership between church and state in the provision of state maintained primary education is subject to change.

The empirical perspective, discussed in chapters four through fourteen, sets out to examine the religious provision of state maintained primary schools in Gloucestershire and the impact of this provision on eleven year old children. Nine main conclusions emerge from this empirical study. The scope and limitations of these general conclusions and the interpretation based on them need to be assessed in association with the methodology and detailed analysis presented in chapters four through fourteen. While they are grounded in a detailed study of one local education authority during 1983-1984, chapter four has argued that it is not unreasonable to regard this area as representative of the shire counties in general.

* Many county schools promote a Christian presence in education and foster contact with the churches.

* Many headteachers are church-going Christians whose personal beliefs influence their professional practice.

* Christian presence in county schools is diminishing as older headteachers are replaced by a younger generation.

* Church of England controlled status promotes neighbourhood schools which are more church-related than county schools.

* Church of England aided status promotes religiously distinctive schools, even in single school areas.

* Catholic aided status promotes very religiously distinctive schools, operated mainly for Catholic pupils.

* Church of England controlled schools have a negative impact on the religious attitudes of their pupils compared with county schools.

* Church of England aided schools have the same impact on the religious attitudes of their pupils as county schools.

* Catholic schools have a positive impact on the religious attitudes of their pupils compared with county schools.

These conclusions show that in many senses the partnership between church and state in the provision of state maintained primary education still functions as it was conceived at the time of the 1944 Education Act. Today many county schools continue to promote a Christian perspective in education and to foster contact with the churches. Christian headteachers and Christian teachers in county schools continue to promote Christian worship and Christian education. Today many Church of England schools continue to serve the whole of their neighbourhood, in the same way as county schools, but additionally they offer a distinctively church-related educational environment for their pupils which is of an unassertive nature.

As long as county schools promote a Christian perspective in education, part of the churches' educational work is being done for them. The data also suggest, however, that county schools are unlikely to remain Christian places indefinitely. The Christian perspective in county schools is diminishing as older headteachers are replaced by a younger generation. As the Christian character of county schools diminishes, the churches will need to rethink their educational strategy.

As county schools become increasingly secular, serious weaknesses may well emerge in the school-related educational policies of the Free Churches, the Church of England and the Catholic church in England. Historically the Free Churches have taken the line that county schools make a significant contribution to the Christian formation of the young and that this contribution can be complemented by the churches' own Sunday school work. Some more recent Free Church thinking has argued that Christian nurture should be entirely in the hands of the home, the churches and the Sunday schools. Not only are county schools unlikely to continue with their side of the partnership, but the Free Churches have found it increasingly difficult to maintain their Sunday school work, especially in rural areas. Parents who are members of the Free Churches and who desire a Christian education for their children may find difficulty in satisfying this requirement, if the local county school has ceased to promote a Christian approach to education and if the local chapel is unable to provide adequate alternative educational facilities during evenings or at weekends.

Part of the Church of England has taken the line that where church schools exist primarily to serve local neighbourhoods in the same way as county schools they should not place an emphasis on providing distinctive church-related education. The survey suggests, however, that most Church of England aided and controlled schools serving local neighbourhoods continue to promote their religious character and identity by offering more characteristics of church-related education than county schools. Another part of the Church of England has taken the line that church schools can make a significant contribution to the Christian formation of the young by providing distinctive church-related education in those neighbourhoods where church schools exist. While the Church of England is operating religiously distinctive neighbourhood schools, many of their pupils are not from church-related backgrounds. The survey suggests, however, that at best these schools are having no distinctive religious impact on the pupils when compared with county schools; at worst they are having a negative impact.

While the Church of England may have found it relatively easy to hold its general and domestic aims in education in tension within a predominantly Christian educational system, it may find greater difficulty in doing so within a more secular educational environment. On the one hand, it is becoming increasingly difficult to justify church-related neighbourhood schools for non-churchgoing pupils within a secular state maintained educational system. On the other hand, there are a number of church-related young people living in neighbourhoods which are not readily serviced by a church school and where it may not be possible for the churches to guarantee the Christian character of county schools. The Catholic church has taken the line of providing distinctive Catholic schools for the children of Catholic parents. The Catholic church has understood these schools to play an important part in the Christian formation of the young, in partnership with church and home. The survey demonstrates that, where Catholic schools exist, they make a positive contribution to the religious formation of young Catholics. Particularly in rural areas, however, the Catholic community is insufficiently strong to maintain separate Catholic schools, leaving half the young Catholics in a county like Gloucestershire without easy access to a Catholic school.

If county schools are unlikely to continue to promote a Christian perspective in education, the churches in the shire counties need to consider seriously alternative ways of providing a Christian future for the children of their active members. The Free Church experience suggests that Sunday schools are not an adequate alternative, since many churches continue to find difficulty in mustering the resources to promote professional voluntary work among children and young people. The Roman Catholic experience suggests that church schools which set out to provide an alternative educational environment for the members of one denomination cannot provide an adequate alternative in a rural area, since large tracts of the country remain unserviced by Catholic schools. The Anglican experience suggests that, if church schools concentrate primarily on serving whole neighbourhoods, they also inevitably neglect the needs of church-going families who do not live within those neighbourhoods served by church schools. During the next decade, the Christian denominations might well be advised to consider the possibility of working more closely together in order to consolidate a network of church-related schools, as a distinctively religious alternative to increasingly secular county schools, for those parents who wish their children to be educated within a Christian environment. Practically, such a network of church-related schools could only be fully possible in a rural area if operated as an ecumenical venture.

STATISTICAL APPENDIX

The following tables are numbered in chapter sequence. They contain additional statistical information and the details about statistical significance testing required by the specialist reader. All other statistical information has been included in the text itself to avoid frequent cross-referencing between tables and text. While space does not permit the inclusion of the questionnaires themselves, copies may be obtained by writing to the Culham College Institute, 60 East St Helen Street, Abingdon, Oxon.

3.1 Pupils attending church schools as proportion of all pupils in maintained schools in England and Wales

Year	Primary		Secondary		Total	
	Anglican %	Catholic %	Anglican %	Catholic %	Anglican %	Catholic %
1947	–	–	–	–	17.8	7.0
1948	–	–	–	–	17.3	7.0
1949	22.5	8.8	3.8	2.9	16.9	7.0
1950	22.2	8.7	3.8	3.0	16.7	7.0
1951	22.0	8.6	3.9	3.1	16.5	6.9
1952	21.6	8.5	3.9	3.2	16.4	6.9
1953	21.0	8.3	3.7	3.3	16.1	6.9
1954	20.5	8.3	3.7	3.4	15.7	6.9
1955	20.1	8.5	3.6	3.6	15.3	7.0
1956	19.7	8.8	3.5	3.6	14.7	7.2
1957	19.4	9.0	3.4	3.8	14.3	7.3
1958	19.1	9.3	3.3	4.0	13.7	7.5
1959	18.8	9.7	3.1	4.4	12.9	7.7
1960	18.5	9.9	3.2	4.7	12.5	7.9
1961	18.3	10.2	2.9	5.1	12.1	8.1
1962	18.1	10.3	2.8	5.6	11.9	8.4
1963	17.9	10.4	2.8	6.0	11.9	8.6
1964	17.8	10.3	2.9	6.5	11.8	8.8
1965	17.8	10.4	2.9	6.9	11.9	9.0
1966	17.7	10.4	2.9	7.2	11.9	9.1
1967	17.5	10.4	2.9	7.6	11.9	9.3
1968	17.2	10.3	3.0	7.7	11.7	9.3
1969	17.0	10.2	3.0	7.9	11.6	9.4
1970	16.8	10.1	3.0	8.0	11.5	9.3
1971	16.6	9.9	3.1	8.1	11.4	9.2
1972	16.5	9.7	3.2	8.1	11.3	9.1
1973	16.4	9.6	3.2	8.1	11.2	9.0
1974	16.3	9.5	3.3	8.2	10.9	8.9
1975	16.3	9.3	3.5	8.3	10.8	8.9
1976	16.4	9.2	3.5	8.4	10.8	8.8
1977	16.4	9.1	3.6	8.4	10.7	8.8
1978	16.5	9.0	3.6	8.7	10.6	8.9
1979	16.6	9.0	3.7	8.8	10.6	8.9
1980	16.7	9.0	3.7	8.8	10.6	8.9
1981	16.7	9.0	3.9	8.8	10.5	8.9
1982	16.8	9.1	4.0	8.8	10.4	8.9
1983	16.9	9.2	4.0	8.8	10.5	9.0
1984	16.9	9.3	4.1	8.8	10.5	9.0
1985	16.9	9.3	4.1	8.8	10.6	9.1
1986	16.8	9.5	4.3	8.8	10.8	9.1

Note

The percentages are computed on the basis of information provided by the Department of Education and Science and the Welsh Office.

Middle schools are deemed either primary or secondary according to the DES classification.

4.1 Shire counties: primary schools, including middle deemed primary

Local education authority	Number of schools	County schools %	C of E aided %	C of E controlled %	Catholic aided %	Other voluntary %
Avon	392	63	6	24	7	1
Bedfordshire	217	77	9	9	6	0
Berkshire	292	63	8	21	9	0
Buckinghamshire	295	71	8	18	3	0
Cambridgeshire	279	71	9	18	1	0
Cheshire	482	64	11	12	13	0
Cleveland	226	75	3	4	18	0
Cornwall	259	76	16	6	2	0
Cumbria	336	51	18	22	8	1
Derbyshire	470	69	7	18	5	1
Devon	451	66	12	17	4	0
Dorset	202	48	23	23	6	0
Durham	316	75	2	8	15	0
East Sussex	221	58	12	22	8	0
Essex	601	73	9	12	6	0
Gloucestershire	274	54	16	27	3	0
Hampshire	609	75	8	15	3	0
Hereford & Worcester	296	48	15	29	6	2
Hertfordshire	468	72	12	7	8	0
Humberside	369	74	2	18	5	1
Isle of Wight	47	55	8	26	11	0
Kent	608	64	8	22	6	1
Lancashire	640	41	27	7	22	3
Leicestershire	343	62	8	26	5	0
Lincolnshire	326	55	11	31	2	1
Norfolk	441	66	9	23	1	0
North Yorkshire	423	51	8	34	6	2
Northamptonshire	270	62	8	25	4	1
Northumberland	148	69	17	7	7	1
Nottinghamshire	433	78	7	10	5	0
Oxfordshire	253	42	15	36	6	0
Shropshire	223	47	10	39	3	0
Somerset	239	46	13	37	3	0
Staffordshire	436	62	7	20	11	0
Suffolk	283	58	7	32	4	0
Surrey	395	66	15	10	9	0
Warwickshire	256	54	7	30	9	0
West Sussex	236	60	12	20	6	1
Wiltshire	300	45	15	35	5	0

Note

These statistics have been computed from the DES returns for January 1984.

Special Agreement schools have been included with aided schools.

Percentages have been rounded to the nearest whole number. This means that some rows may add up to 99 or 101, and that when a county has only one or two 'other voluntary' schools these may not appear in the table.

4.2 Shire counties: primary school pupils, including middle deemed primary

Local education authority	Number of pupils	County schools %	C of E aided %	C of E controlled %	Catholic aided %	Other voluntary %
Avon	75790	70	4	20	5	1
Bedfordshire	47433	83	4	5	7	0
Berkshire	65248	75	5	13	7	0
Buckinghamshire	65181	79	6	10	5	0
Cambridgeshire	59692	77	9	12	2	0
Cheshire	96803	71	10	6	12	0
Cleveland	88654	79	2	2	17	0
Cornwall	47298	78	14	5	3	0
Cumbria	46462	64	12	14	9	0
Derbyshire	85774	79	6	10	5	1
Devon	76999	77	8	11	4	0
Dorset	40149	66	13	14	6	0
Durham	64808	81	2	6	11	0
East Sussex	53796	69	9	14	8	0
Essex	127402	80	6	8	6	0
Gloucestershire	40190	62	12	21	4	1
Hampshire	130164	80	4	12	4	0
Hereford & Worcester	47278	64	10	18	6	2
Hertfordshire	104368	79	9	4	9	0
Humberside	87274	83	1	12	4	0
Isle of Wight	6412	64	9	20	8	0
Kent	121014	72	6	15	7	0
Lancashire	123006	51	21	6	19	3
Leicestershire	88252	77	4	15	4	0
Lincolnshire	48131	64	8	24	2	2
Norfolk	67618	76	6	16	2	0
North Yorkshire	60208	71	4	17	6	1
Northamptonshire	50364	76	4	14	4	0
Northumberland	23928	82	8	4	6	1
Nottinghamshire	121887	88	3	5	4	0
Oxfordshire	41586	59	11	25	5	0
Shropshire	37675	65	6	25	3	1
Somerset	32655	54	12	31	4	0
Staffordshire	90712	73	4	15	9	0
Suffolk	46472	76	6	15	4	0
Surrey	86150	73	11	8	8	0
Warwickshire	50377	64	7	20	9	0
West Sussex	47016	71	12	11	6	0
Wiltshire	44997	57	9	27	6	0

Note

These statistics have been computed from the DES returns for January 1984.

Special Agreement schools have been included with aided schools.

Percentages have been rounded to the nearest whole number. This means that some rows may add up to 99 or 101, and that when a county has only one or two 'other voluntary' schools these may not appear in the table.

Part-time pupils have been included as .5 pupils.

4.3 Survey response rate

	Number of schools approached	Schools where headteachers participate %	Schools where pupils participate %
County	111	96.4	86.5
C of E aided	41	100.0	82.9
C of E controlled	73	93.1	78.1
Catholic	8	100.0	62.5
Other voluntary	1	100.0	100.0

Note

The table refers to primary and junior schools; infant schools are excluded.

12.1 Scale of church-related education

Scale item	Corrected item total correlation
Frequency of clergy contribution to assemblies	.4254
Frequency of clergy contribution to RE lessons	.5076
Frequency of clergy visits to school	.5808
Relationship between assemblies and church's year	.2826
Relationship between hymns in assemblies and local churches	.2362
Religious emphases of assemblies	.2854
Class sets of modern bibles	.1982
Visit church to look at the building	.2608
Visit church to talk with the clergy	.3810
Visit church to study the purpose of the church	.2545
Take part in a weekday church service	.3545
Take part in a Sunday church service	.2405
Hold a school service	.3826
Make a display of pupils' work in church	.2381
Present music, dance or drama in church	.3940
Use copies of the bible in RE lessons	.3448
Visit Christian churches as part of RE	.4572
Pupils read their own prayers in assemblies	.3304
Pupils say the Lord's Prayer in assemblies	.3423
Pupils sing psalms or canticles in assemblies	.3285
Pupils hear passages from the bible in assemblies	.4124
Pupils hear Christian stories in assemblies	.3603

Note

The scale items list the issues which most clearly distinguish between the schools which adopt a church-related approach and those which do not.

The corrected item total correlations show the strength of the relationship between the individual items and the product of the rest of the items.

The internal consistency and unidimensionality of this scale are indicated by an alpha coefficient of .7777.

12.2 Mean scores on scale of church-related education

Groups	Mean	SD	N
Foundation of school			
County	50.7	8.3	107
C of E controlled	57.5	6.1	68
C of E aided	64.0	6.6	41
Catholic	73.0	7.9	8
Headteachers' preferred type of school			
County	51.2	8.6	85
no preference	56.8	7.7	67
C of E controlled	57.0	6.2	24
C of E aided	62.5	8.3	31
Catholic	74.6	7.1	7
Headteachers' religious affiliation			
Humanist or Agnostic	48.4	7.7	22
Free Church	54.4	6.1	40
Church of England	57.1	9.2	141
Catholic	65.7	14.8	11
Headteachers' church attendance			
Never or once a year	48.2	7.5	39
Major festivals	54.6	8.0	31
At least once a month	58.7	8.9	144

Note

Potential scores on this scale range between 21 and 90.

Some headteachers did not divulge personal information.

N   indicates the number of schools within each category

SD   indicates the standard deviation

12.3 Multiple regression significance tests for path model 1

Criterion variable	Predictor variables	R^2	Increase in R^2	F increase	P< increase	Beta
Church-related education	church attendance	.1534	.1534	36.97	.001	+.2546
	age	.1541	.0006	0.15	NS	+.0072
	sex	.1566	.0026	0.62	NS	−.0391
	controlled status	.1775	.0208	5.09	.05	+.3080
	aided status	.3821	.2046	66.22	.001	+.4985
	village area	.3823	.0002	0.08	NS	+.0283
	suburban area	.3826	.0003	0.09	NS	+.0206

13.1 Scale of attitude towards Christianity

Scale item	Corrected item total correlation
I find it boring to listen to the bible	.5180
I know that Jesus helps me	.6964
Saying my prayers helps me a lot	.6565
The church is very important to me	.6372
I think going to church is a waste of my time	.6344
I want to love Jesus	.7322
I think church services are boring	.5729
I think people who pray are stupid	.5679
God helps me to lead a better life	.7154
I like school lessons about God very much	.6441
God means a lot to me	.7790
I believe that God helps people	.7000
Prayer helps me a lot	.7328
I know that Jesus is very close to me	.7311
I think praying is a good thing	.7507
I think the bible is out of date	.5400
I believe that God listens to prayers	.7029
Jesus doesn't mean anything to me	.6665
God is very real to me	.7720
I think saying prayers in school does no good	.6326
The idea of God means much to me	.7563
I believe that Jesus still helps people	.7189
I know that God helps me	.7476
I find it hard to believe in God	.5477

Note

In order to compute corrected item-total correlations negative items are reverse scored.

The corrected item total correlations show the strength of the relationship between the individual items and the product of the rest of the items.

The internal consistency and unidimensionality of this scale are indicated by an alpha coefficient of .9552

13.2 Semantic differential attitude scales

Adjectival pairs	Corrected item – total correlation							
	English	Maths	School	Religion	Music	Church	Assembly	Games
Pleasant/unpleasant	.7209	.7499	.7354	.7638	.7938	.8038	.7402	.5921
Good/bad	.7119	.7634	.7333	.7645	.8173	.8020	.7642	.6748
Interesting/boring	.6999	.7385	.6921	.7372	.7938	.7650	.7163	.6395
Nice/nasty	.7428	.7741	.7283	.7640	.8126	.7866	.7662	.7026
Happy/sad	.6568	.6903	.6820	.6481	.7071	.6654	.6485	.6106
Important/unimportant	.4322	.3862	.4644	.6185	.6243	.7145	.6073	.4489
Friendly/unfriendly	.5937	.6317	.5849	.6671	.6897	.6939	.6578	.5648
Alpha Coefficient	.8724	.8864	.8780	.9006	.9175	.9172	.8957	.8390

The corrected item total correlations show the strength of the relationship between the individual pairs of adjectives and the product of the rest of the adjectival pairs.

The internal consistency and unidimensionality of the scales are indicated by the alpha coefficients.

13.3 Sex difference

Scale	Boys		Girls		F	P<
	Mean	SD	Mean	SD		
Christianity	81.8	20.2	89.1	17.6	178.1	.001
English lessons	35.4	9.6	39.0	7.8	201.4	.001
Maths lessons	38.2	9.8	38.3	9.1	0.1	NS
School	38.1	9.1	41.1	7.3	153.9	.001
Religious education	34.8	10.3	37.5	9.3	87.7	.001
Music lessons	33.9	11.5	40.6	8.7	511.2	.001
Church	34.2	11.0	38.1	9.6	164.7	.001
Assemblies	35.9	10.1	38.8	8.8	103.5	.001
Games	45.0	5.7	44.6	6.0	6.7	.01

Attitude scale scores

Note

Scores on the Likert scale of attitude towards Christianity can range between 24 and 120.

Scores on the semantic differential attitude scale can range between 7 and 49.

The statement 'NS' indicates that the difference between the mean scale scores for boys and girls is not statistically significant.

13.4 Home difference

Parental church attendance	By fathers' attendance		By mothers' attendance	
	Mean	SD	Mean	SD
Never	79.8	19.6	78.3	19.9
Once or twice a year	84.4	17.7	81.2	18.1
Sometimes	92.7	15.5	89.9	16.1
Monthly	93.1	16.8	93.6	15.4
Weekly	100.5	16.3	99.5	15.3
r	+.3379, P<.001		+.3701, P<.001	

Attitude towards Christianity

13.5 Church-going difference

Pupil church	Boys		Attitude towards Christianity	Girls	
attendance	Mean	SD		Mean	SD
Never	72.4	20.2		79.4	18.7
Once or twice a year	79.5	18.0		81.5	16.4
Sometimes	86.8	16.7		90.7	15.2
Monthly	89.0	16.9		94.7	13.2
Weekly	98.0	15.8		100.2	13.9
r	+.4199, P<.001			+.4202, P< .001	

13.6 Environmental differences

Scale	Villages		Attitude scale scores Suburbs		Towns		F	P<
	Mean	SD	Mean	SD	Mean	SD		
Christianity	86.0	18.6	84.1	19.8	85.4	19.0	3.8	.05
English lessons	37.2	8.8	36.9	9.3	37.4	8.7	1.8	NS
Maths lessons	38.7	8.8	38.0	9.9	38.2	9.3	1.9	NS
School	40.4	7.6	38.9	8.8	39.6	8.3	9.1	.001
Religious education	36.5	9.6	35.3	10.1	36.2	9.9	5.3	.01
Music lessons	37.5	10.2	36.5	11.1	37.7	10.6	5.6	.01
Church	37.2	10.0	35.3	10.8	36.1	10.5	10.8	.001
Assemblies	38.1	9.1	36.7	9.8	37.5	9.6	7.0	.001
Games	44.3	6.3	44.8	5.8	45.0	5.7	4.2	.05

14.1 School differences

Scale	Attitude scale scores								F	P<
	County		C of E aided		C of E controlled		Catholic			
	Mean	SD	Mean	SD	Mean	SD	Mean	SD		
Christianity	84.7	19.4	87.7	17.8	84.2	19.7	99.2	14.5	26.1	.001
English lessons	37.3	9.0	37.5	8.7	36.6	8.8	37.6	8.3	1.8	NS
Maths lessons	38.3	9.6	38.3	8.7	38.0	9.4	39.2	9.0	0.6	NS
School	39.5	8.5	40.2	7.9	39.0	8.4	40.3	7.1	3.2	.05
Religious education	36.0	10.0	36.9	9.4	35.0	10.2	40.5	7.8	12.7	.001
Music lessons	37.1	11.0	37.9	10.0	37.3	10.2	34.2	11.5	4.1	.01
Church	35.9	10.6	37.0	9.6	35.6	10.8	40.6	9.1	9.8	.001
Assemblies	37.4	9.6	37.7	9.0	36.6	9.7	39.0	9.4	3.3	.05
Games	45.0	5.6	44.4	6.3	44.5	6.3	44.3	5.3	3.0	.05

14.2 Catholic pupils

Scale	Attitude scale scores				F	P<
	Catholic schools		Other schools			
	Mean	SD	Mean	SD		
Christianity	101.2	12.8	94.5	18.2	9.7	.01
English lessons	38.1	7.8	39.1	7.0	1.0	NS
Maths lessons	39.6	8.0	37.8	10.1	2.1	NS
School	40.7	6.5	40.8	7.2	0.0	NS
Religious education	41.6	7.2	38.7	9.1	6.5	.01
Music lessons	35.8	10.9	37.1	10.6	0.8	NS
Church	41.9	7.5	39.2	9.2	5.2	.05
Assemblies	38.3	9.2	40.3	7.8	2.7	NS
Games	44.6	5.1	45.1	5.7	0.4	NS

14.3 Multiple regression significance tests for path model 2

Criterion variables	Predictor variable	R^2	Increase in R^2	F increase	$P<$ increase	Beta
Mothers' church	mothers' social class	.0425	.0425	81.4	.001	−.2062
attendance	fathers' social class	.0652	.0227	44.6	.001	−.1625
	C of E aided school	.0674	.0022	4.2	.05	+.0465
	C of E controlled school	.0682	.0008	1.6	NS	+.0294
	Catholic school	.1016	.0334	68.1	.001	+.1844
	village area	.1078	.0061	12.6	.001	+.0806
	suburban area	.1092	.0014	2.8	NS	−.0416
Fathers' church	fathers' social class	.0512	.0512	99.0	.001	−.2263
attendance	mothers' social class	.0651	.0139	27.2	.001	−.1270
	C of E aided school	.0701	.0050	9.8	.01	+.0700
	C of E controlled school	.0708	.0007	1.4	NS	+.0269
	Catholic school	.0828	.0120	23.9	.001	+.1103
	village area	.0856	.0028	5.7	.05	+.0548
	suburban area	.0870	.0014	2.8	NS	−.0419
Pupils' church	sex	.0288	.0288	54.4	.001	+.1697
attendance	mothers' church attendance	.4610	.4322	1469.9	.001	+.6597
	fathers' church attendance	.4744	.0134	46.6	.001	+.1607
	fathers' social class	.4763	.0019	6.6	.01	−.0447
	mothers' social class	.4767	.0004	1.4	NS	+.0219
	C of E aided school	.4769	.0003	0.9	NS	+.0160
	C of E controlled school	.4776	.0007	2.3	NS	−.0263
	Catholic school	.4782	.0006	2.0	NS	+.0245
	village area	.4788	.0006	2.2	NS	+.0261
	suburban area	.4789	.0001	0.3	NS	−.0110
Attitude towards	sex	.0373	.0373	137.5	.001	+.1931
Christianity	pupils' church attendance	.2349	.1977	916.9	.001	+.4508
	mothers' church attendance	.2447	.0097	45.7	.001	+.1336
	fathers' church attendance	.2490	.0044	20.0	.001	+.0926
	size of school	.2491	.0000	0.2	NS	−.0062
	C of E aided school	.2494	.0004	1.7	NS	+.0192
	C of E controlled school	.2523	.0028	13.5	.001	−.0557
	Catholic school	.2535	.0013	6.0	.01	+.0367
	village area	.2538	.0003	1.4	NS	−.0237
	suburban area	.2539	.0001	0.5	NS	−.0115

BIBLIOGRAPHY

Chapter 2   Church and State

Beck, G.A. (ed) (1950) *The English Catholics 1850-1950*, London, Burns Oates.

Brooksbank, K., Revell, J., Ackstine, E. and Bailey, K. (1982) *County and Voluntary Schools*, Harlow, Councils and Education Press.

Brown, C.K.F. (1942) *The Church's Part in Education 1833-1941*, London, National Society.

Burgess, H.J. (1958) *Enterprise in Education*, London, National Society and SPCK.

Butler, R.A. (1971) *The Art of the Possible*, London, Hamish Hamilton.

Cliff, P.B. (1986) *The Rise and Development of the Sunday School Movement in England 1780-1980*, Nutfield, National Christian Education Council.

Cruickshank, M. (1963) *Church and State in English Education*, London, Macmillan.

Dent, H.C. (1947) *The Education Act 1944: provisions, possibilities and some problems*, London, University of London Press.

Ferguson, J. (ed) (1981) *Christianity, Society and Education*, London, SPCK.

Iremonger, F.A. (1948) *William Temple*, London, Oxford University Press.

Kelly, S.E. (1978) The schools of the established church in England: a study of diocesan involvement since 1944, unpublished Ph.D. dissertation, University of Keele.

Kemp, E.W. (1959) *Kenneth Escot Kirk*, London, Hodder and Stoughton.

Louden, L. (1983) The managers of Blackburn diocese and the implementation of the 1944 Education Act in Lancashire, *Journal of Educational Administration and History*, 15, 1, 10-21.

Murphy, J. (1971) *Church, State and Schools in Britain 1800-1970*, London, Routledge and Kegan Paul.

Murphy, J. (1972) *The Education Act 1870*, Newton Abbot, David and Charles.

Phillips, R.J. (1986) *Church and State: Hereford diocesan schools*, Hereford, Hereford Diocesan Council of Education.

Rich, E.E. (1970) *The Education Act 1870*, London, Longmans.

Temple, W. (1942) *Christianity and the Social Order*, Harmondsworth, Penguin.

Tirrell, L.B. (1976) *The Aided Schools Handbook*, London, National Society and SPCK.

Chapter 3   Religion and Education

Abbott, W.M. (ed) (1966) *The Documents of Vatican II*, London, Geoffrey Chapman.

Abrams, M., Gerard, D. and Timms, N. (eds) (1985), *Values and Social Change in Britain*, London, Macmillan.

Aspin, D.N. (1983) Church schools, religious education and the multi-ethnic community, *Journal of Philosophy of Education*, 17, 229-240.

Berry, L.C. (1946) *The Teacher's Handbook to a Book of Morning Worship*, London, J.M. Dent.

Birmingham (1962) *Agreed Syllabus of Religious Instruction*, Birmingham, City of Birmingham Education Committee.

Birmingham (1975) *Agreed Syllabus of Religious Education*, Birmingham, City of Birmingham Education Committee.

Birmingham (1975) *Living Together: a teacher's handbook of suggestions for religious education*, Birmingham, City of Birmingham Education Committee.

Brierley, P. (ed) (1986) *UK Christian Handbook 1987/88*, Bromley, MARC Europe.

British Council of Churches (1976) *The Child in the Church*, London, British Council of Churches.

British Council of Churches (1981) *Understanding Christian Nurture*, London, British Council of Churches.

Cambridgeshire (1949) *The Cambridgeshire Syllabus of Religious Teaching for Schools 1949*, Cambridge, Cambridge University Press.

Cambridgeshire (1970) *Religious Education: suggestions for teachers*, Cambridge, Cambridgeshire and Isle of Ely Education Committee.

Carlisle Commission (1971) *Partners in Education: the role of the diocese*, London, National Society and SPCK.

Catholic Commission for Racial Justice (1984) *Learning from Diversity*, London, Catholic Media Office.

Cox, E. (1983) *Problems and Possibilities for Religious Education*, London, Hodder and Stoughton.

Cruickshank, M. (1972) The denominational school issue in the twentieth century, *History in Education*, 1, 200-213.

Dummett, A. and McNeal, J. (1981) *Race and Church Schools*, London, Runnymede Trust.

Durham Report (1970) *The Fourth R: the report of the commission on religious education in schools*, London, National Society and SPCK.

Earl, W.J.H. (1984) The 1944 Education Act: forty years on, *British Journal of Religious Education*, 6, 88-92.

Essex (1970) *Interchange: working papers in religious education*, Chelmsford, Essex Education Committee.

Felderhof, M.C. (ed) (1985) *Religious Education in a Pluralist Society*, London, Hodder and Stoughton.

Francis, L.J. (1979) Theology and education: a research perspective, *Scottish Journal of Theology*, 32, 61-70.

Francis, L.J. (1983) The logic of education, theology and the church school, *Oxford Review of Education*, 9, 147-162.

Francis, L.J. (1985) *Rural Anglicanism: a future for young Christians?*, London, Collins Liturgical Publications.

Francis, L.J. (1986) *Partnership in Rural Education*, London, Collins Liturgical Publications.

Free Church Federal Council Education Committee (1984) *Church Schools*, London, Free Church Federal Council.

Gay, J.D. *et al* (1982) *The Debate about Church Schools in the Oxford Diocese*, Abingdon, Culham College Institute.

General Synod of the Church of England Board of Education (1984) *Schools and Multi-cultural Education*, London, Church House.

Gilbert, A.D. (1980) *The Making of Post-Christian Britain*, London, Longman.

Goldman, R.J. (1964) *Religious Thinking from Childhood to Adolescence*, London, Routledge and Kegan Paul.

Goldman, R.J. (1965) *Readiness for Religion*, London, Routledge and Kegan Paul.

Green, R.H. (1982) *Church Schools: a matter of opinion*, London, Southwark Diocesan Board of Education.

Habgood, J. (1983) *Church and Nation in a Secular Age*, London, Darton, Longman and Todd.

Halstead, J.M. (1986) *The Case for Muslim Voluntary Aided Schools*, Cambridge, The Islamic Academy.

Hampshire (1971) *Approaches to Religious Education: a handbook of suggestions*, Winchester, Hampshire Education Committee.

Hampshire (1978) *Religious Education in Hampshire Schools*, Winchester, Hampshire Education Committee.

Hampshire (1980) *Paths to Understanding*, Basingstoke, Globe Education.

Harding, S., Phillips, D. and Fogarty, M. (1986) *Contrasting Values in Western Europe*, London, Macmillan.

Hay, D. (1982) *Exploring Inner Space*, Harmondsworth, Penguin.

Hirst, P.H. (1972) Christian education: a contradiction in terms? *Learning for Living*, 11, 4, 6-11.

Hirst, P.H. (1976) Religious beliefs and educational principles, *Learning for Living*, 15, 155-157.

Hirst, P.H. (1981) Education, catechesis and the church school, *British Journal of Religious Education*, 3, 85-93.

Holm, J. (1975) *Teaching Religion in School*, London, Oxford University Press.

Hull, J.M. (1975) *School Worship: an obituary*, London, SCM.

Hull, J.M. (1976) Christian theology and educational theory: can there be connections? *British Journal of Educational Studies*, 24, 127-143.

Hull, J.M. (ed) (1982) *New Directions in Religious Education*, Barcombe, Falmer Press.

Hull, J.M. (1984) *Studies in Religion and Education*, Barcombe, Falmer Press.

Jebb, P. (ed) (1968) *Religious Education: drift or decision?* London, Darton, Longman and Todd.

London (1984) *Religious Education for our Children*, London, Inner London Education Authority.

Louden, L. and Urwin, D.S. (1984) Aided school governors: their role and training, *School Organisation*, 4, 245-264.

Lyon, D. (1985) *The Steeple's Shadow*, London, SPCK.

Manchester (1985) *Multifaith Manchester*, Manchester, Manchester City Council.

Moss, T. (ed) (1986) *In Search of Christianity*, London, Firethorn Press.

National Society (1984) *A Future in Partnership*, London, National Society.

Partners in Mission Consultation (1981) *To a Rebellious House?* London, CIO Publishing.

Plowden Report (1967) *Children and their Primary Schools*, London, HMSO.

Report to the Bishops of England and Wales (1981) *Signposts and Homecomings: the educative task of the Catholic community*, Middlegreen, St Paul Publications.

Sacred Congregation for Catholic Education (1977) *The Catholic School*, Abbots Langley, Catholic Information Office.

Schools Council (1971) *Religious Education in Secondary Schools*, London, Evans Brothers and Methuen Educational.

Smart, N. (1968) *Secular Education and the Logic of Religion*, London, Faber.

Smart, N. (1969) *The Religious Experience of Mankind*, New York, Charles Scribner's Sons.

Smart, N. and Horder, D. (eds) (1975) *New Movements in Religious Education*, London, Temple Smith.

Socialist Education Association (1981) *The Dual System of Voluntary and County Schools*, London, Socialist Education Association.

Socialist Education Association (1986) *All Faiths in All Schools*, London, Socialist Education Association.

Souper, P.C. and Kay, W.K. (1982) *The School Assembly Debate: 1942-1982*, Southampton, University Department of Education.

Souper, P.C. and Kay, W.K. (1982) *The School Assembly in Hampshire*, Southampton, University Department of Education.

Swann Report (1985) *Education for All*, London, HMSO.

Thiessen, E.J. (1985) A defense of a distinctively Christian curriculum, *Religious Education*, 80, 37-50.

Tilby, A. (1979) *Teaching God*, London, Collins.

West Riding of Yorkshire (1966) *Suggestions for Religious Education*, Wakefield, West Riding County Council.

Wilson, B. (1966) *Religion in Secular Society*, London, Watts.

Wilson, B. (1982) *Religion in Sociological Perspective*, Oxford, Oxford University Press.

Yates, J. (ed) (1986) *Faith for the Future*, London, National Society and Church House Publishing.

Chapter 4   Research Design

Edwards, A.L. (1957) *Techniques of Attitude Scale Construction*, New York, Appleton Century Crofts.

Francis, L.J. (1976) An enquiry into the concept 'Readiness for Religion', unpublished Ph.D. dissertation, University of Cambridge.

Francis, L.J. (1978) Attitude and longitude: a study in measurement, *Character Potential: a record of research*, 8, 119-130.

Francis, L.J. and Kay, W.K. (1984) Attitude towards religion: definition and evaluation, *British Journal of Educational Studies*, 32, 45-50.

Greer, J.E. (1983) Attitude to religion reconsidered, *British Journal of Educational Studies*, 31, 18-28.

Guttman, L. (1944) A basis for scaling qualitative data, *American Sociological Review*, 9, 139-150.

Likert, R.A. (1932) A technique for the measurement of attitudes, *Archives of Psychology*, 140.

Osgood, C.E., Suci, G.J. and Tannenbaum, P.H. (1957) *The Measurement of Meaning*, Urbana, University of Illinois Press.

Thurstone, L.L. (1928) Attitudes can be measured, *American Journal of Sociology*, 33, 529-554.

Chapter 9   Village Schools

Cambridge Policy Study in Education (1981) *A Positive Approach to Rural Primary Schools*, Cambridge, Institute of Education.

Comber, L.C., Joyce, F.E., Meyenn, R.J., Sinclair, C.W., Small, M.A., Tricker, M.J. and Whitfield, R.C. (1981) *The Social Effects of Rural Primary School Reorganisation in England*, Birmingham, University of Aston.

Department of Education and Science (1985) *Better Schools*, London, HMSO.

Forsythe, D. *et al* (1983) *The Rural Community and the Small School*, Aberdeen, Aberdeen University Press.

Gay, J.D. (1985) *The Size of Anglican Primary Schools*, Abingdon, Culham College Institute, Occasional Paper Number 7.

Nash, R. (1980) *Schooling in Rural Societies*, London, Methuen.

Chapter 13   Meeting the Pupils

Argyle, M. and Beit-Hallahmi, B. (1975), *The Social Psychology of Religion*, London, Routledge and Kegan Paul.

Batson, C.D. and Ventis, W.L. (1982) *The Religious Experience*, New York, Oxford University Press.

Brierley, P. (ed) (1980) *Prospects for the Eighties*, London, Bible Society.

Gay, J.D. (1971) *The Geography of Religion in England*, London, Duckworth.

Strommen, M.P. (ed) (1971) *Research on Religious Development*, New York, Hawthorn Books.

Chapter 14   School Influence

Boyle, J.J. and Francis, L.J. (1986) The influence of differing church aided school systems on pupil attitude towards religion, *Research in Education*, 35, 7-12.

De Vaus, D.A. (1981) The impact of Catholic schools on the religious orientation of boys and girls, *Journal of Christian Education*, 71, 44-51.

Egan, J. and Francis, L.J. (1986) School ethos in Wales: the impact of non-practising Catholic and non-Catholic pupils on Catholic secondary schools, *Lumen Vitae*, 41, 159-173.

Fahy, P.S. (1980) The religious effectiveness of some Australian Catholic high schools, *Word in Life*, 28, 86-98.

Flynn, M.F. (1975) *Some Catholic Schools in Action*, Sydney, Catholic Education Office.

Flynn, M.F. (1985) *The Effectiveness of Catholic Schools*, Homebush NSW, St Paul Publications.

Francis, L.J. (1979) School influence and pupil attitude towards religion, *British Journal of Educational Psychology*, 49, 107-123.

Francis, L.J. (1983) Anglican voluntary primary schools and child church attendance, *Research in Education*, 30, 1-9.

Francis, L.J. (1986) Roman Catholic secondary schools: falling rolls and pupil attitudes, *Educational Studies*, 12, 119-127.

Francis, L.J. (1986) Denominational schools and pupil attitude towards Christianity, *British Educational Research Journal*, 12, 145-152.

Greeley, A.M., McCready, W.C. and McCourt, K. (1976) *Catholic Schools in a Declining Church*, Kansas City, Sheed and Ward.

Greeley, A.M. and Rossi, P.H. (1966) *The Education of Catholic Americans*, Chicago, Aldine Publishing Company.

Hornsby-Smith, P.M. (1978) *Catholic Education: the unobtrusive partner*, London, Sheed and Ward.

Macdonald, K.I. (1977) Path Analysis, in C.A. O'Muirchcartaigh and C. Payne (eds), *The Analysis of Survey Data*, volume 2, chapter 3, New York, John Wiley and Sons.

Neuwien, R.A. (ed) (1966) *Catholic Schools in Action*, Notre Dame, Indiana, University of Notre Dame Press.

O'Keeffe, B. (1986) *Faith Culture and the Dual System*, Barcombe, Falmer Press.

Rhymer, J. and Francis, L.J. (1985) Roman Catholic secondary schools in Scotland and pupil attitude towards religion, *Lumen Vitae*, 40, 103-110.

INDEX